Also by Radek Sikorski

Dust of the Saints:
A Journey to Herat in Time of War

FULL
CIRCLE

A Homecoming
to Free Poland

Radek Sikorski

SIMON & SCHUSTER

SIMON & SCHUSTER
Rockefeller Center
1230 Avenue of the Americas
New York, NY 10020

Copyright © 1997 by Radek Sikorski
All rights reserved,
including the right of reproduction
in whole or in part in any form.

SIMON & SCHUSTER and colophon are registered
trademarks of Simon & Schuster Inc.

Designed by Virginia Norey

Manufactured in the United States of America

1   3   5   7   9   10   8   6   4   2

Library of Congress Cataloging-in-Publication Data
Sikorski, Radek.
Full circle : a homecoming to free Poland/Radek Sikorski.
p.   cm.
Includes index.
1. Sikorski, Radek.   2. Politicians—Poland—Biography.
3. Poland—History—20th century.   I.Title.
DK4452.S55A3 1997
943.805'092—dc21   97-5661
[B]   CIP

ISBN: 1-439-10132-9
ISBN-13: 978-1-439-10132-2

Contents

Acknowledgments

Chobielin has been rebuilt thanks to my wonderful parents, Teresa and Jan, who lived through it all: the long winters without central heating, the digging of cars out of snowdrifts, and the burglaries.

Andrzej Szmelter encouraged my parents in looking for a listed ruin. Olga Romanowska found Chobielin and was a guardian angel for the project throughout. I am also very grateful for the advice and help from the keepers of listed buildings: Maciej Urbańczyk, Maciej Obremski, and Tadeusz Zielniewicz. Tadeusz Czerniawski and Jacek Wiśniewski put their good taste to the cause of reconstruction. Thanks to the Polish Cultural Foundation for permission to quote material from Pan Tadeusz.

Bob Asahina and John Riley nurtured the book in its early stages, while Sarah Pinckney and Rebecca Wilson saw it through to publication. Thank you Gill Coleridge, for your professionalism and good humor in representing me.

Several friends kindly read an early version of the manuscript: Dave Mehnert, Adam Zamoyski, Jan Parys, Matthew and Veronica Leeming, James Sherr, Jay Reddaway, Hannah Kaye, and Ed Lucas. Naturally, any mistakes are mine alone.

19th-century Poland
under Partition

Baltic Sea

Gulf of Danzig

POMERANIA

Danzig ●

Elbing ●

Marienburg ●

WEST PRUSSIA

Neustettin ●

Vistula

Kulm ●

Schneidemuhl ●   Nakel ●

Bromberg ●   Thorn ●

Schubin ●

POSEN

Posen ●

RUSSIA

GERMANY

0 10 20 30 40 50
kms

SWEDEN

The Polish-Lithuanian
Commonwealth

RUSSIA

Windau • LIVONIA

*Baltic
Sea*

KURLAND

• Polotsk

LITHUANIA Vitebsk •

Kovno • • Smolensk

• Vilna

Beresina

POMERANIA Gdansk • Konigsberg
EAST
PRUSSIA
Grodno

Niemen

Mohilev •

Bydgoszcz • • Torun Pultusk

POLAND

Dnieper

Minsk •

PODLESIA

Bug

Brest Pinsk •
Litovsk

Priper

Poznan • GREAT
POLAND Warsaw •

SILESIA

Kalisz •

• Radom

Lublin •

• Chernigov

HOLY
ROMAN
EMPIRE

Tschenstochau

LITTLE
POLAND

VOLHYNIA

• Jitomir

Cracow •

• Lemberg

GALICIA

• Zurawno

• Bar

• Chigirin

PODOLIA

Dniester

OTTOMAN
EMPIRE

Black Sea

*Adriatic
Sea*

0   100   200   300   400   500

kms

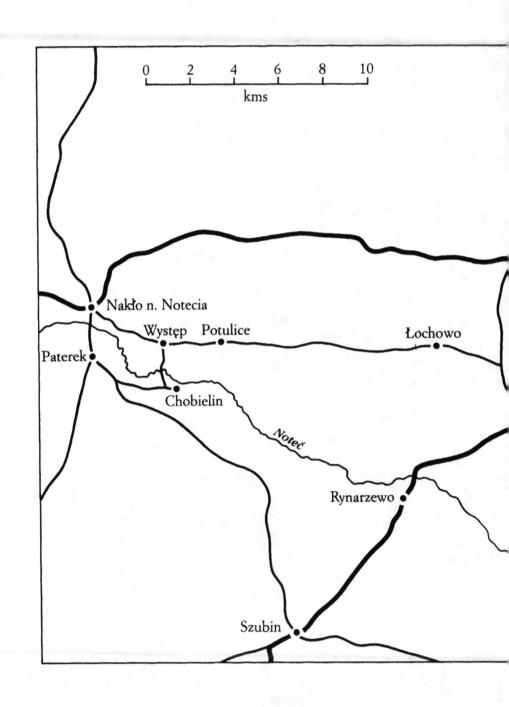

0   2   4   6   8   10

kms

Nakło n. Notecia

Występ   Potulice   Łochowo

Paterek

Chobielin

Noteć

Rynarzewo

Szubin

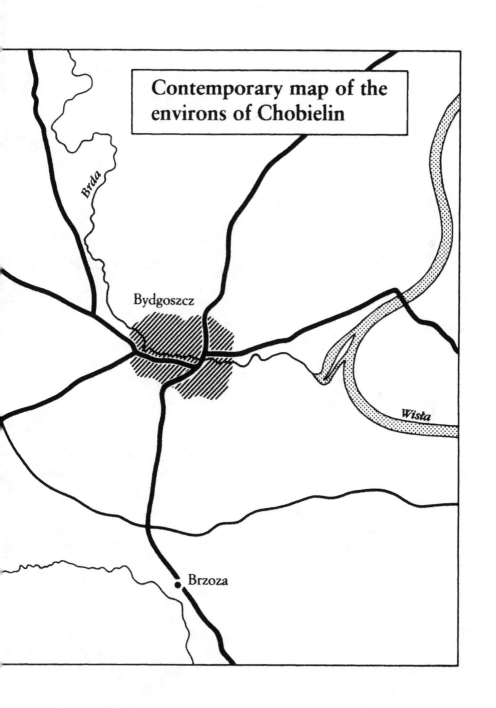

Contemporary map of the environs of Chobielin

Brda

Bydgoszcz

Wisła

Brzoza

Road to Wystep

Keepers
Lodge

0   50   100   150   200
metres

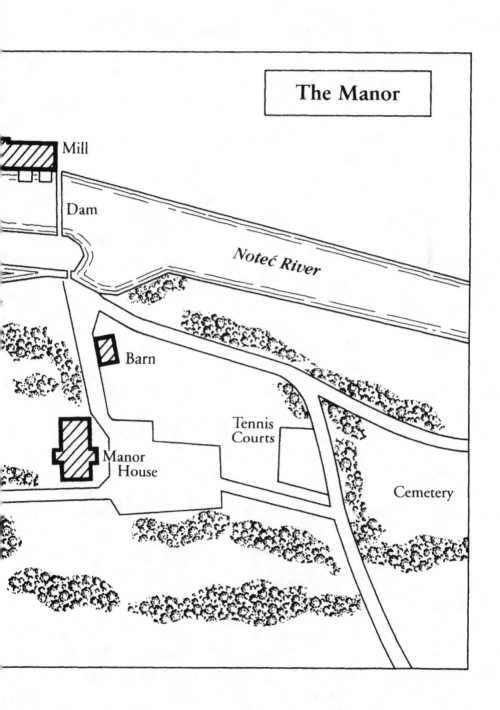

The Manor

Mill

Dam

Noteć River

Barn

Tennis
Courts

Manor
House

Cemetery

Selective Chronology of Polish History

1939	British guarantee to Poland (March 31); Nazi-Soviet Pact (August 23); World War II (September 1); Poland partitioned by Germany and USSR (September 28)
1941	German invasion of USSR
1943	Warsaw Ghetto rising (April)
1944	Lublin Committee formed by Stalin's puppets (July 22); Warsaw rising (August–October); Beginning of liquidation of resistance to Soviet supremacy
1946	Chobielin's confiscation by Communist authorities (August 12)
1947	Rigged elections to the first postwar Sejm
1948	Formation of the Polish United Workers' Party (PZPR) and the launch of one-party state
1948–1956	Stalinism
1955	Formation of the Warsaw Pact
1956	October events and the election of Władysław Gomułka as Communist Party leader
1966	Celebration of the millennium of the Polish state
1968	Anti-Semitic purge in the Communist Party and beyond
1970	Baltic riots: fall of W. Gomułka: Edward Gierek, First Secretary
1976	June riots and the rise of political opposition
1978	Cardinal Karol Wojtyła elected Pope John Paul II (October 16)
1980	Strike at the Lenin Shipyard at Gdańsk and the start of Solidarity's self-limiting revolution
1981	The beating up of Solidarity activists in Bydgoszcz (March) and the imposition of martial law (December 13)
1989	Rountable negotiation between a part of the opposition movement and the Communist authorities; Chobielin's purchase by Jan and Terest Sikorski; First semi-free elections since World War II (June 4); Swearing-in of first noncommunist prime minister since the 1940s (August)
1990	"Shock therapy" economic reforms by finance minister Leszek Balcerowicz (January 1); The Communist Party transforms itself into the Social-Democracy of the Republic of Poland; election of Lech Wałęsa as president

1991   First completely free parliamentary elections;
        Jan Olszewski forms the first government appointed by a freely
        elected Sejm including the first civilian and noncommunist minis-
        ter of defense (December)

1992   Olszewski's minority government brought down over the issues of
        Russo-Polish Treaty and lustration

1993   Post-Communist Parties win a general election and form a govern-
        ment

1995   Aleksander Kwaśniewski beats Lech Wałęsa to the presidency

Die fehlenden wirklichen, doch nicht vorhandenen zu
haben, genehmigten den Regreß in allen Punkten unwidersprechlich
dabei ausdrücklich.

Daß außer den durch den gegenwärtigen Regreß zur Abli=
sung gekommenen Reallasten zwischen dem Berechtigten
und dem in §.4 .... aufgeführten Grundstücke
keinerlei Leistungen oder Gegenleistungen mehr bestünden,
deren Ablösung durch Vermittelung der Rentenbank zu
folgen müßte.

Die Interessenten beantragen, den gegenwärtigen Regreß
für den Berechtigten und für dem Pflichtigen
aufzustellen, und oblegen hierzu die Verhandlung zur Zeit
der Genehmigung, wie folgt.

Ausstellung der fehlenden	Unterschrift der fehlen.
der Königliche Joseph von Hulewicz zu Chodzież	Joseph v Hulewicz
der Pflichtige August Falkenberg zu Chodzież	August Falkenberg

Erste Abteilung.

Eigentümer.	Laufende Nummer der Grundstücke	Grund des Erwerbes. Verzicht.	Erwerbspreis. Wert. Feuerversicherungssumme.
1.	2.	3.	4.
Dem Rittergutsbesitzer Friedrich Albrecht Falkenberg zu Chobielinen Mühle.		Aufgelassen und eingetragen am 9. Dezember 1892. gez. [illegible]	
der Landwirt Julian Reysowski aus Nakel a/N.	1.	Aufgelassen am 17. Dezember 1919 und eingetragen am 8. Januar 1920. Binkowski. Fiedler	
Skarb Państwa Polskiego	1	W wykonaniu art. 2. ust (1) lit. b. c. d. e. dekretu z dnia 6. IX. 1944 r. o przeprowadzeniu reformy rolnej (D. U. R. P. z roku 1945 nr. 3 poz. 13) i art. 1 dekretu z dnia 24. VIII 1945 r. (D. U. R. P. nr. 34 poz. 204) na wniosek Wojewódzkiego Urzędu Ziemskiego Pomorskiego z dnia 12 czerwca 1946 wpisano dnia 12 sierpnia 1946 r. (-) Nosal (-) Lesiński	

Niniejszą księgę wszystkę zamknięto dnia 23. Stycznia 1947.

Nosal Lesiński

PART
I

PROLOGUE

ON THE FOURTH OF JUNE 1989, the day of Poland's first partly democratic election since the Second World War, I was deep in the Angolan bush, not far from the strategic Benguela railway. I had joined a unit of Jonas Savimbi's UNITA guerrillas on a long trek from his base at Jamba to the battleground in the central highlands. They had been fighting a Cuban-supported Communist government in Luanda since the 1970s and I admired them. Later, Savimbi's personality cult, the dishonesty of my minders, and the atmosphere of voodoo superstition were to change my mind.

But for now, we were still comrades in the cause of fighting Communism, so when the unit I was with ambushed a Luanda-regime convoy, I was glad I could report it in the Western press. The road ran along a little dike rising out of the cornfields. Our assault party struck with mortars, machine guns, and rocket-propelled grenades, and several trucks immediately caught fire. The armored personnel carriers from the convoy swept our side of the road with heavy machine guns.

I was filming, keeping one eye on the camera's tiny screen, in which soldiers were looting the burning trucks, and watching my step with the other. Suddenly, I saw a soldier a dozen yards from me tip to the side. A bullet from a heavy machine gun had torn off his leg. Mortar explosions, screams from inside the inferno, and the low crackle of burning scrub drowned the voices of soldiers shouting contradictory orders. Smoke began to sweep the battlefield, giving the illusion of safety. Huge cans of tuna fish, cases of ammunition, and a couple of typewriters on their heads, the soldiers were beginning to make for the low hills behind us. There was to be a prize among the loot—the archive of a Communist Party organization in one of the local towns, which contained lists of collaborators.

In revenge for the ambush, the Communist air force bombed us. The guerrillas tuned a radio to the jets' frequency and we eavesdropped on the conversation between the pilots and the base. They spoke Spanish, probably Cubans:

"I'm at five hundred feet now," one squeaky voice rose excitedly. "Bandits straight ahead. A very large band. Releasing bombs now. Release!"

"Direct hit!" the other pilot joined in, just as excited. "They are running. Running away."

"Well done." A steady voice of the control tower came in. "Come back to base. Back to base." All along, the planes were tiny sparks thousands of feet above us. The pilots kept well out of range of our antiaircraft missiles. The bombs fell uselessly several kilometers away.

We reached camp at midnight and feasted on the liberated tuna fish. At dawn the next day the rest of the camp was still asleep when I woke up. Around me, the soldiers shivered in the dawn chill under their light blankets. Guards huddled around campfires. Without leaving the sleeping bag, I added wood to the dying fire and reached for the radio. The clear voice of a BBC speaker emerged from the static. It was past the hour and I had missed most of the bulletin but caught the summary at the end. One item was bad, one good, and one so superb I rubbed my face to make sure I was not dreaming: Chinese tanks had stormed into Tiananmen Square; the Ayatollah Khomeini was dead; and in Poland, Solidarity had won a landslide victory in the first almost free elections since the Communist takeover of my country nearly half a century before.

I looked around me with new eyes. The sleeping soldiers, the camouflaged foxholes, and the guards pacing in the distance suddenly seemed strange. Only the day before we were all comrades in the same cause. Now my mind was far away. What was I doing here, in the middle of Africa?

The Solidarity victory was the beginning of the end for Communism. For me, it meant one thing. After eight years of exile, I could go home.

Coming home and restoring Chobielin, the dilapidated manor house my parents had recently acquired, was likely to be a journey in time, as well as space. I had been born and educated in Poland, Communist Poland, but at eighteen, when I left, I did not appreciate my homeland as an adult. Years of exile had cut me off from normal contact with family and friends. Just at the age when one ceases to think that one's elders' reminiscences are a bore and begins to find them fascinating, I was deprived of them. I wanted to pick up the threads of half-remembered history to see how I came to be the way I was.

In England, I had gotten used to being thought of as something of an exotic animal, coming from a strange, faraway country so prone to invasion and disaster as to be positively careless. The unspoken assumption was that there must be something wrong with us—hopeless romantics ever ready to charge tanks on horseback—which makes us deserve our bad luck. Was it true?

I hoped the rebuilding would inspire me to delve into the history of the manor house and families connected with it. The history of Poland I had learned at school left me frustrated, and not just because of the lies of official propaganda. The picture of our past in my mind's eye was too broad, too distant. It was almost disconnected from the actual Poland I grew up in—perhaps because so few events, people, or buildings in my home city were ever mentioned in history books. Perhaps if I focused on my house and my region—what the Germans call my *Heimat*—I could fill centuries past with real people and actual places.

My excitement at going back was tinged with apprehension. Poland had spent half a century under totalitarian regimes, first the Nazis, then the Communists. Most people are not heroes and mine was a pretty ordinary family. What would I find when I looked closer?

CHOBIELIN

I HAD ALWAYS WANTED TO LIVE in a *dworek*. Every Pole does. An expatriate Englishman may dream of returning to a Georgian Old Rectory in the home counties. An Irish-American may long to go back to a mythical little white cottage. A German or a Frenchman may dream of retiring to a stone farmhouse in Bavaria or Provence. A Pole sees himself as the proud resident of a *dwór,* a manor house, or *dworek,* a little manor house. A classic *dworek* is eighteenth- or early nineteenth-century, neoclassical, and falls halfway between an aristocratic palace and a prosperous peasant house, with an obligatory white porch, pillars, and at least a hint of a park. It need not be grand—most used to be wooden—and in England an average *dworek* would qualify as little more than a spacious cottage. Thousands used to dot the length and breadth of Poland.

A *dworek* is not just a nice house to live in, but a calling. Nations which have not lived under occupation perhaps cannot imagine the aura surrounding the places where national aspirations were once preserved. In the nineteenth century, when Poland was wiped off the map of Europe, Polishness was preserved in two places: in church by the peasants, and in the *dwór,* the manor house, by the nobility. It was from their manor houses that Polish nobles set off on their hopeless nineteenth-century insurrections and it was the manor houses which the czarist authorities confiscated as punishment after each failure. Until a couple of generations ago, Polish romantic novels—the best reflection of popular imagination—always centered on a *dworek.* Every Polish child learned at school, even in Communist schools, this setting for Arcadia by our national poet, Adam Mickiewicz, written in exile in Paris:

> *There stood a manor house, wood-built on stone;*
> *From far away the walls with whitewash shone,*
> *The whiter as relieved by the dark green*
> *Of poplars, that the autumn winds would screen;*
> *It was not large, but neat in every way,*
> *And had a mighty barn; three stacks of hay*
> *Stood near it, that the thatch could not contain;*
> *The neighbourhood was clearly rich in grain;*
> *And from the stooks that every cornfield filled*
> *As thick as stars, and from the ploughs that tilled*
> *The black-earthed fields of fallow, broad and long,*
> *Which surely to the manor must belong,*
> *Like well-kept flower beds—everyone could tell*
> *That plenty in that house and order dwell.*
> *The gate wide open to the world declared*
> *A hospitable house to all who fared.*[1]

Mickiewicz's celebration of the *dworek* may have been on the school curriculum, but real manor houses hardly flourished in Communist Poland. Aristocratic palaces were too big to ignore and most were saved under the wing of the Catholic church, as schools, or as old people's homes. Those estates and manor houses that were turned over to agricultural or scientific institutes were also lucky—the institutes' staffs were more sophisticated than the average collective farm director. Many palaces were turned into "houses of creative endeavor" for the use of the regime's crony writers and journalists. The really magnificent houses were preserved for show: the socialist state takes care of the nation's treasures. Others served Party bosses for well-deserved holidays under the tender appellation of "Cadres' Improvement Centers."

Your average *dworek,* on the other hand, once the heart of most large villages, has virtually disappeared from the Polish landscape. Out of over ten thousand manor houses in Poland before the war, less than a thousand survived Communist rule, perhaps half of them in a salvageable state. There was no campaign to raze them, as in Russia; they perished through stupidity and sloth. Under the Communist land reform decree of 1944 (of which more later) parcels of land over fifty hectares were confiscated and turned into collective farms, or shared out among the peasants. The remaining fifty hectares and the family houses were not supposed to be taken away from their owners. But, as a rule, Communists did not respect even their own laws. Squads of police or Party militants ejected landlords, law or no law. The landlords were sent packing and the local peasantry encouraged to help themselves to the contents. For years afterward, you could find bits of grand pianos fulfilling a multitude of useful functions in peasant pigsties. The looted manor houses were turned over to local authorities, collective farms, or state companies, who often found it cheaper to raze the manor house altogether.

Perhaps exiles are particularly prone to long for a home of their own. I developed my obsession in Britain where I arrived in 1981. I had thought of spending just a few months there between secondary school and university. During my stay General Jaruzelski crushed Solidarity and imposed martial law. Rather than go back to Poland and face possible arrest—my friends had been imprisoned—I chose exile and made myself as irritating as I could be to the guardians of People's Poland. My presence abroad, which was illegal according to Communist law, and my role as a journalist always meant extra work for the overworked officials in the local security police office: more tapping of my parents' phones, more censoring of their mail, more worry about what I might be writing about socialist Poland in the capitalist press. One of the favorite methods that the security police used to apply pressure was the withholding of a passport for travel abroad. My father had tried to slip out to see me under the pretext of attending the World Cup—but the police saw through it. Another ploy was to pretend to go to Rome for a religious pilgrimage. My parents spent several days and nights queuing in front of the passport office to hand in the application forms. Needless to say, the authorities saw through that, too. Finally, at the eighth or ninth interview, just a week before the proposed date of their departure, the overfed police major lashed out at my mother, "Unless your son shuts up, you will never see him again." My mother left his office in tears, only to be summoned back the next day and told that the merciful People's State would, after all, give her this one last chance to persuade me to mend my anti-socialist ways.

We spent our hard-won vacation in a remote stone cottage in rural north Wales, high above the cliffs of Hell's Mouth Bay, and it was there that we first talked about restoring a ruined manor house. We were at the tip of a hilly peninsula, divided by stone walls between which sheep grazed and bleated. My mother liked the cottages and farmhouses which dotted the countryside. "They don't belong to rich people," she observed, "because the cars beside them are mostly old. But each house is painted properly and every garden is well tended. You can tell each has an owner, not like with us." The more well-kept farms and beautifully preserved stately homes we saw, the sadder we became at the desolate state of the Polish countryside. Poland was still Communist and we expected Communism to endure. But perhaps the system was by now sloppy enough to turn a blind eye if someone took care of an old pile of bricks. My parents volunteered to start looking for a ruin that would not be too far from Bydgoszcz, our native city in western Poland.

A few months later, a friend passing through London brought me a videotape. My parents had called on the office of the keeper of listed buildings in our home city, who had recommended a few sites. My parents liked best a house called Chobielin. It was by a river, which was essential for my father's angling hobby. Like most houses in the register of ruins, it was in a terminal state of disrepair. But Chobielin had several advantages: it was only half an hour's drive from the city, situated in beautiful land away from a village, and, above all, it housed only one family of squatters. The video picture was of poor quality, but good enough to suggest that Chobielin must once have looked like a traditional Polish *dwór*.

We had only the vaguest idea of the estate's history, gleaned by my parents from the tales of the local peasants. They were told that a German who owned Chobielin at the turn of the century (and who was responsible for the ill-fitting wing) went bankrupt in the hyperinflation of the end of World War One. His Polish manager bought out the house and a few thousand acres of land for the price of a few sacks of grain. After the Communist liberation in 1945—so the tale went—the manor was taken over by the thugs from the Interior Ministry and saw some spectacular orgies. Then, when the mess became too much, it was given over to the estate farmhands, who finished the destruction. Interned Solidarity leaders were said to have been kept in the ruin for several freezing nights when martial law was imposed in December 1981. Distant family of the prewar owners were said to be still alive, in Canada, and occasionally even came to see Chobielin. We were told, however, that they had no thought of rebuilding the house. At that time the sale of ruins had been permitted for over ten years, but few former owners made inquiries. While socialism lasted, fear still held them at bay. Most were pleased when someone took care of their former property.

Several days later I finally managed to get through to Bydgoszcz on the telephone.

"How much do they want for it?" I shouted into the receiver.

"What did you say?" My father's voice was barely audible in the static.

"I said how much do they want for it?" I screamed.

"What? I can't hear you. The line is very bad. It's always like that when it's raining. Did you say how much they want for it?"

At that moment the Polish operator interjected. "Have you finished?"

"No, I have not—"

The line went dead.

My letter confirming my commitment—necessarily without knowing the price—was sent by express mail. It arrived in Bydgoszcz six weeks later. As usual, an attached note explained how it was accidentally damaged in the post. The letter had been crudely cut open and arrived wrapped in a plastic bag. I should have known then that the end of the regime was near when the security police could no longer be bothered to conceal their rummaging anymore.

As a listed building, the manor had been protected by law, theoretically at least. But the Communists' appreciation of our national heritage may be judged by the way the price was set: the local authority delegated a builder to estimate the value of bricks, beams, and other usable material at demolition prices.

At the last moment, there was a hitch. The local authority clerk who had steered the paperwork for a year suddenly remembered: "Do you realize that if you go through with this, you lose all rights to ration cards?" She looked up at my parents, despondent, expecting the deal to be off. Surely, nobody would be so reckless as to voluntarily deprive himself of ration cards?

As far back as I could remember, there had always been "temporary" shortages of such luxuries as soap, shoes, toilet paper, or sausage. Now, in the 1980s, even vodka, sugar, and butter were only available with ration coupons. However, the farmers—defined as anybody who owned more than a hectare of land—were excluded from most entitlements. Those whose cards identified the countryside as their permanent place of residence were assumed to be keeping a pig or some chickens in the garden and could surely barter their produce for everything else.

"No more ration cards then," said my father. For all he knew, he was resigning himself to spending the rest of his life raising pigs and chickens.

Thus we acquired a ghost estate with a couple of hectares of land near a major city for under a thousand pounds. The deed sold for 6,849,899 old zlotys, to be precise, at a moment when the dollar sold on the street for 5,500 zlotys. In early 1989, when the paperwork was completed and the money handed over, this was no small sum. An average Polish monthly salary edged only just above 100,000 zlotys. In fact, we overpaid. We were paying the equivalent of a couple of Polish cars at a time when the Ministry of Culture recommended giving away properties in a similar state for a single symbolic zloty. There was another circumstance which lowered Chobielin's value: the ruin was still inhabited by the last family of farmhands. In theory, the authorities had the duty to rehouse them. In practice, there was nothing one could do to evict squatters and we realized we might end up having to lure them away by buying them an apartment.

It might have been years before I saw Chobielin. By the very act of claiming political asylum in Britain, I had broken Communist law and could not safely visit Poland. In February 1989 I watched the Soviet Army withdraw from Kabul, but I still expected the war I privately declared on the evil empire to be a long march. It proved a sprint. By August, I was to sit in the gallery of the Polish parliament, watching the swearing in of the first non-Communist prime minister of Poland since the war. Like the Afghans, we too had finally won, but unlike them, I could start enjoying the fruits of our victory.

❀

A couple of weeks after returning from Angola, in London, I found myself talking to a Polish consul. The same man had told me a couple of years earlier that the authorities would be sympathetic if an undesirable like myself were to apply to renounce his Polish citizenship. This time, he was solicitous: *"Paszporcik będzie w try miga."* We'll have a lovely little passport for you in a flash.

A fortnight later, I was in West Berlin, driving across the Wall into the East. It was dawn before my father and I crossed East Germany and entered Poland. I was seeing Poland for the first time as an adult. In one village a woman dressed in white drowsily took iron shutters down from the windows of a flat-roofed shop. A shivering queue had already formed. In another, a policeman dozed inside his car, his head cast back at the headrest, a blue radar dish on a tripod beside the road. He did not stir, even though we had definitely broken the limit. Milk collectors stood atop their horse-drawn carriages, arching their backs as they lifted zinc canisters off little wooden stalls in front of each house. Men with wild faces, still or already drunk, swerved violently onto the road.

As we drove on, I tried to imagine an earlier landscape behind the modern architectural mess. In one village, a broken stone tablet and a plaster wing of a fallen angel peeping out of the greenery explained what a hillock beside the road had once been: a German cemetery. In another, granite foundations supported a modern barn covered with asbestos. The place must once have had a manager who planned his buildings with centuries in view. By following the cobbled roads off the asphalt, to lumps of greenery in the distance, my eyes sometimes spied out the battered porch of a still extant manor house, or a few bits of stone where one had once stood.

Three hours from the border we reached home territory near my native city of Bydgoszcz. The Jarużyn bus stop, where we finally turned off the main road, was a concrete hut, half submerged in weeds. Its old coating of brown paint was peeled by frosts and daubed with obscenities. Trailing dust, the car groaned over the potholes as we covered the last few kilometers on a bad country lane. We were approaching Chobielin.

The contours of the old estate were still distinguishable. We passed the smithy, its wooden portico stooped with age. By a clump of barns and cottages—the old farm buildings—children with faces like chimney sweeps waved to us. Then, suddenly overcome with shyness, they stuck their fingers in their mouths and looked away. Past the farm we drove in the shade again, in a long avenue of slim chestnuts. There were spaces in it like gaps after pulled-out teeth. Stones which once made up a cobbled road now tickled my feet as they struck against the suspension. It was the old drive leading to the manor itself.

The park came into view at the top of a little hill. Gnarled oak and elm trees in sober green rose from a gay field of ripe corn dotted with poppies—old men among blond grandchildren. Soon, the car was creaking down a dark tunnel made by trees whose crowns joined overhead. We stopped to clear boulders and stumps which blocked the way. At the bottom, light shone through the leaves. We emerged into the sun and there, a hundred yards away, on a rise between the park and a river, we saw a picturesque ruin.

In the sharp rays of morning light, a steep roof hunched with age, its tiles mellowed to the color of ripe orange, stood out against the backdrop of rich green leaves. The walls were made of weathered bricks of outmoded size, covered with gray where old plaster remained. Four square columns, also shorn of plaster, supported a balcony without balustrade—an effusion of bushes. To the left of the porch, the panes were smashed and birds flew in and out, but on the right there were still curtains in the windows. Above, tin replaced several rows of missing roof tiles. Smoke issued from a chimney and I smelled burning coal. The ruin was still inhabited.

The view was cluttered by wooden shacks clinging to the house and others built against the remains of the entrance gate. To the main body of the manor house someone had stuck a tall, square town house which gave the compound the look of a steam engine.

The ground in between was thick with rubbish. Glass fragments crunched under my feet as I picked my way between rusted agricultural implements, barrel staves, a trough, a bottomless steel bucket, bits of wire, old tires, and plaster fragments fallen from the gate.

At that moment two little mongrel dogs emerged through a hole in the balcony door and began yapping viciously. A flock of geese took fright. Screeching, they wobbled away, taking shelter in one of the shacks by the gate.

Probably alarmed at the sounds of animal terror, a peasant woman holding a rolling pin emerged onto the porch. Wearing an apron, she was as broad as she was tall. Grim determination on her face gave way to a testy smile when she saw what alerted the dogs and frightened the geese.

"*Dzień dobry panie Sikorski,*" she welcomed my father as we came closer.

"*Dzień dobry pani Erlichowa,*" he replied. "This is my son." He turned to me. "Returned from England just today and the first thing he wanted to do was to come here."

After a quick, sharp look at me from top to bottom she said: "*Witamy młodego pana dziedzica.*" Welcome to the young master. Her fleshy face opened in a broad, somewhat overzealous smile. Was it a genuine expression of quaint obsequiousness, or was she mocking me? I could not tell.

On my first visit to Chobielin on my first day back in Poland I was not sure what the etiquette of asking permission to enter my own house should be. My house, but Mrs. Erlich's home.

"May I?"

"Please, please," Mrs. Erlich gestured earnestly, gratified to be asked, and moved out of the way.

I pushed on a bulky brass handle and the heavy wooden door gave way. Before my eyes adjusted to the darkness in the hall, I heard birds twittering from an overhead nest. It was built around a hook in the ceiling from which a chandelier must once have been suspended. A shaft of light coming through a hall window focused on an open can of brown paint standing on a wooden staircase. The brush was petrified inside. Dense black cobwebs shrouded what should have been the fuse box. Wires drooped from a board with bare bits of copper crudely twisted together.

The woman followed me inside and removed a padlock on a double door with the number 7 scratched crudely on peeling paint. We entered the former drawing room. In the middle stood a large wooden case filled with rotting fruit. An electric switch, ripped out of the wall, dangled on the wires. A heap of rubble waist high filled a corner. Broken bits of tile indicated where a glazed stove had once stood. It was dark. The French windows which had once led on to the terrace and the garden had been bricked up.

I followed the woman from room to room. None of the doors retained original handles. Brass had given way to aluminum or holes had been punched through the wood and kept together with wire. It was the same story everywhere: stoves smashed up, floorboards ripped out, cobwebs in the corners, peeling paint, chickens.

"Look what they did." She pointed at a large hole in the ceiling of the dining room. A wooden beam as thick as a tree, black with rot, hung dangerously in the air over our heads. It was the fault of the squatters who had lived upstairs, she said with indignation. Water poured in through the slits and corroded the ceiling beams. If it hadn't been for the supports in the dining room, the roof and the first floor would have fallen down.

The outside walls were also damaged. A crack, in some places the size of an arm, split one wall from the top of the roof to the middle of the ground floor. The linden tree beside the house was the prime suspect. Its roots had penetrated beneath the foundations and forced the wall up. Repair would mean stripping down the whole wall and building it up again brick by brick.

Even the cellars—a maze of cool chambers with stone walls and vaulted ceilings—threatened to collapse. Keystones in many of the ceiling arches were loose. Remove one and a whole section of the house might cave in. Even if their vaults could be repaired, the cellars were deep and the river was near. Once central heating was installed and the walls began to draw in ground moisture, damp could be a danger. Waterproofing the foundations would be laborious and expensive.

The grounds were no less melancholy. The keeper's lodge, a handsome little villa in which people had lived as late as 1982, was a mere shell. All the windows and doors had been wrenched out. A rusting steel line noosed around its wooden roof beams—someone had attempted a final demolition.

The hiss of water against brick and stone grew louder as I approached the river. A large brick barn rose on the opposite bank—the old mill. As I came close, a boy clad in only loose shorts jumped off a pile and plunged into the rapids. His head peeped out of the water and he was safely carried downstream, toward the shallows. The mill was just about standing although the wooden beams in the Tudor-style construction were bent with age. As I was to learn later, the local carp farm used it as a warehouse. The piles in the river had once carried turbines. A couple of giant iron wheels red with rust and shrouded in cobwebs nestled against the mill wall, testifying to what must once have been an engineering venture of some sophistication.

Straight ahead from the porch, across the road which had brought us, a clump of spruce trees marked the cemetery. Remains of the boundary walls indicated that it must have been enlarged several times to accommodate successive generations of Chobielin owners. Not a trace remained of the iron railings which must once have bounded it. Pious local peasants had likewise demolished the chapel and looted the graves. Only granite frames and holes in the sandy ground remained. The gravestones—of black marble, we were later told—had been carted off for recycling. It was better not to think of what happened to the corpses. But was it wise to live in the vicinity of grave robbers?

"My Lord, wasn't it beautiful here once." The woman sighed and her eyes glazed over as she thought back to distant times. "Here," she pointed to two holes in the ground in front of the porch, "two chestnuts once stood, one on this side and one on the other side of the stairs." The trees once shaded carriages pulling up onto a stone pediment. "But they cut them down for firewood." She accented the "they," meaning other squatters, with disgust. There had been strange trees in the garden, she said, lawns, workshops, a carriage house, and a large hole in the ground lined with granite boulders—the ice house.

"I suppose you'll be wanting to pull it down for the bricks?" The sudden look of craftiness on her face betrayed that this was what she really wanted to know. "Because if you were, you know, that's fine with us."

"I was thinking rather of rebuilding it."

She looked surprised. "That's fine with us too. Just give us a replacement apartment, but mind, a proper one, in a tower block not in some cottage, and we'll be gone in no time." The battle lines were drawn. I was soon to discover that Polish law made eviction virtually impossible.

Mrs. Erlich was only being sensible. Most sane people would say that Chobielin was a hopeless case: bulldoze it down before it collapses by itself and buries some innocent prowler. Was there much to save? To an estate agent the enterprise would have seemed ludicrous. It would have been easier, faster, and cheaper to build a similar house from scratch.

But for me, rebuilding Chobielin was not to be a real estate invest-ment. In moments of doubt I thought of it as a folly—my way of tilting at windmills. Other times I hoped it would be my contribution to re-building Poland, and a last battle against the Communists. Just as pre-viously I had fought them with a telephoto lens, a word processor, and one or two bursts from an assault rifle, now I would fight their legacy with bricks, mortar, and furniture polish. I wanted to purify a few acres of Poland from the filth, actual and metaphorical, of their rule. Instead of being forced to build their glorious future, I wanted to rescue some-thing of Poland's past. My greatest reward, I told myself, would be if, in a few years' time, my guests would come, look around, and think that Communism had somehow spared this remote spot.

MY COMMUNIST CHILDHOOD

IT WAS BECAUSE COMMUNISM tried to abolish history that I revered old things. And it was precisely because I had been taught that manor houses were a feudal relic that made me want to live in one. Like every major religion, Communism imposed not only a new politics, a new morality, and a new language, but also new aesthetics, not least in architecture. I went to a primary school which was a typical lump of concrete built in the late 1960s to a standard design as part of the authorities' campaign "One Thousand Schools for Poland's Millennium." We lived on a typical Communist housing estate, bastardized Le Corbusier built to socialist standards of craftsmanship. In fairness, our 1960s house was not as bad as later constructions: it was built of brick, each apartment had two balconies, and the space between the blocks allowed for a proper-sized playground on each side. This was no coincidence. Both my parents had acquired the apartment as members of a building trade co-op. Because they were building for themselves, the architects circumvented the rules in order to give the block more space and the builders gave it their best. Thus human nature triumphed over state-imposed altruism.

Thanks to this, the block still stands while many others, all over the Communist world, are collapsing with increasing frequency at the slightest earth tremor or explosion of leaking gas. Indeed, you can trace the vitality of the Communist faith in Poland by the standards of buildings the regime erected: sub-Mussolini heroic style with stone facades in the 1950s, sober brick in the 1960s, shoddy concrete blocks in the 1970s, and nothing at all in the 1980s.

But it was not just the ugliness with which we were surrounded but the crudeness of the brainwashing that made me rebel. My first political memory dates from about the age of five; it was my first May Day demonstration. A huge crowd filled our city's main street, the May Day Avenue. To get a better view I used my father's shoulders as a platform and pulled myself up onto the branch of a tree. Below me, I saw a sea of smiling spectators. It was a parade; it was fun. There were bands playing marching music, songs broadcast through loudspeakers, floats and flowers. I had been given lollipops and cotton candy, and a little red flag to carry. Earlier that morning, there had been a television broadcast from the Moscow May Day parade, complete with tanks, and missiles pulled by enormous trucks through Red Square. A live link-up showed other marches in other friendly countries; we were told that workers in capitalist countries were too afraid to march as we did. Images of the capitalist police dispersing demonstrations with tear gas filled the television screen.

Politics continued at my primary school. Indoctrination began at the age of six. Our primer taught us to feel socialist brotherhood with the oppressed in the Third World. With hindsight the rhyme sounds remarkably racist:

The little Negro lives in Africa
He has black skin, our comrade.
He studies hard in the morning
From his first Negro primer
And when he comes home from school
He plays and frolics—that's his work.
His mother shouts—Bambo, you imp—
But Bambo just puffs up his black mouth.
His mother says: Drink some milk,
But Bambo escapes up a tree. . . .

Later, I played with the Communist version of Trivial Pursuit. This was a book of quiz games which came in a shiny, colored package. One succeeded or failed at the quizzes depending on one's knowledge of fraternal Communist countries and production statistics. In one of them, the idea was to match the leader, for example Nicolae Ceausescu, with the country, Romania, and with its flag; in another, I had to enumerate Soviet achievements in space, or guess the level of Polish steel production.

My favorite comic strip was the *Adventures of Matolek the Goat,* who goes around the world in search of the town of Pacanów where, he believes, he may acquire goat hooves. It was a prewar children's classic eventually adapted into a cartoon film. *Matolek* literally means "little imbecile" and the goat—wearing shorts and with a fool's face—is lovable precisely because he makes endearing slipups. Only later did we realize how much it had been adapted for the new era by the censors. In his peregrinations *Matolek* is whisked away to the moon, to be deposited back on earth by a star, surviving the flight by sitting on the star's comet-like tail. In the prewar version, the star is six-pointed—the standard Christmas star of the Bethlehem provenance. In the version I read, the star had dropped one point so as to resemble the great emblem of the Russian revolution.

Coming down to earth, near Warsaw, the original *Matolek* looked down on the city center with the old Royal Castle, the King Sigismund III memorial, and the spire of a church. In my new version the only object on the Warsaw skyline the goat sees is the ghastly skyscraper built by the Soviets in the 1950s, the Joseph Stalin Palace of Culture and Science. Where prewar policemen dressed in long trench coats swing a baton at *Matolek* for infringing traffic regulations, nice socialist militiamen politely point him in the right direction. While crossing the United States, *Matolek* finds a golden treasure, which he hands to the Polish embassy "to pass on to poor children in Poland." In the new version, the embassy is no longer "Polish embassy" but simply "Embassy." Its neoclassical building metamorphoses into a clone of the Lenin mausoleum. *Matolek's* gift is no longer passed on to poor Polish children—poverty, especially among children, having been eradicated by socialism—but to "dear" Polish children.[2]

My favorite television serial was called *Czterej Pancerni i Pies,* or Four Tankmen and a Hound. It was screened on Sunday mornings—in order to make it difficult for families to tear children away from the box to go to mass, we suspected. The Four Tankmen television club ran quizzes and competitions. Those who answered correctly questions relating to the Polish army's battles on the Eastern front took part in a draw. Each Sunday one name was drawn from a huge wicker basket of correct answers. The first prize was every boy's dream: a real tank helmet, complete with ribbed padding, headphones, and a connection cord, which one could dangle nonchalantly from one's head. I remember going green with envy when I saw one of the boys in my neighborhood parade in one. (Only later did I learn that he was the son of an army colonel. Daddy probably "organized" one from surplus stock in his unit.)

The story of the tankmen began with the youngest, Janek, with whom we all identified, who lived in Siberia in 1943. He had become a crack shot by hunting bear. One day a newspaper arrived in his remote hut: a Polish army was being created in the Soviet Union. He joins it without hesitation and, after many adventures, comes to liberate Poland together with his good-natured Soviet comrades-in-arms. Only much later, in London, reading émigré books, did I ask myself what Janek was doing in Siberia in 1943. The veiled part of the story was that Janek's family had been deported east, together with about a million other Poles, when the Soviet Army moved into Poland in collusion with Hitler in 1939.

In Polish classes, we read short stories and wrote about Lenin: Lenin as a model pupil, Lenin the revolutionary, Lenin in prison writing to his mother using an inkpot made of bread. Up to a certain age, the indoctrination obviously worked because at eleven I wrote the following essay on the set theme "Describe Lenin":

> *Vladimir Ilyich Lenin was born in 1870 in a working-class family. After finishing secondary school he studied at the Imperial University in Kazan. In 1917–1918 he directed the Great October Revolution. Lenin was a modest, unassuming man. He always walked about pensively. He was the author of many works about economic and social life. He was a talented commander of the Revolution. He was a patriot already in his youth. He hated the Czar. He was always sensitive to human suffering. He was caring. He was a very noble and good man and that is why the Czar's stooges killed him.*

Lenin also lived on in our obligatory Russian classes. Our Russian primer taught us a poem:

When the sun rises,
and looks into our classroom
It lights up brightly
a portrait on the wall.

Like a word of greeting
for a good day
Ilyich, as if alive,
is looking at me.

I learned by heart Mayakovsky's revolutionary poetry. I remember reciting in front of the class: "The individual is nothing, the individual is nil. The Party is everything," or words to that effect. On that particular occasion I knew that if I recited it well, I could lift my marks for that term. For the same reason, I sung the "Internationale" in singing classes.

At twelve, I was still malleable. In fact, my old school notebook shows alarming levels of early opportunism. An entry for April 30, 1975, shows homework on the subject of "May Day in K.I. Gałczyński's poem 'A March Through the Streets of the World.'" The task was to pick out quotations from the poem and to contrast May Day parades in socialist and capitalist countries. I executed my task exemplarily:

IN SOCIALIST COUNTRIES

The sun gilds the red; flags flutter in the
streets and on bridges; the procession
marches and with it—spring.

The parade is bright, ceremonious;
people of all trades take part; everyone
is celebrating the great day.

IN CAPITALIST COUNTRIES

*Thus though the world marches toward
a new age. With every year the march
swells. As if by a campfire, downtrodden
peoples warm their hands by the red flag.*

In capitalist countries May Day is
banned. Demonstrations are dispersed
by the police and the army. May Day is
a day of struggle for equal rights and
brotherhood.

In between classes we joined "Peace Campaigns." One could get special points and higher marks for helping to make posters to place on school bulletin boards. These might depict Vietnamese people wearing wide straw hats being crushed by American bombs, or perhaps just American bombs: big, nasty black objects, crossed out with a large red X, and the word NO, written on top. Children in nice socialist countries, on the other hand, were painted holding hands and dancing in circles, with a dove flying above them.

School elections were another important extracurricular activity. The class council, our "Student Self-Government Committee," was supposedly chosen by free election. School voting, we were told, was to be a small example of socialist democracy at work—and indeed it was. There were no campaigns, no speeches, no promises of better school food, however bogus—not even a committee to nominate candidates. Somehow, the top name on the ballot was always Jacek W., the least popular boy in the school. Jacek W. was a classic teacher's pet, who was especially good at dressing up in a red tie and coming up to the podium to parrot slogans at rallies. We didn't like him; nobody ever admitted having voted for him, but Jacek W. always won. The ritual was something we all went through, just as our parents went through the ritual of voting for unopposed candidates in national elections.

Despite their obvious artificiality, all patriotic occasions—voting, rallies, marches—were treated with the solemnity of a religious ceremony; and every time one occurred some poor wretch had to stay after hours and record them in the school chronicle. My primary school chronicle

(I had a look at it again recently)—several thick volumes bound in fake leather—starts with the photograph of the school's opening, in September 1967. Newspaper clippings show the ribbon being cut by Comrade W. Soporowski, first secretary of the Communist Party's Bydgoszcz City Committee, and Comrade T. Filipowicz, the director of the propaganda department of the regional Communist Party Committee. Barely a month later, while the pavement outside was still unfinished, the school was already celebrating the fiftieth anniversary of the October Revolution. Under a red star, a hand-painted portrait of Lenin, and a drawing of two rifles, someone inscribed a citation whose clumsiness makes me think that it was written with deliberate insincerity:

> *Fifty years ago the Great October Revolution triumphed. Its victory brought freedom to many countries. Unfortunately, the Polish reactionary regime did not permit our fatherland to become free too. Only after the hard experiences of World War Two did the Soviet Union lift up our fatherland from defeat and poverty. For twenty-three years now we have been free; we breathe freedom, and we owe this to our friends from the east.*

Rallies for the October Revolution, the Polish People's Army, May Day, Victory Day, International Women's Day, the Militia and Security Service Day, and a few others belonged like Christmas and Easter to the official Communist calendar. We also supposedly volunteered for special galas. For example, we celebrated forty years of the Polish-Soviet Friendship Society (the chronicle points out that the ceremony was attended by no less a dignitary than the director of the Gdańsk branch office of the Soviet House of Culture), the Lenin Year, fifty years of the Soviet Union, forty years of the International Brigades in Spain, and, for some reason, the twenty-second anniversary of the creation of the Polish United Workers' Party. Each event was marked with a big rally. We organized a festival of Soviet songs and our scouts organization received a banner from the Union of Veterans. We sent greetings to Comrade Wojciech Jaruzelski, at the time still a humble minister of defense, to congratulate him on his elevation to three-star general. "The 25th Congress of the Communist Party of the Soviet Union made a big impact in our school," records the chronicle. "Every class prepared displays in the glass cases on the walls and the school self-government sent a telegram to the Soviet embassy. Scouts laid flowers and stood guards of honor in front of the monument of the heroic Soviet Army." For another rally we made a big banner which was hung on the wall in the gymnasium: "The Party's Program—Is Our Program."

On one occasion we sent 1,379 notebooks to the children of Vietnam, appended with a message:

Dear Vietnamese brothers,

We, the children of the Number 20 school from Bydgoszcz . . . wish you victory against the American aggressor which is destroying your country and your people. Your struggle is ours and that's why it must lead to victory. . . . We want the sun of freedom to shine over your country and for your faces to beam with smiles of happiness. We wish peace for all the children of the world and so that all children are as happy as we are in Poland.

On another, we passed a spontaneous resolution:

We, the children of the Number 20 elementary school in Bydgoszcz, join our voices against the neutron bomb. We want to learn and work for the benefit of our country. We know that we cannot achieve anything without peace. For this reason we firmly oppose those forces which would like to disrupt the security and cooperation of the nations of the world. . . .

At the age of ten, when I supposedly applauded this resolution, I had no idea what a neutron bomb was.

However, by far the biggest rally, and the biggest lie, of my school career was in 1974, when we marked the thirtieth anniversary of the People's Militia and Security Service. Because our director's husband was a security service bigwig, the Militiamen's Day was always solemnly celebrated. With unintentional irony, the chronicle commemorated each rally with drawings which featured fierce-looking Alsatians, their teeth dripping with blood. Now our school was to receive a great honor: it was to be renamed after an esteemed Communist, Second Lieutenant Zdzisław Wizor. He was a dedicated security officer who lost his young life fighting counterrevolutionary bandits—that is, anti-Communist rebels—in our area in 1946. We read newspaper articles about him, such as this in the local Party mouthpiece, *Gazeta Pomorska:*

> *The thirtieth anniversary of the foundation of the People's Militia and Security Service is the day of people deeply committed to the task of building our people's fatherland. In the first years after the war, the time of the laying of the foundations of People's Poland, officers of the People's Militia and Security Service took up arms to defend their socialist ideals. Many of them gave their lives fighting against reactionary bands. Today, popular esteem surrounds their memory.*

In our Polish classes we wrote stories about the hero and described the school's preparations for the glorious day of receiving his name: "The poetry ensemble and the choir are preparing a montage of words and music," reads my notebook. "All the students are rehearsing their parts. The school building is being spruced up. Both the inside and the outside walls have been painted. We are decorating our classrooms. A selection of children's paintings about the People's Militia is on show in the upper hall. A commemorative plaque celebrating our hero has been put up in the main entrance hall." The paintings in fact took part in a competition on the theme "Thirty years of the People's Militia in the eyes of a child." The ten best paintings were to be honored by being taken to Warsaw to be displayed at the Culture House of the Interior Ministry itself.

On the day, the rally in the schoolyard was bigger than usual. A large slogan hung on the wall: "He did not die—he lives in our hearts." Everyone was dressed in uniforms and scarves—each class had its own color. Great men were in attendance: the local police commandant, our hero's widow and his daughter, a secretary of the local Party committee, the head of the county educational department, the head of the Communist veterans union, all the regional grandees. The militia orchestra played the "Internationale" while we took the oath to follow faithfully in Lieutenant Wizor's heroic footsteps.

And while the teachers' attention was on the momentous events in the center, we practiced tossing coins into cracks in the pavement. You had to try to get your coin as near as possible to the crack and then flick it closer with your thumb. As in golf, whoever managed to do it with the least number of flicks won, and took everybody else's coins.

The photographs from that ceremony are still in my school's chronicle, as is the plaque in the hall. But the school's name is now going to be changed and the plaque will be removed. It appears that Lieutenant Wizor's heroic curriculum vitae was largely fabricated. It is now suspected that he never finished secondary school. Worse, even his revolutionary ardor is now in some doubt as well. Rumors have emerged that his zeal had less to do with his Communist beliefs and more with collaboration with the Nazis during the war, which he tried to expiate by serving the new regime. But no one told us anything about this in 1974.

From the point of view of indoctrinating us, the most self-defeating school activities were "voluntary works," which were of course nothing of the sort. We usually picked potatoes at collective farms. The trips were organized by the school and were supposed to imbue in us, the future intelligentsia, respect for the toil of our comrades: workers and peasants. And we did indeed learn the socialist work ethic. When picking potatoes we followed a machine that dug them out of the ground; our task was to put them into wicker baskets which we then emptied into the back of a truck. After a couple of hours, however, when our backs ached from constant leaning down, we would press every other potato into the ground with a sharp kick. After our passage, the field was empty, yet the truck only half full. The farm managers knew what was up and had the same field lifted and picked by teams from different schools over and over again; I doubt whether our contribution was worth the gasoline expended on busing us out to the farm.

At factories, we stole. Once, we were sent to a nearby subsidiary of Romet, Poland's largest bicycle manufacturer. After a day's shirking everyone emerged with a stolen set of spare parts for his or her bicycle, which were often unobtainable in the shops.

Later, when we were somewhat older, the brainwashing was packaged in a single class, called "Citizen Training." We learned about the socialist constitution, the ABCs of class struggle, and the evils of capitalism. One year, our teacher in this class was an unusually tall woman who wore pink, orange, and violet clothes, and believed what she taught. We called her "Skarpeta," which means sock, because she once took a sock out of her pocket and blew her nose with it. We used to leave the front row of desks free in her classes, because she had a missing tooth: that meant when she got excited, as she often did, she spat on the unfortunate students in the front row. When challenged on any political subject she would grow furious. "How can you say that? My parents were peasants, and I am a teacher. Look at what socialism has done for us all."

My secondary school, also in Bydgoszcz, was housed in a solid red-brick building in the center of town and was also named after a Communist, a nineteenth-century activist called Ludwik Waryński. While there I wrote a history exam paper which my mother preserved for posterity at the back of a closet:

1. *DISCUSS: The problem of private ownership of land 1947–1956; after 1956; today.*
2. *DISCUSS: Social Policy toward the countryside 1971–80.*
3. *What decisions and actions by the authorities can ameliorate the situation of agriculture and increase the level of national food consumption?*
4. *DISCUSS: Organizational forms of rural self-government.*

My answer to the first question began like this: "After the land reform proclaimed by the London government in exile on August 1, 1944, the Communist government was obliged to announce land reform for political reasons. . . ."

There is still a bold red line on the paper under the reference to the London government, which was not supposed to be mentioned, together with the following annotation: "This is a totally ludicrous statement!"

Looking back on that exam paper I began to wonder how it was that I knew about the London government in exile, which was dismissed in our curriculum as an émigré irrelevancy. After all, I was to visit collective farms in the Soviet Union in 1990 where they would ask me, quite seriously, whether it was better there, or in the West. Thinking back on my childhood, however, I realized that my official education was only a part—and a much smaller part—of my education as a whole.

Unlike my first political memory, that of the May Day march which I cannot date precisely, my second political memory I can pinpoint to

December 1970. I was seven and a half. One day my father brought home the newspapers, which were thicker than usual. Inside there were lists of new prices—for everything, from toothpaste and potatoes to toilet paper and tractors—set by the government. A long list of items filled several columns of newsprint. "There will be trouble," my father said. "In the fifties they handled it differently. They would have raised the prices of consumer goods and lowered the price of locomotives and tanks, so that overall, they would have said, prices remained the same."

In those days, our apartment had two rooms. I shared one with my mother. She slept on the bed, and I slept in a nearby cot, which I later destroyed by jumping onto it from the top of the piano. My father stayed in the other room and every night he fell asleep listening to Radio Free Europe. From my cot, I could hear the sound of voices fading in and out through the thudding, repetitive noise of frequency jamming. It was said that one frequency was always left clear so that a transcript could be prepared for members of the Communist Party's central committee. But it was difficult to tune in to that frequency. Our primitive radio was little more than a large wooden box, an achievement of socialist technology from the days before transistors.

Shortly after the price increases appeared in the newspapers, I became aware that bad news was coming on Radio Free Europe. My father was trying very hard to tune to it—much harder than usual. When we could hear it, the Polish news readers in Munich spoke of riots, people dying in the shipyards of Gdańsk. For several days, the official media wrote nothing about it—and then suddenly the news appeared on our television (another wooden box): black-and-white pictures of rioting, people looting shops. But you could see that the local party committee building was on fire, that soldiers were shooting. When we tried to call my father's brother in Gdańsk, we found that the telephones were cut off.

The crisis continued. Władysław Gomułka, the Communist Party leader, resigned "on grounds of health." After Christmas, Edward Gierek, the new leader, made an address to the nation. I said to my father that there would be a lot of work for photographers. Portraits of the leader hung in classrooms, offices, everywhere one went. Now there would have to be new ones. My father laughed when I asked how long it would take to make all the replacements.

But Radio Free Europe—hard to tune in to, difficult to hear, vital to my father nevertheless—was only one of many sources of information which came into direct conflict with what was taught at my school and in the official media. Nobody ever gave me political lectures; nobody ever encouraged me to take to the underground, to print illegal newspapers, or to agitate against the government. But in various ways, different members of my family and different aspects of our lives made it clear to me, even at a very early age, that life did not end with the state, the schoolteachers, and the newspapers.

My favorite relative was and is my uncle Klemens, my father's elder brother, a master gunsmith in Gdańsk. We only visited him a couple of times a year but each time was a treat. His workshop was on Mariacka Street, the prettiest in Gdańsk, a stone's throw away from the medieval cathedral and town hall. Houses which could have been in Amsterdam with carved and gilt facades still hinted that Gdańsk was once as wealthy as Venice. My uncle's workshop was on the ground floor of one such merchant house, with a forecourt and a stone stairway. His forecourt was defended by two iron cannon; two halberds framed the door. Inside, walls were covered from top to bottom with hunting knives, pistols, swords, powder horns, bugles, antlers, shotguns, and rapiers. The smell was of hides, oils, metal shavings, and polishing paste. After winning several heroic battles with the local bureaucracy, Uncle Klemens dug deep under the house and arranged a small shooting range. A little stairway with antler banisters led to a cavern where I helped my cousins keep up a steady cannonade with air guns.

During the decades when it was chic to replace wood furniture with varnished plywood, my uncle collected unfashionable old junk. His apartment was filled with oak credenzas and tables, traditional Gdańsk furniture stained black. Crossed swords hung on Oriental carpets on the walls. Hand-beaten tin plates and jugs lined the shelves. In the cellars, he kept odds and ends: sabers, military drums, bits of statues, raw cattle horns, millstones. He had moved to Gdańsk just after the war, when the city still lay in ruins. Like its sister Baltic port of Königsberg, the Soviets had needlessly shelled and stormed Gdańsk in the spring of 1945 when the battle for Berlin was already raging. Unlike Königsberg, however, Gdańsk was not being razed, but rebuilt, and my uncle accumulated his collection mostly on his walks between his home and his workshop across the old town. The canals were being dredged and the workers often fished things out. My uncle would offer them a bottle of vodka for a medieval baptismal plate, a silver spoon, or a coin. What the workers did not know was that when Gdańsk burned and the Germans were taking the last ships out, they threw their most valuable metal antiques through the windows into the canals, hoping to recover them on their return.

Each object came alive in Uncle Klemens's hands. From their markings, he could tell from which Gdańsk workshop, sometimes from which craftsman, it had come. A scratch was enough for him to deduce or invent its entire history. "Craftsmanship!" he railed. "That was what made this city rich once, but now all they can do is talk." Uncle Klemens must have been good at his job because huntsmen flocked to his workshop from all over Poland. His hunting stories kept the whole company transfixed, even when we knew that they were vastly exaggerated.

The extent of Uncle Klemens's political interests was Gdańsk old town. Instead of displaying amber for tourists, he argued, the forecourts should resound with craftsmen banging metal and scraping wood. He helped to revive an ancient rifle fraternity, lobbied the authorities to reopen the arsenal, and was always on hand to parade in a traditional gentry *kontusz* during the summer Dominican Fair. Only when asked would he talk about how larger politics had interfered with his life. He served in the army for twenty years, organizing workshops and training gunsmiths. Most officers were Communist Party members but he belonged to the small percentage who did not join and got away with it—specialists were hard to replace. The 1968 Communist Party purge is best known for the wave of anti-Semitic hysteria which one wing of the party whipped up to get rid of the other, but other undesirables were targeted as well. Uncle Klemens was given the choice to sign up for the Party or quit—he left the profession he loved a year before he was eligible for an army pension. Relatives remonstrated with him to hold his tongue, and be more realistic. It did not help. A few years later, after he dared to protest at Party bosses shooting deer from helicopters in his district, he was deposed as master of the hunt. The two blows did not make Uncle Klemens into a dissident. He just opted out of Communist Poland and confined his ambitions to the workshop and the antiques collection. He is the best example I have that you could live under Communism and keep a clear conscience.

Another uncle, my great-uncle Stefan, fought in the victorious Polish-Bolshevik war of 1920. Uncle Stefan had first marched with

Józef Piłsudski, Poland's great military commander, all the way to Kiev. Later, when the Red Army invaded Poland, and tried to set it up as a Soviet republic, Uncle Stefan had fought near Warsaw. He never said much about it, but the very fact that he had been engaged in a war against the Red Army—and spoke about it with pride—made it hard for me to assume, as I was taught in school, that the Red Army was a Polish child's best friend.

My childhood also coincided with Communist Poland's period of unusual prosperity. Policies such as allowing millions of people to travel to the West were meant as a safety valve through which frustrations could be discharged. Edward Gierek, the Communist Party leader in the 1970s, miscalculated when he thought that in return grateful citizens would grant him social peace and a measure of legitimacy. Eventually, the artificial boom of the early 1970s turned into a bust of the late 1970s and a wave of bloody riots swept him from power. Today free Poland is still rolling over the credits which clever Western bankers granted by the billion on the assumption that a socialist economy is as much or more creditworthy than a capitalist one because planners can always arbitrarily allocate resources to debt servicing.

However, thanks to Edward Gierek's easygoing recklessness, my generation enjoyed something akin to a normal Western youth. Gone were the days when jazz was banned as a dangerous bourgeois corruption: Marlboro cigarettes and Coca-Cola appeared in the shops. If you had hard currency, you could even buy the dream of dreams: real blue jeans. My parents both worked in state architectural firms, earning well above the average, but their monthly salaries, when exchanged into hard currency on the black market, still amounted to no more than several dollars. Hence, every Western object acquired the status of a relic, as in one of those cargo cults where simple-minded natives worship pieces of rubbish thrown away from ships and washed up on the shore. A pair of jeans was a gift one could dream of getting at Christmas. For several months I was the object of universal envy for being the first in the school to own an electronic watch—a primitive job half an inch thick, which one had to press hard to display the digits. To this day I have a fascination for frivolous Western gadgets and will happily spend money on flip-flops with lights in them or a talking toothbrush.

We held parties at which it was the height of cool to drink genuine vermouth. Each Pink Floyd album—worth a couple of average monthly wages—was welcomed like a piece of the True Cross. We learned English by translating the texts on the jacket and thought we felt the same angst. Only later was I to discover that the anxiety of our Western contemporaries was in fact the opposite of our own: they were fed up and bored with consumerism while we craved and wallowed in its meanest manifestations. I remember my sixteenth birthday party; my parents coolly went away for the weekend, leaving me the keys; dark room, couples dancing on the parquet floor rubbing their hips to the sounds of "Dark Side of the Moon," their faces flickering in the candlelight; me on the sofa, timidly putting my arm around Beata, a blonde I had been courting all term, a glass of vermouth in the other hand, thinking to myself with self-satisfaction: "How Western, how sophisticated!"

Even more subversive than vermouth and Pink Floyd was our ability, alone in the Soviet bloc, to travel to the West. The difficult bit was procuring the hard currency. Each Polish family could apply once a year for an allocation of dollars exchangeable at a rate higher than the fictitious official one but lower than the black market one. Each spring we waited anxiously to know what our vacations would be: a month under foreign sun, or getting drenched at a campsite by a Pomeranian lake. It was a time of fearful soul searching. Has someone informed on my father for telling political jokes? Maybe "they" have run out of dollars and the number of allocations would be drastically reduced? Or perhaps "they" will punish my parents for nonattendance at the last general elections? The authorities deliberately spread the rumor that political compliance was closely related to the likelihood of being favored with a hard currency allocation and this was probably the main reason for most professional families' compliance with the official rituals.

The days each spring on which the letters granting the allocation arrived were the happiest moments of my childhood. My parents and I would reach for atlases and road maps, and plan the summer itinerary down to each day. In those days "the West" to us meant any non-Communist country. We usually chose Turkey or Greece. Those destinations made sense because we could drive to their very borders through the Soviet Union, Romania, and Bulgaria fueled on cheap, socialist gasoline. Most important, however, both countries offered the possibility that far from spending our allocation, we could hope to trade our way through the vacation and bring some of the precious dollars back.

Before the day of departure, the whole family called in old favors to collect a suitable trading stock. My parents were embarrassed, but my commercial instincts blossomed. As the vacation approached, a heap of goods rose on our kitchen floor. In Turkey itself, the grapevine had it, Polish electrical appliances such as mixers, irons, and vacuum cleaners were in demand. I also bought several pieces of Polish-made cut crystal: ashtrays, vases, sugar bowls. At customs one could claim, however implausibly, that the former were a part of our camping equipment whereas the latter were presents for dear friends whom we were visiting in Turkey. (As with so many things under socialism, normal border rules were reversed. Customs officials tried to prevent goods from being taken *out* of the country, rather than smuggled in.) It was even more profitable to take goods which could be sold in the Soviet Union: chewing gum, nail polish, perfume, jeans, bed covers, and, for some reason, wigs. Just like us, the Soviets craved anything that was suggestive of consumerism, except that for them Gierek's Poland was already one foot in paradise. On the other hand, Soviet shops were still stocked with items in demand in Turkey and things we did not have in Poland: cameras, car accessories, and, in particular, perfectly decent DIY tools. One could also try to smuggle rubles out of the Soviet Union (a heinous crime, punished by the confiscation of the sums involved and the smuggling instrument—the family car) so as to exchange them later into Bulgarian leva, which were in demand in Turkey from sheepskin merchants. To minimize our travel costs, we also took kilos of dry sausage, dozens of packets of pureed potatoes, boxes of canned soups and vegetables; all this in addition to the essentials: tents, mattresses, portable gas stoves, and spare car parts. My father would spend a couple of weekends trial-packing everything into the trunk, onto the top rack, and into the back seat of our Polski Fiat 125. I inevitably ended up with just a little cavity on the back seat with a tent pole or a spare spring poking into my side.

For the sake of company, and for mutual assistance with inevitable car breakdowns, we always traveled in groups of three or four families, each car weighed down on its suspension from the load of our wares. The first shock was the Polish-Soviet border at Medyka. After a cursory examination by Polish customs—who might at most confiscate for themselves a crystal bowl or a vacuum cleaner—the cars entered a no-man's-land on the Soviet side delimited by watchtowers and a barbed-wire fence. It was not quite the "border that united" which I had read about in school textbooks and newspapers. The queue always lasted several hours, sometimes days. The crossing was often closed without warning and there was nothing for it but to swear and wait. There were no shops, no cafés, and no toilets—just a sheer field broken by ditches or clumps of bushes. We slept inside the car, running the engine for warmth.

When we finally made it to the Soviet side, the circus began. Far from being treated like the internationalist brothers and sisters that we officially were, Soviet customs and immigration treated us with the utmost suspicion. The routine was always the same. First, our passports were taken away and disappeared inside the immigration building for some hours. Then each car had to drive onto an inspection ramp and a man with a hammer knocked on each part of the undercarriage. Another young soldier stuck a long rod inside the fuel tank. We had to unpack all our luggage so that the customs men could make sure there was no spy secreted inside the seats. Often, they asked for little presents: my father's yellow-tinted driving glasses or a pack of razor blades. Alienating one of them could have meant having the car subjected to a special search which involved almost total dismantling—with the reassembly left up to the owners. We learned to leave small items from my trading stock lying invitingly on the dashboard. They invariably disappeared.

Sometimes there were tense moments. One year we traveled with a color picture of the Pope stuck behind the windshield—put there by my father shortly after his election out of patriotic bravado.

"Who is this?" asked a customs officer, pointing at the figure in white with a hand raised in benediction.

"That?" My father suddenly remembered that our customs declaration stated categorically that it was forbidden to bring any religious objects into the Soviet Union. "That is one of our generals." He smiled weakly.

"A general?" The soldier gave my father a searching look.

"Actually, an admiral, the commander of our Baltic fleet," said my father, keeping a straight face.

"I see. He has a very smart uniform."

The road through the Soviet Union was lined with tall trees—probably to protect the surface from blizzards—but everyone was convinced that it was to block the view, so motorists could not see that fields lay fallow. We could only follow the prescribed route over which sinister-looking concrete watchtowers rose up by every major crossroads. We could see that the policemen in them wrote down each foreign car's registration number. Straying was inadvisable. A patrol car or a policeman would soon stop us and long arguments would ensue.

The route took us through Lwów, once an easternmost outpost of Austro-Hungary, which had belonged to Poland until 1773 and between the world wars. At school, history teachers had told us that the Soviet Union was justified in taking it in September 1939. Lwów and all of eastern Poland were, we were taught, ancient Russian lands (no one mentioned Ukraine) and the Soviet Union merely moved in to protect its people from the Germans. In fact, like most border disputes in mixed areas, the issue was very complicated. While the countryside was predominantly Ukrainian, Lwów itself had spoken mostly Polish for centuries. Every Polish child knew that it was in the Lwów cathedral that our unlucky King Casimir pledged to better the lot of the peasants after they helped him regain his throne from the Swedish "deluge" of 1655. And now, even under Soviet rule, the city hardly looked Russian. Two stone lions, celebrated in Polish songs, still stood at the entrance to its neoclassical town hall. The town hall square was Renaissance, with a house that once belonged to John III, the deliverer of Vienna. The lion of St. Mark still guarded the porch of another one, probably once the Venetian consulate, a relic of Lwów's commanding position on one of the trade routes to Asia. We laid flowers on the steps of a large monument to the poet Adam Mickiewicz. It did not seem odd to me that a man born in today's Belarus, claimed as a Jew by the *Encyclopedia Judaica,* whose most famous poem, written in Paris, began in Polish with the sentence "Lithuania, my Fatherland, you are like health," should have had a statue built in his honor in what is now a Ukrainian city when it was part of the Austro-Hungarian empire.

We also examined the statue of Lenin at the other end of the same square. The monument was supposed to have been made out of fragments of a statue of the Virgin Mary and, if you looked closely, you were supposed to see the lilies on the Virgin's robe appear from underneath Lenin's coat. I looked hard but just could not see it. (Years later, in

1991, I had the satisfaction of seeing Lenin removed from the square and the tale—with an odd twist—received a sort of confirmation. The pediment on which the statue stood turned out to have been made of gravestones from a Jewish cemetery.)

In Lwów, the buildings themselves contradicted official history. The facade of the Jesuit monastery contained a large coat of arms of the Old Commonwealth—the Polish eagle and the Lithuanian knight in chase. Polish names peeped out from underneath peeling plaster on Jugenstil department stores. A half-rusted plaque with the house number and Polish street name Kanonia remained in Rosa Luxemburg Street, probably because slothful Soviet workers could not be bothered to remove it—it had been placed too high for ladders to reach. Hearing us speaking Polish in the street, old men would often greet us and drag us inside a porch for a surreptitious conversation. They were people who had missed the boat and did not leave for Poland in the official ethnic cleansing of the 1940s and 1950s. "Do you have any Polish stamps?" one of the old men once asked me. He was white-haired, stooped, and looked at me, barely a teenager, with solicitous humility. "I just want to have something that comes from Poland." There was a religious reverence in the way he pronounced "Poland."

The official lie in Lwów's case was particularly blatant because Lwów, unlike most of eastern Poland, had never belonged to Russia, not even during Poland's nineteenth-century partitions. It had medieval city walls, Renaissance, Baroque, and neoclassical churches, and an Armenian cathedral with a cemetery of Armenian nobles with Polish coats of arms. A sumptuous Uniate basilica looked down at the city from a hill. A square remained empty where the synagogue used to stand. Lwów had always been rich, from trade in the Middle Ages, and in the nineteenth century as the center of a minor oil boom. It had an American consulate, a fashionable hotel (The George—run by a Frenchman), and an opera house which was a scale model of La Scala. Its streets still evoked a fiercely bourgeois spirit. Closing my eyes I imagined stately motorcars driving along its cobbled streets, women promenading in fur coats, and men rushing about their affairs in top hats. Opening my eyes, I saw the new Soviet inhabitants who stuck out against the city's architecture, oblivious to its stylish past: earthy faces of peasant women in scarves and stocky men carrying fake leather briefcases.

Lwów's Gothic cathedral was founded by King Casimir the Great, the very one who gave a charter to my native Bydgoszcz. Marble tombs of famous Polish nobles adorned its naves. Frescoes and paintings recalled scenes of the city's heroic past: defense against the Tartars, the sacking by the Swedes. But despite the historic glory, the once great Catholic cathedral was now threatened with closure at the whim of a Soviet bureaucrat. We always visited the cathedral during our journey south, particularly so in 1979, the year following the election of Karol Wojtyła as Pope. After mass I pushed on toward the altar, to a side door in the presbyter which led to the sacristy. I was with Jacek, the son of family friends accompanying us on the trip. We carried a bundle whose existence I only revealed to my parents once we had safely crossed the Soviet border. It could have gotten us into trouble: it contained several hundred pictures of the new Pope. To tell the truth, I had brought them as part of my trading stock and hoped to sell them for a profit. But now, in the cathedral, the only decent thing to do seemed to be to give them away. The sacristy was paneled with wood darkened with age. An old woman, who probably remembered Austro-Hungarian as well as Polish times, sat behind a large desk and wrote in a ledger. She looked up and I laid the box in front of her.

"I brought these from Poland. I thought they might be scarce here. I hope you find use for them."

She looked inside, spread a few of the pictures on the desk and went silent for a long while, her head down. Then she looked up: her face was solemn but her eyes were shining brightly. She was crying. "God has sent you. We have had people coming here from hundreds of kilometers away. They have heard that the Pope has been elected but have not seen his face because the newspapers or television have not shown it. We couldn't give them anything because we didn't have any pictures ourselves. Now we will. Many people will pray for you for a long time."

It was nothing, just doing my duty, I mumbled, and we shuffled away toward the door, moved but embarrassed.

"Panowie!" Her voice was suddenly firm and it brought us up when we were almost in the doorway. We straightened, flattered by being called gentlemen for the first time in our lives. "When will you come back to Lwów?" she asked.

"Probably next year, on our way to Turkey, as usual," I replied.

"I mean, in uniforms, gentlemen. We want you to come back to Lwów in uniforms."

We all assumed that Lwów was now a Soviet city and would be so forever. But Lwów taught me reverence for Poland's past. The tangible experience of a forbidden truth inoculated me against lies. Later, in exile, when I read of the slaughters that had really happened there after the Soviet Army moved in in 1939, I remembered the old man asking me for Polish stamps in Lwów streets and tried to imagine what he must have gone through before he was able to venerate even Communist Poland.

After Lwów, our intermediate destination was usually the same campsite on the Black Sea in southern Bulgaria called Nestinarka. This was the jumping-off point for the journey to Turkey. It had a filthy whitewashed public lavatory which we called "the white house" but compensated for it by being right on a golden, mile-long beach. It was occupied almost exclusively by tourists from other Communist countries: East Germans, Hungarians, and Czechoslovaks—all of whom envied us Poles, the only ones allowed to continue their journey beyond the fraternal frontiers of the Warsaw Pact. On each side, the beach was bounded by volcanic crags which formed secluded little enclaves. These were occupied by nudists. Some were no doubt local gigolos in search of foreign trade but most of them seemed to be German families—from wrinkled grandmothers to puffy granddaughters—baring themselves unself-consciously, wind-surfing and snorkeling. Poles were timid. At most, the women bared their breasts to the sun, which they quickly covered up when they heard the sound of teenagers commenting on them in their own language.

The reality of Bulgaria sometimes intruded upon our holidays. On one expedition to the crags a couple of friends and I walked further than usual, until the beaches were empty of even the most privacy-conscious nudists. A large stone barn built on top of a rocky promontory which jutted into the sea in the distance intrigued us. It was almost dark by the time we were climbing up a steep path to the barn, grabbing lumps of pumice in the rock. The building was of indeterminate age, made of the same rock on which it stood. A heavy wooden door was secured with a rusted iron chain. We fiddled with the door and the chain gave enough so that, as we were slender, we could sneak in through a hole at the bottom. Inside, it was dark; only two shafts of light came through slits high up near the ceiling. Before our eyes adjusted, I stumbled on a heavy piece of wood on the floor. Suddenly gold appeared. Large circles, ovals, and squares glowed on the walls and gold bars lay on the floor. Slowly, as our eyes saw more, pink faces appeared inside the gilt frames. "It's a church," someone whispered. We suddenly felt frightened and stood motionless in our swimming trunks and bare feet, gaping at the awesome sight around us. It had been desecrated. The piece of wood over which I had stumbled turned out to be a broken bench. The gold bars were in fact hacked off pieces of altars jumbled on the floor with other bits of church furniture. Most of the paintings were torn or slashed, probably with bayonets. The largest, on the ceiling, a huge Christ with a halo, holding a sword, had a neat row of bullet holes gashed across his Byzantine face. When our first astonishment subsided, one of us said that we should look for icons.

For a brief moment, we imagined ourselves like Tom Sawyer and Huck Finn, bearing treasures back to the campsite. But the call was weak. The sight inspired terror rather than exhilaration. We skulked off and stayed somber all the way back. We returned to our supper well after dark to an angry reception from our parents. We tried to pacify them by saying that they should come with us to the church the next day. Perhaps the paintings were some lost masterpieces whose discovery would make us famous. But the grown-ups had different ideas. We all got a stern earful and that side of the beach was proclaimed out of bounds for the rest of our stay.

In Istanbul, we struck our tents on a large field at the foot of one of the outer Roman walls, like a besieging army. The campsite office displayed a large sign, in Polish, stating that trading was forbidden in the grounds, but nobody seemed to take any notice. A constant stream of visitors came through, demanding to see our wares. Streetwise as we gradually became, we knew that it was better to go to the bazaar ourselves rather than deal with such small-time intermediaries.

We did the sights such as St. Sophia's, the Blue Mosque, and the underground Roman water reservoir but what excited me was the sight of a NATO army base in one of the suburbs. We took a wrong turn and, by accident, drove inside an army barracks. Suddenly, we were driving along rows of American tanks. We stopped apprehensively, expecting to be arrested or at least questioned. Instead, a black soldier—the first black man I'd seen in real life—opened his mouth in a warm smile. Encouraged, I got out and insisted on photographs of myself with him against a tank. The grown-ups wondered for a long time how the West expected to win the Cold War with security like that.

The high point of the trip was the visit to the bazaar. This was what decided whether we would make a couple of hundred dollars on the holiday, break even, or lose a couple of hundred—which was the difference between having savings for next year's vacation and my parents saving up for the entire coming year to make up the shortfall. For amateurs such as we were, our paltry stock represented all we had, so security was tight. Not only were our crystal bowls, electric appliances, or wallets liable to be stolen but, as several friendly traders warned my parents, there were places deep inside Asia Minor where there was still demand for blondish boys like me. "Hold his hand all the time," they said.

The shops which bartered goods from Poland were easily recognizable because their windows were adorned with fake notes of recommendation from Poland's famous soccer players. Those were the days when our national soccer eleven was at the peak of its performance. The authorities offered the players rich inducements—Poland was rife with rumors that players were given Fiats for each successful game! The idea seems to have been that if people's attention was on soccer, their minds were off shortages and politics. Perhaps thanks to such a capitalist approach, Polish elevens did well, qualifying to the top games in the World Cup and winning medals at the Olympics. As a result, each conversation in Turkey started with a recitation of the names of famous Polish soccer players:

"Lubański—good, yes?"

"No, Gadocha more good."

"Lato, okay?"

"Yes, Lato okay."

In those days, the early and mid-1970s, this trade was a small-time affair—thousands of middle-class families like ours simply trying to supplement their incomes. In the 1980s, it was to become a giant business, with professional traders oscillating between Poland and the eastern markets all the year round. For millions of Polish families, those shops in the bazaar where you exchanged Polish crystal vases and kitchen appliances for hard currency or gold were their first introduction to applied capitalism. In the 1990s the same people, or their children, would be launching the small businesses which are the driving force of our economic boom. But it was back then, in the bazaars of Istanbul and, later, the marketplaces of West Berlin and Vienna, where Poland's popular capitalism was born.

The experience of real existing capitalism helped open cracks in my understanding of real existing socialism. But even more important as an antidote were books, not necessarily smuggled émigré books, but even widely available teenagers' classics. I must have read fifteen times or more our nineteenth-century epic, Henryk Sienkiewicz's *The Trilogy*, which spans the dramatic years 1648–1684, when Poland suddenly lost greatness. Official Poland taught us to identify with a dead ideology, to aspire to things like higher production figures, and to admire boring fanatics. Sienkiewicz taught different values and a different code: courage, honor, gentlemanly conduct. He took my imagination back to a time when Poles, even in adversity, could be confident and proud. In *The Trilogy* the heroes of the wars with the Cossacks, Tartars, and Swedes were flesh and blood: rakish noblemen, faithful retainers, crafty peasants, and virginal women. When I read *The Trilogy* today I see its flaws. Most of Sienkiewicz's characters are simplistic, superficial, and unlikely—in fact, deeply immature. We know all along, for example, that Pan Zagłoba, the fat, buffoonish nobleman, a Harry Flashman thirty years on, really has a heart of gold, will remain loyal to his friends, and will come out on top in every crisis. On the other hand, Jan Skrzetuski, severe and unbending like a Roman, never strays from the path of virtue and would therefore be reunited with the bride he had counted for dead. Pan Wołodyjowski, the little knight and master swordsman, is bound to do the honorable thing and blow himself up in a tower rather than surrender the fortress of Kamieniec Podolski to the invading Turks. My favorite was Andrzej Kmicic, one of the few characters who struggle between vice and virtue. A bit of a bounder, he is tricked into serving the treasonous Prince Janusz Radziwiłł when the Swedes invade in 1655. Kmicic's beautiful fiancée, Oleńka, however, being one of those ridiculously patriotic Sienkiewicz women, would rather end up in a convent than marry a collaborator. Their breach is almost total when she is told, by another renegade aristocrat, that Kmicic had in fact attempted to assassinate the legitimate monarch—this at a time when Kmicic, having returned to the path of virtue, daily risks his life in defense of the Monastery of Jasna Góra, the site of the miraculous Black Madonna icon. They get it together in the end, of course.

The Trilogy, with its old-fashioned patriotism, hardly figured in the school curriculum, but was always widely available (to this day it is Poland's all-time bestseller). To have banned it was about as conceivable as banning Shakespeare in England. In a translation, such as the recent one into English by W. S. Kuniczak, *The Trilogy* reads much like any other historical epic. Had Poland been free when it was written it would have been its answer to Walter Scott. Instead, it's a holy book, a bible of Polish patriotism. Every Polish teenager secretly identifies with one of *The Trilogy*'s heroes, which is why so many soldiers of the wartime underground took their names as pseudonyms. For an idea, or a country, to hold men's loyalties, it must not merely be true or good but also attractive. Communism's dreariness could not compete with the elan of Sienkiewicz's old Poland.

The other nineteenth-century Polish epic, *Pan Tadeusz,* was on the school curriculum. Set in a manor house in Lithuania, it is a tale of minor and major nobles dining, hunting, flirting, quarreling, and plotting. *Pan Tadeusz* ends with Polish volunteers chasing the Russians away and greeting Napoleon as a liberator, something which from the context appeared fortuitous. So, in one class we would be taught about the eternal Polish-Russian friendship, and in the next class we would memorize a poem in which the gallant thing for a Polish noble to do with the Russians is to take to them with their swords. Only a moron could have failed to spot inconsistencies.

A defender of the theories of totalitarianism could justly object that Poland was never fully totalitarian because the Party never eradicated all organized sources of competing authority, most important the Catholic church. In fact, the last two decades of Communist rule in Poland, the 1970s and 1980s, the years of my growing up, might someday be remembered as the golden age of the Polish Catholic church. Communist persecution was no longer so strong as to pose a threat to the church's survival, but real enough to make it seem like a victim, and the one free institution around which people could unite. For me, it was another antidote against the propaganda of official Poland.

To start with, two of my great-uncles were priests. One, Uncle Władek, was the keeper of ancient manuscripts in the library of the Gniezno cathedral: his official title was canon of the Gniezno Archdiocese. Gniezno was the cradle of Polish Christianity, the first capital of Poland; the archbishopric of Gniezno was the oldest in Poland, its very name, derived from *gniazdo* (nest), touching an ancient reverence. The library where my uncle worked sprawled all over the vaulting above the cathedral nave. When I came to visit, my uncle would take his enormous iron key ring and open the narrow doors into the crooked rooms, to show me what was there. We walked on narrow pathways over the vaults of the cathedral below us. I remember illuminated vellum manuscripts in leather bindings stacked neatly on shelves in the gloom; sheets of medieval church music; prewar parish records; books of sermons; foreign works of theology. My uncle would complain that for every zloty spent on restoration, the Gniezno library had to pay a zloty and a half to the state in taxes. As a result, much of the collection was deteriorating, which to me seemed a great pity.

After visiting the library, we would go back to the church compound where he lived. The buildings were not old—I suppose they were prewar—but their style was traditional: sloping roofs, red tile, stucco walls, very different from the sort of building which the Communists taught us to admire. We would have our midday dinner in the compound dining room, where we sat beneath a holy picture, on tables covered with white cloth. The nuns, smiling merrily beneath their wimples, brought us watery soup and overcooked dumplings, and we said prayers before and after eating.

After dinner, we repaired to my uncle's flat. His rooms were neat and small, furnished with prewar, solid wood furniture. The nuns living in the building kept them very clean. My uncle made tea, and showed me family photograph albums. There were pictures of my grandmother before the war, in a long fur coat and a hat; pictures of himself at the seminary, wearing long robes, surrounded by other smiling young men; even pictures of himself in Germany, during the war. He had been brought there as a slave laborer, but was well treated, and spent much of the war in a university library. In the pictures, people's faces looked different. They were livelier and happier than the faces one saw on the street in Bydgoszcz.

Later, my Uncle Władek was entrusted to transcribe Cardinal Wyszyński's memoirs from manuscript. Cardinal Wyszyński, who died in 1981, had been imprisoned by the Communists in the 1950s and after his release presided over the Catholic church's campaign of quiet resistance. My uncle carried out the transcription work with the aid of two nuns. All were sworn to secrecy. The diaries will only be revealed in the year 2011, thirty years after Wyszyński's death.

Uncle Władek's brother, Uncle Roman, was an energetic parish priest in the town of Inowrocław. Over twenty years, he persuaded half the town to help him restore Inowrocław's Romanesque church, which had been a ruin since the Middle Ages. My father, an incorrigible religious skeptic, helped to design the heating system for the church for free, "just to spite the Commies," as he put it. I often visited Uncle Roman with my grandmother and we stayed in the rectory, looked after by his housekeeper. In the morning, my uncle disappeared early to prepare for mass. We would next see him standing on the altar of the large, nineteenth-century church in the center of town, cloaked in silk-embroidered vestments. Afterward we would visit the Romanesque church, then under restoration. Over the vestry entrance of the ancient church, devilish faces, complete with horns, were carved in the granite; one of them looked like my teacher Skarpeta, the Sock.

As for my father, he had been an altar boy before the war but lost his faith, apparently after he witnessed a priest appropriating money donated by the faithful during mass. On Sundays he preferred to go fishing, on one of the lakes that dot the countryside around Bydgoszcz. My religious education was largely carried out by my grandmother. She taught me to cross myself and I woke up and went to bed with a prayer to my guardian angel. While my father struggled with pike or carp, my grandmother and I often stayed behind and joined the long lines of the faithful going to mass.

Our parish church was the Bydgoszcz basilica, started before the war with donations from Poles in America and run by missionaries from the order of St. Vincent de Paul. Its vast dome, topped by a cross, was visible for miles around. It accommodated thousands of people at any time; each mass attracted hundreds of families, who walked toward it in droves from all directions in their Sunday best. While the men pushed baby carriages, the women, with solemn faces, discreetly searched the crowds to see if any friends and acquaintances were noticing their presence and their neat appearance or new clothes. It always seemed as if the whole city had come together. You would think that the country was in the midst of a religious revival rather than living under Communism. Although there was plenty of space for everyone to come to the main services in mid-morning, mass was also said at outlandishly early hours, 5:30 or 6:00. Those masses were, my grandmother pronounced, for Communist Party members who wanted to avoid being noticed.

Early in the morning they could attend discreetly, lurking behind a pillar in the empty church.

Although the basilica was very large—two multistory wings spread from the colonnaded porch—the outside walls were unplastered brick and the inside was austere, with a whitewashed cupola and a rude concrete floor. Giant plaster saints sheltered underneath arches in the round nave. My grandmother particularly favored St. Jude, the patron of lost causes; and I spent many hours saying the rosary beside it. My conscience struggled with my greed as I dropped coins of my pocket money—earned the hard way, taking deposit bottles to a refund kiosk—into a dark wooden box by the side of his altar.

While the school tried to brainwash me, I was taught traditional moral values at catechism classes after hours. It took a solid half hour to walk to the basilica, and we were squeezed to capacity in small rooms—but we did not resent it. Catechism was something we were doing in spite of our schoolteachers, and it gave us a delicious feeling of contrariness. We waited patiently in the corridor on the fourth or fifth floor of one of the basilica's wings, until a priest or a nun let us take our places behind old-fashioned wooden desks. We were told biblical stories, but we never actually read the Bible itself. We also memorized the catechism, a children's variant of the grown-up version written in the 1590s, wrapped in a blue cover. On only one occasion do I remember being intellectually stimulated by what was being said. Our priest, whom we called "Alcoholic" on account of his unnaturally red cheeks, taught us proofs for the existence of God which were meant to steel us against the Darwinian nonsense we were told at school. He was particularly keen on the argument from design (the argument, that is, that the world is so complex that it must have been designed). On that occasion, Alcoholic added a clinching proof of his own. "Look," he said enthusiastically, standing up straight and spreading out his arms, "God sends us proof of his existence even in the very shape of our bodies," and he swept the class with a triumphant eye. "Remember that your very body is shaped like the cross!"

At the age of ten, like most of my friends, I took First Communion, for which I had my first suit made. We were taught which sins were major and disbarred one from taking Communion, and which were venal, and could be forgiven without revisiting the confessional. A week or so before the great day, we queued on both sides of a wooden neo-Baroque confessional. It had niches on both sides of the priest's cubicle so that while the person on one side said his contrition and final prayers, the priest was already listening to another litany of sins on the other side. Even though writing down one's sins was frowned upon as equivalent to cribbing, we reckoned that the confession was anonymous and that even if we chanced on one of our teacher-priests, he could not tell one whisper from another.

So, like everyone else, I prepared for my first visit by writing down my misdemeanors on a sheet of paper, adding all the formulas just in case my memory failed me. I clutched it inside my pocket all the way to the church, horrified lest it should fall out and be found by one of my classmates who could probably identify my handwriting. Would God forgive me for smoking cigarettes during a long break in the school lavatory? And what about several instances of truancy? If only God would let me have a fresh start, I would be good from now on! I really wanted to become a reformed character. I heard a knock on the wooden wall of the confessional, and Latin phrases being whispered on my behalf. After a gentle admonition I heard my penance. I rose up on trembling feet and staggered out so overcome with bliss and repentance that I almost forgot to pick up the piece of paper lying on the shelf of the priest's cubicle, which was my certificate of eligibility for the First Communion ceremony. I imagine that a good confession cleanses the mind better than months of psychoanalysis.

The ceremony was a spectacular occasion. Lines of us—boys in identical suits and girls in white dresses, each holding a large candle—sailed to the balustrade like a troop of dancers in a vast ballet production. On the way home, I struggled with innocent impure thoughts.

Most people dropped out of religious education at secondary school but I continued of my own volition. While our contemporaries in the West rebelled by joining anarchist groups or sampling dope, we rebelled by going on pilgrimages, building street altars for the Corpus Christi procession, or helping to tidy up a chapel. At another solemn ceremony I stood in a long line of youths while a bishop wearing a pointy hat and carrying a crozier confirmed me by rubbing holy oil into my temple. I also attended the standard premarital counseling, entirely theoretical for me at that stage, at which we were taught, among other useful things, that if one has quarreled with one's spouse, one should never go to sleep without making up. The teaching of contraception, however, could not have been very good, either at school or in the church, for when I arrived in England at the age of eighteen and first heard the term "rhythm method," I naturally assumed it consisted in catching the right rhythm during lovemaking.

The Church always had an upper hand in the struggle for my soul. Where the schoolteachers who tried to drum Communism into our heads used abstruse jargon—long words which they themselves barely understood—the priests used traditional Polish, with words that grabbed the heart rather than the brain. Where the teachers taught theories, the priests told human tales, even if of men long dead. The school's lukewarm efforts could not compare with my grandmother's fierce zeal and crafty methods. She stimulated Pavlovian reflexes in me by bestowing her approval—and bars of chocolate, a rare delicacy at the time—after I'd been to confession or performed some prescribed good deed.

One day in 1978 the church's victory in my soul became irreversible. I was in my room, hoping to finish writing my homework in order to be allowed to watch the evening film, when I heard my mother's squeal from the other room. I rushed in and saw my parents glued to our black-and-white television set. Like almost everyone in Poland, they were watching the 7:30 evening news. The announcer, the same one who daily recited the same old lies, was dressed more solemnly than usual and had a bouquet of flowers on the desk in front of him. Normally stony-faced, he seemed to be moved by something. The very slight emotion in his voice was, unmistakably, pride. To this day I wonder whether it was genuine or put on. I still did not know what had happened when the picture switched to Rome, the balcony of St. Peter's, and then to an official clad in vestments above a huge crowd filling the square.

The official announced: "The Pope is elected," and the crowd went silent. He looked at a cue card to read out the name and, twisting his tongue, pronounced, almost correctly: "Karol Wojtyła." The crowd hesitated for a split second—obviously puzzled by the choice—and then exploded into applause and a barrage of camera flashes. A few seconds later the familiar face of the archbishop of Kraków was smiling and blessing the square. My parents, even my father, cried with joy. The phone kept ringing late into the night, with friends and relatives commenting on the glorious news.

It was the next morning, as I stood in the aisle of the No. 52 bus taking me to school, that I felt for the first time the division between "us," the people, and "them," our rulers. "We" were the majority of the people on the normally dreary bus, who were smiling, chatting to strangers, sharing our delight. "They" were a few morose faces on the back seats, those who alighted at a bus stop by the huge white building of the regional headquarters of the secret police.

The next year, the Pope came to Poland and I traveled to see him at an airfield in Gniezno. His white helicopter descended near a crowd of over a million people, elated but perfectly disciplined. Volunteer officers with armbands in the papal white and yellow politely showed us to our sector. Regular police were absent, withdrawn so as not to provoke political demonstrations, yet no incidents of any kind were reported. After the open-air mass the crowd walked several kilometers to Gniezno. Halfway there, my friend Wojtek and I climbed a tree on top of a small ridge. In each direction, the road brimmed over with people as far as the eye could see. We felt the unthreatening power of the crowd. The people who voluntarily came here were more numerous than participants in involuntary May Day parades. We realized for the first time that "we" were more numerous than "them."

Later we stood and cheered on the square in front of the archbishop's palace in Gniezno, waiting for the Pope to come out. A meeting with youth was scheduled; student bands played guitars and sang songs. Suddenly, two men came out onto the balcony: the Pope in white and, in cardinal's crimson, Primate Wyszyński, the man who had preserved the church's independence even in its worst years of persecution in the 1950s. The Pope's face was jolly; one could tell he would have most gladly joined us down below with our guitar playing. Wyszyński was of the prewar school, severe. He stretched out his open palm level with his silk belt and cut through the air in a sideways movement like a Roman emperor. The unruly crowd of teenagers fell silent as if by the touch of a magic wand. I cannot remember what Wyszyński said, but the impression of steely authority emanating from that austere figure is with me to this day.

Later, when we returned home, our parents thought we exaggerated the size of the crowds. Television pictures had showed that the mass was attended exclusively by nuns and old-age pensioners. This time, the lie was particularly inept. Millions of people who might not have given much thought to the official media's manipulation now experienced it firsthand. It was partly from that feeling of millions of people coming peacefully together and feeling their strength that Solidarity grew the very next year.

BYDGOSZCZ,
1981

MY FIRST SEMIPUBLIC EXPRESSION of rebellion was at fourteen. We loved being marched from school to see Soviet war films because it meant we didn't have a mathematics or a history class. Soviet soldiers were always heroic to the point of idiocy while the Germans were denied even the compliment of being efficient. If they won for a time, it was only through sheer evil. Such crudeness jarred. On one occasion, when the lights were out and teachers could not see, I recall that the whole theater burst out into laughter and clapping when a Soviet submarine surfaced into the guns of a German destroyer.

I fought with the teachers, especially our history teacher, Mrs. Hojan, who was the author of the dismissive comment about the London government's reform plans. Most teachers would tell us the official line but hint that the truth was different. Mrs. Hojan, like Skarpeta, was one of the minority who actually believed. We asked her provocative questions, such as who was really responsible for the Katyń massacre of Polish officers (Communists claimed the Germans had done it; in fact, as almost everyone in Poland knew, the culprit was Stalin, who signed the orders, and the Soviet NKVD, who carried them out) or what was in the secret protocols of the Ribbentrop-Molotov pact (which the Communists denied existed and which in fact contained an agreement on the Nazi-Soviet occupation of Poland and the Baltic states). Instead of arguing, she would just dig her heels in and defend the Communist lie. We argued back. She walked with a limp and today I feel ashamed for having been so stubborn. At the time, it seemed as if her disability was like an unfair attempt to win the argument, and it just egged me on. More than once I was ordered out of the classroom when she was on the verge of tears. I thought of Mrs. Hojan years later, in London, when reading a book by Janina Bauman, a survivor of the Warsaw ghetto, who became a Stalinist after the war, and who also sincerely believed that it was the Germans who were responsible for Katyń. I was reviewing her book, published only months before Communism's collapse, in which she restated her faith in German guilt and reminisced about how much she cried when Stalin died. The added twist was that Janina Bauman's own father was among the Katyń victims. Ideological prejudice was enough, it seems, to blind people to reason.

But whereas arguments with Mrs. Hojan were intellectual and she was personally decent, the supervisor of our class, a Mrs. Karpińska, was a different sort. We called her "Blada Jula" (Juliette the Pale) on account of her paper-white, mummy-like face. Unlike Mrs. Hojan or the Sock, Blada Jula did not seem to have convictions. Rather, she was the type who simply supports those in authority. Before the war, she might have belonged to the Catholic Action, and persecuted girls for wearing dresses above the knee. She taught chemistry but it was generally known that, unlike most teachers, she never finished college. During classes, she was inseparable from a yellow-bound notebook filled with chemical formulae, which she frequently looked up. Many a plot was hatched to try to snatch the notebook from her to see how she would fare. The chip on her shoulder about the lack of a degree was assumed to be the source of her insecurity and unpleasantness. Only later did I learn that other teachers tried to avoid her, suspecting she was a secret police informer of the sort found in most institutions in People's Poland. She seemed to hate humanity, particularly us, her students, and found solace in tracking and exposing our misdemeanors.

It was open warfare between her and me. I was now older and more cunning and made it a point of honor to try to get through four years of secondary school without attending a May Day parade. I avoided other official galas on the grounds that my parents were too poor to be able to afford a suit for me, a blatant lie. She summoned my mother to an interview, ostentatiously looked over my mother's clothes, and said: "Well, you skimp on a suit for your only son, but you can obviously afford a sheepskin coat for yourself!" By the time my mother emerged into the corridor, she was crying from anger and humiliation.

My absence at the May Day parade in junior class cost me a mere reprimand but as she got to know me better, and as May Day approached in our second term, her vigilance grew. She checked whether I took part in the official preparations: rehearsing songs, making banners, and learning the Party slogans. I pretended to go along just like everyone else. And then, on the day, I just did not turn up. I went camping by a lake with my parents instead. The next day, Blada Jula's usually pale face was red with fury. The whole class went silent in anticipation of the storm that was about to break. She summoned me to the blackboard, the ironic smirk on her face betraying the pleasure she expected from giving me a drubbing. Coolly, I took out a certificate of medical incapacity for May Day, given to me by our family doctor, Dr. Mierzwiński, who knew exactly to what fraudulent use it would be put. Stunned for a few seconds, she looked at me with even more hatred than before. "Yesterday, you could not get out of bed to attend the march and today you are fully recovered?" She looked around the class as if calling on everyone to testify to the absurdity of the proposition.

"I really wanted to, but the doctor just would not let me. It was an attack of a rare kind of fever." I pointed to Dr. Mierzwiński's long, inscrutable Latin diagnosis. She shouted, ordering me to sit down, but I won the day.

The worst was the third May Day of my secondary school. I did not turn up, as usual, and this time Blada Jula summoned both my parents to the school director's study, which was usually the last warning before expulsion. My parents sat nervously in deep armchairs in front of the director's desk while Jula, standing, recited a long list of my iniquities. Each was discussed in detail, my parents offering weak excuses. Finally, as the clinching argument which confirmed my being a bad egg, she suspended her voice and whispered menacingly: "In fact, we suspect that your son may be anti-Soviet!"

This was no light charge and, as my mother later told it, you could hear a pin drop as Jula eyed them. They looked at the director, and the director looked at Jula. And then, in one of those attacks of reckless-ness to which my father was prone, he looked back at her, irony in his eyes and voice, and replied: "Really? Impossible!"

The interview was at an end. Thirty years before the director might have reached for the telephone and had all of us sent to jail. Now, in 1980, they just let it pass, stunned at my parents' attitude, but resigned. In fact, Blada Jula laid off me after that. If her strongest charge did not work, what else would? Friendly teachers told me that our whole fam-ily now had *żółte papiery* with the school authorities, literally, a yellow file, the color prewar hospitals assigned to mentally ill patients. If one's parents are crazy, it was a waste of one's breath trying to reform the off-spring. And by the time the last May Day of my secondary school career came, in 1981, Solidarity was in full swing. Blada Jula went all quiet, and nobody dared force anyone to go to May Day parades anymore.

By my final year of secondary school, at seventeen, I was a hardened anti-Communist. On September 1, 1980, the ceremony marking the be-ginning of my last academic year at secondary school was as tedious as always: the same Communist slogans on the walls, the same wooden speeches. But in the boys' lavatory, which we called Hades because it lay in a dungeon in the basement, you could feel a changed mood. There were excited whispers.

"Who is this man Wałęsa?" boys asked. "And why did he need such a huge pen?" Television pictures had showed him the night before sign-ing the historic Gdańsk Agreements with a pen in the shape of a huge cigar. We had just come back from vacation. Now we exchanged the bits of information we picked up from official media, foreign broad-casts, and the grapevine.

Outside school, the very streets had changed. Normally, the mood of a crowd in a Communist country was sullen and hostile. Tired, gray people shuffled from shop window to shop window in the hope of hunting down a piece of meat or a roll of toilet paper, treating others as competitors for scarce goods. People vented their frustration and anger with acts of petty rudeness.

But now the crowds were smiling; queues reverberated with chatter. Incredibly, I noticed a driver stop at a zebra crossing and motion pedestrians to go first instead of charging ahead, horn blaring, as usual.

I had experienced that mood briefly before. It was the same glorious feeling of togetherness, of authentic participation in something greater than ourselves, which we had felt twice before: first, when the world's media announced the election of Karol Wojtyła as Pope, and then when the Pope had come to Poland the previous summer.

It was the same everywhere. My parents told me that work had almost stopped. Everybody was talking politics. My father, known for his unorthodox views, became the organizer and was later elected head of the Solidarity branch in his architectural office. My mother traveled to Gdańsk, to the Solidarity headquarters, and brought uncensored newspapers to her co-workers. Then we saw Wałęsa in the flesh. He had a brother in Bydgoszcz, and Wałęsa's rally there was one of his first public appearances outside Gdańsk. The largest hall in the city was full to capacity. Crowds stood outside and listened to the proceedings through loudspeakers.

We came away charmed and impressed. Nobody could repeat what Wałęsa actually said—he spoke ungrammatically, in a proletarian jargon—but what came shining through the blabber was an impression of authenticity. We guessed what he meant because we assumed that his were the same thoughts as ours, long stultified by lies and censorship.

In Bydgoszcz, as in the rest of the country, Solidarity branches sprang up spontaneously in virtually every factory and office. Even the people's militia formed one. Within days, the regional Solidarity headquarters (by the river Brda, in the same building in which my grandmother lived) became a power in the city. Bydgoszcz had two leaders who complemented each other through their opposing characters. Antoni Tokarczuk, the nephew of a patriotic bishop, was stockily built and had a steady temper to match. He was outshone by Jan Rulewski, who became one of the dozen best known national Solidarity figures, with a reputation as a radical. A tall, commanding figure, he had a history of resistance to Communism as early as his army service where, it was said, he had refused to swear an oath of allegiance because it contained an undertaking to defend socialism and the Soviet Union. In an effort to victimize him, the authorities made a fatal mistake in giving him, an engineer, a lowly job at Romet, Poland's biggest manufacturer of bicycles and one of the largest factories in Bydgoszcz. This put Rulewski in touch with the workers, who chose him to lead their revolt. The sixteen months of Solidarity's legal existence in 1980 and 1981 have correctly been described as a "self-limiting revolution"—Wałęsa and his advisers in Gdańsk moderated their demands hoping to work out a coexistence between the free trade union and the Communists. But "our" Rulewski would have none of it. His fierce speeches rang with patriotic rhetoric. In interviews he brushed aside talk of a possible Soviet intervention. The Soviet Union was a paper tiger, he declared. At a rally, he claimed that he would march on Moscow barefoot if need be. Afterward, it was said that the local Communist governor sent him a box with a pair of sneakers.

Needless to say we, the schoolboys, loved "our" Janek. This was my final year of secondary school and I should have been cramming for my *matura,* the final exams, but it was much more fun to hang around the Solidarity headquarters. My English, already good, came in handy and I translated newspaper clippings for the press review in our local Solidarity paper, called *Wolne Związki, Free Trade Unions.*

Several of us from the same school—Wojtek, Stefan, Piotr, Krakus, and others—also started an underground organization, modestly called Związek Wyzwolenia Narodowego, the National Liberation League. Even as underground movements went we were poorly equipped. At first, our only fighting equipment was a printing press which I made myself in my parents' cellar. It was a square wooden bracket on a large stand. You pinned a special permeable plastic sheet in the bracket, and pushed black paint through the perforations in the sheet onto paper underneath. When the paper with the imprint in black had dried out, we put it underneath the bracket again, to be printed again with a new sheet and red paint.

Like every self-respecting underground movement, we had a news bulletin entitled (not very originally) *Orzeł Biały (The White Eagle),* which consisted of two pages of typescript. We held forth about the evils of Communism, the truth about the Katyń massacre of Polish officers, and the perniciousness of Soviet domination. We obtained the stencils at the Solidarity headquarters and a friendly printer ran them off for us in the dead of the night. When the posters and the leaflets were ready, we bought buckets, wide brushes, and glue, and then spent a deliciously exciting night pasting them all over town. Socialist sloth was for once our ally: the streets were dark, lit only with the weak light of poor-quality bulbs, half of them missing. One person pasted glue onto a wall, a shop window display, or a square mailbox, another pressed on the poster, making sure to squeeze out air bubbles from underneath the paper. The poster was then smeared with glue all over, which made it nearly impossible to tear off. We worked swiftly and systematically: one team moving along the May Day Avenue, another in Długa street, a third in Dworcowa.

When it was well past midnight and we had still not been interrupted, we decided to risk the ultimate dare: to stick posters right on the wall of the regional Communist Party headquarters itself. It was an imposing building standing back from a large traffic circle, distant and well lit, but you could approach to within several steps of the front door through a subway which led underneath the traffic circle. We organized our lines of retreat: one team guarded the underground maze itself and one an exit well away from the Party building. Our hearts pounding and our hands shaking, Stefan and I went forward to apply the posters. The plaster on the building was uneven, and the job took longer than usual. I pressed the paper into the sunken surfaces, but it would not stick. Finally, having applied half a bucket of glue, the poster stayed. We rushed back along the secured route, to be greeted with relieved congratulations.

The next day I could not wait for the end of our classes at school, to see the impact we had made in town. Our campaign had been a great success. You could not cross any of the main streets without spotting our leaflets. We must have given the authorities quite an idea of our numbers and sophistication. Now we joined groups reading our texts, pricking our ears for their comments. They were mostly friendly. One or two complained that we had defaced freshly painted facades—something we had overlooked in the dark. One elderly lady, following Stefan's particularly radical text about the presence of Soviet troops in Poland, said, "Those who wrote this have their heads screwed on right."

"Yes, they do." We nodded among ourselves in agreement. "They still do."

Another night we spray-painted graffiti. In fact, after some research behind my father's garage, we chose cans with a bright silver undercarriage anti-rust spray which was much more difficult to paint over. Teams again went into town and the next day the streets proclaimed boldly: *Wolność dla konfederatów* (Freedom for the Confederates—we meant the imprisoned members of the anti-Communist Confederation for Independent Poland) and *Polska dla Polaków,* Poland for Poles. This last might sound chauvinist but that was not the intention. We meant merely that the Soviet Army should pack up and leave us to run our own affairs. More controversially, one team disobeyed orders and painted a series of unauthorized slogans: *Kraj Rad* = *Raj Krat* (The Soviet Union = Prison Bars) and, most appallingly, *Kraj Rad Polskę Zjad* (The Soviet Union has eaten Poland). These slogans rhymed but the last one in particular did so, very badly, and only through a deliberate introduction of a spelling mistake. We had a furious row with the rogue team for bringing the budding underground movement into disrepute. The police spent several days trying to cover the graffiti with thick paint but, sprayed directly on brick, the fluorescent letters always shone through. For years afterward, including during martial law, you could still see the slogans I had painted on the outer wall of my school, my mother reported to me in London. They faded only when the reason for painting them, Communism itself, faded too.

Hanging around the Solidarity headquarters, I gained access to a typewriter (something which, incredible to think now, required permission from the secret police) and wrote my first short story. It was called *Stacz,* "Q-Man," about a professional queuer, and was later published in the Polish émigré press. The *stacz,* a pensioner, made his living by being paid to queue for other people. The idea may seem outlandish but Q-men became quite common in the 1980s. (They appear occasionally even now, in the 1990s, except that now they are paid to queue for shares in privatized companies rather than for meat or soap.) My Q-man one day fails to notice that the shop to whose door he clings at dawn has closed down. The mistake is only discovered several hours later, at opening time, and the crowd behind him grows furious at having wasted the time. Someone stabs an umbrella into his side and an ambulance collects him unconscious from the street. Upon arrival at the hospital he joins a long queue waiting for admission. He dies lying on a gurney wondering whether there really is a hospital at the end of the queue or whether the queue shrinks only thanks to the removal of the corpses.

Grim as it sounds, it was really only an exaggeration of our daily lives. The idea occurred to me after visiting my grandmother in hospital around that time, lying on a stretcher, waiting several days for an operation in a long line of patients along a corridor. My English friends argued with me later that at least under Communism we had free health care.

Almost every month of Solidarity's existence was punctuated by some confrontation with the authorities. Some were no doubt deliberately provoked in order to sap the movement's energy and portray it as militant. Others happened simply because the authorities were only learning how to deal with something they encountered for the first time: an entity they did not control and people who spoke plainly and made demands that had not been cleared in advance. Some of the Party bosses pressed for confrontation, positively longing for a Soviet invasion, which would have given them an opportunity to ascend to power. They still controlled the security services, the army, radio, and television. Having conceded the legal existence of Solidarity, for example, the authorities then dragged their feet in granting it legal registration, provoking a wave of protests and strikes. One printer got hold of a confidential document which outlined how Solidarity was to be undermined and ran off thousands of copies. His arrest again brought the whole country to the boil with strikes and rallies.

In March 1981 Bydgoszcz became the focus of such a confrontation, the biggest during the peaceful Solidarity revolution. Low-level protest action started when several farmers occupied a building near the railway station which belonged to ZSL, the United Peasants' Party (a bogus "ally" of the Communist Party, and in reality its faithful stooge). Like the workers, the farmers set up a genuine organization to represent their interests, which they called Farmers' Solidarity; they intended to occupy the ZSL building until it was granted recognition. The Bydgoszcz Solidarity branch backed their demands and Rulewski joined in the protest. After a few days it looked as if the dispute might be resolved. Rulewski, several of his top associates, and representatives of the striking farmers were invited to a sitting of a regional assembly where their grievances were supposed to be addressed.

On March 19, in the evening, an acquaintance from the Solidarity office phoned me at home saying that something fishy was going on near the building. My father and I drove into the center of town. It was already dark and the streets were emptier than usual but there were noises coming from the square in front of the regional assembly. A loose crowd of a couple of hundred people stood in front of the building and listened to people shouting something from large windows on the first floor. As we approached another noise drowned their voices. A score of blue trucks, their windows protected with metal bars, turned a corner and drove past us. For the first time in my life I saw ZOMO, the riot police. They sat on benches inside the trucks holding truncheons and shields. I tried to catch their gaze but they looked away. The convoy turned the corner but was back again in a few minutes. It kept circling the block, heightening the tension.

The people in the first-floor windows were Solidarity representatives. Every few minutes one of them would look out and tell the crowd what was going on. That afternoon the leaders of the legislature had broken their promise—instead of debating the farmers' demands, they abruptly closed the session. Outraged, Rulewski and his associates, the farmers, and some of the counselors had refused to leave the chamber. The authorities called in the police, plainclothes secret servicemen among them, who threatened to eject them by force. Eventually they reached a compromise: the Solidarity delegation would leave after issuing a joint communiqué with the remaining counselors. When I arrived the communiqué was already being finished and the crisis seemed past its peak.

My father and I thought of going back home but after another quarter of an hour we became aware that nobody had spoken to us from the first-floor window for some time. The front door was locked, and the riot police convoy kept circling round and round. Cut off from news, the crowd began shouting to those inside to open up. We began fidgeting. Then, some people ran up from behind the building, gesticulating wildly, screaming. I saw several people running, carrying something, a body. It was Rulewski's. "The police! It was the police that beat them up!" someone shouted. I rushed into the park behind the building, which I knew well because it bordered on the other side with my school. Two more people were carried past, an old farmer and a young assistant of Rulewski's. In a little courtyard at the back of the assembly building dozens of uniformed and un-uniformed men held some of the Solidarity men and women by the arms. Other activists were still resisting. Curses, the tearing of cloth, and the sounds of fighting pierced the darkness. Some people climbed over the fence; the rest were pushed out through a narrow gate.

People rushed to and fro; someone shouted that we should go to the defense of the Solidarity headquarters. We ran, making the narrow streets echo with the noise of our heels on the cobblestones. The office was not under attack; rather, there were already ambulances waiting to take the three worst-injured men to hospital. They looked terrible. Rulewski's face was smeared in blood, his front teeth missing. Before they were carried into the ambulances the night brightened with camera flashes.

Only later did we hear what had apparently happened. The secret police had made a video recording of their action and under union pressure it was eventually made public. Toward the evening, when Rulewski and the counselors kept dragging their feet in writing their communiqué, the SB (Security Service) major in charge of the operation gave the protesters a fifteen-minute ultimatum to finish and clear out. In the fashion of the day, which was to use Communist turns of phrase to taunt the Communists, Rulewski asked him, "You're not one of those Western policemen who truncheon people at the behest of the bourgeoisie?" The deadline was extended several times and finally the communiqué was completed. And then, just as the text was being read out, minutes before the protesters would presumably leave, the major gave the order to charge. The unexpected attack caused panic. Someone screamed: "Make a circle, women in the middle!" Above the din of boots on the parquet floor and the crash of furniture breaking, people pulling and pushing, the words of the national anthem rose out of the protesters' throats, punctuated by truncheon blows. One of the police ordered, "Get Rulewski!"

The next morning photos of the battered men and reports of what had happened reached Solidarity cells all over Poland. Magnified by rumor that Rulewski had died in the hospital, the news caused fury. It was received as the declaration of war on Solidarity.

The incident has entered history books as *prowokacja bydgoska*, "the Bydgoszcz provocation," the theory being that the authorities deliberately induced the crisis. General Jaruzelski had just been installed as prime minister and had called for ninety days of social peace. If this succeeded, the theory went, the idea of a political compromise between the regime and Solidarity might take hold and this endangered the interests of those who had the most to lose by such a deal: the security apparatus and Party bureaucrats. Egged on by hard-liners in Moscow, they were supposed to have incited the crisis to prove that coexistence between the Communist Party and Solidarity was impossible and sterner measures were needed to bring back order. The theory gained plausibility from the slant of the official media, which taunted Solidarity further with outrageously distorted reports of the incident.

The circumstances were indeed suspicious. Why did the authorities block, in such a provocative manner, the local assembly debate on the farmers' demands? Why did the police attack just as the protesters were ready to withdraw? Why did they beat them up even after removing them from the local assembly chamber, in the corridors and in the courtyard? And why did this happen now, on the very day when the Warsaw Pact began the largest ever maneuvers on Polish soil, codenamed "Soyuz 81"? These were questions that all Poland was asking. The authorities drove even level-headed people to fury when they published a government report about the incident which stated that, yes, on balance, it looked as if the wounds sustained by the Solidarity men "were not self-inflicted." This could not be allowed to pass.

Briefly, Bydgoszcz became the political capital of Poland, as Solidarity's top leaders and advisers, including Wałęsa, descended on the city, trailing the world's media. Soviet bloc media heightened the tension by disseminating reports of Solidarity seizures of post offices and a television transmitter. A confrontation with Solidarity meant a possible Soviet crackdown. A Soviet crackdown meant possible resistance. Resistance meant armed conflict in Europe. How would the West respond? Ronald Reagan had assumed the presidency just a few months before. Anything was possible. We were in the center of an international crisis, with geostrategic implications. Bydgoszcz was on the front pages of newspapers and in TV bulletins around the world.

Throughout, I was in the very eye of the storm, in our local Solidarity headquarters. The building was now guarded by the workers' militia, an uncle of mine among them. As is supposed to be the case with the center of hurricanes, it was relatively quiet. In what I later learned was his political method but at the time regarded as refreshing populism, Wałęsa kept himself aloof from the negotiations with the government commission. While others argued with government delegates in a smoke-filled conference room, he mingled with the crowd of journalists and activists in the corridor. Smoking a pipe, his face jolly despite the air of crisis, his very posture gave us confidence. I lapped up

Wałęsa's every word and translated them to the various Western television teams. After several hours someone brought a huge vat with frankfurters floating in boiling water. Wałęsa got the first fork, I grabbed the second, and we fished for the catch. I was first. Wałęsa smiled and winked.

The government would not come clean, so Solidarity was going to show it what would happen when it assaulted its people. After a stormy meeting of the National Commission in a railway social building, Solidarity decided to hold a four-hour warning strike to be followed, if need be, by an unlimited general strike. So, on Friday, March 27, 1981, just as we were sitting down to our lessons at 8:00 in the morning, we heard sirens sounding all over the city for work to stop. During breaks we walked into town. It was an eerie sight. Not a kiosk was open, not a streetcar or a bus moved. Buildings were draped in the national red-and-white flag, people wore red-and-white arm bands. It was the same all over Poland. By nature unruly, we Poles can be amazingly disciplined in moments of national emergency and this was just such an occasion. By now Solidarity had almost ten million members in a workforce of twelve and a half million. Barring schools, some armaments factories, and emergency services, compliance was almost total. All Poland, from the Silesian coal mines to the Pomeranian shipyards, came to a halt that morning. This proved to be the largest ever strike in the history of the Soviet bloc.

But the government would still not budge, so the union geared up for the unlimited general strike. The mood became tenser still. I helped move our local Solidarity headquarters from the defenseless building by the river to a block at the railway repair yard, where it was protected by a maze of workshops, office blocks, and a cobweb of rails with trains on them. If the tanks came, workers were to weld carriages to the rails to serve as barricades. The railway police, armed with rifles, were already on our side. We set up telexes and ran off strike instructions on duplicating machines. In case of a general strike worker guards were to keep order, making sure that nobody got drunk and nothing was damaged or stolen. In case of the imposition of emergency rule the union was to resist, forming shadow committees to continue the strike if the original committees were arrested. In case of an invasion, we were to offer passive resistance such as changing street signs and signposts. As if to concentrate our minds on the latter option, the nightly television news bulletins showed pictures of Warsaw Pact tanks revving their engines on maneuvers already inside Poland.

In anticipation of the general strike, we geared up for action at school. I was elected president of the Uczniowski Komitet Strajkowy, a Students' Strike Committee, and we walked about the corridors wearing smart identification tags stamped with an official red seal which I personally made out of a large piece of rubber. We sent letters to Parliament and to the Politburo that today sound embarrassingly naive. We demanded the removal from the Party of people who "opposed reforms out of selfishness," "disinform the public," and, worst, "try to create barriers between the government of General Jaruzelski and society." Like most of the country, we were convinced that the incident at the regional council was "a provocation" against the general inspired by hardliners, and we demanded their punishment. Only if our demands were met, we wrote, could the Party hope to regain the public trust.

We were going to occupy the school just in the same way factories and offices were going to be occupied: everyone would bring his or her own sleeping bags and food, and we would live in the school building for as long as it took. We called a meeting of representatives of similar committees from other secondary schools in the city so as to coordinate our actions. We had no idea of what the outcome of the strike should be. Solidarity could not take over the government. We just felt that the Communists should not get away with beating our people. They had to be brought to heel. We were going to show them.

If the Soviets invaded, I decided I would personally fight back. I would have the means thanks to Dr. Józef Mierzwiński. A large man, he reminded me of Pan Zagłoba, the ebullient knight from *The Trilogy*. When in a good mood, he regaled the company with graphic descriptions of gynecological examinations and stories of his exploits in the Warsaw uprising. His father, a well-known Warsaw doctor, was supposed to have knocked out a German tank by hurling a demijohn of methylated spirit from his surgery window. Dr. Mierzwiński had attacked tanks with Molotov cocktails: the number he claimed to his name went up as the evening progressed and as the number of empty bottles increased. He telephoned me on one of these days and, instead of asking for one of my parents as usual, told me to come to his surgery in town, without telling anybody. It was important, he said. When I turned up, in the early afternoon, the patients had already been cleared from the waiting room and he was ready. We were going for a trip outside town. We rattled down the May Day Avenue, driving over the cobblestones in his Fiat, across a railway track and past the red-brick army barracks. We turned left by an imposing building with cannons in front of its porch and armor and spears on top of its gate—the headquarters of the Pomeranian military district. We stopped by another railway track with a pine wood on the other side. We got out of the car—Dr. Mierzwiński carrying his doctor's bag with him—and crossed the track.

On the other side of the track, Dr. Mierzwiński counted several hundred steps into the woods and then stopped. He turned around. "The trees were much smaller when I was here last time, thirty years ago," he said. The garrison, whose exercise ground we could see through the trees, had grown as well and was now only about three hundred yards away. Soldiers were running an obstacle course, watched by guards on a couple of watchtowers in the corners of the compound. Although I still didn't know what we were looking for, I hoped they would take no interest in two civilians strolling in the woods.

After we had traversed a section of the wood several times, Dr. Mierzwiński suddenly gave a yelp of pleasure: there was a sign on a tree which he recognized. He stopped, opened his doctor's bag, and took out a portable shovel. He counted several steps from the tree with the sign and pointed to a spot. We dug alternately. The ground was light, more dirty sand than soil, but hard roots impeded our progress. After ten minutes, when the hole was as deep as my arm, it was obvious that it was the wrong spot. We went back to the tree and counted the steps again, casting furtive looks toward the soldiers.

It was only in the fourth or fifth hole that the shovel hit something hard which was not another root: the sound was metallic. Several energetic digs later, we uncovered a metal box the size of a gasoline can. Blocking the view from the watchtowers with our own bodies, we pulled it up. The box was rusted, and corrosion had bitten into its lid so that earth had seeped inside. Dr. Mierzwiński boldly shoved his hand into the dirt and pulled out what at first I took to be a stick covered with soil and fiber. His face lit up: this was obviously what we had come for. He started cleaning the stick with the bundle of rags from his bag, and soon pale steel began to show from underneath the dirt. It was a gun. I took another quick glance behind me, but there was no apparent danger: the soldiers in the watchtowers continued to watch their friends sweating through the course.

It was a prewar standard-issue Polish Mauser, with the crowned eagle of the 1930s armory deeply etched onto the top of the barrel. The butt was rotten and the steel had begun to corrode, but it was still in working order. Intriguingly, the barrel had been shorn off, as if the weapon had been prepared for use at close quarters. I sifted the dirt inside the can. There was just one cartridge.

Dr. Mierzwiński wrapped the gun in the rags and motioned me to dig again. "There should be more ammunition," he said. "There was a large bottle, sealed with wax, containing armor-piercing cartridges. You will be able to use them to hit cisterns containing fuel." I dug again, but without luck. He racked his memory and measured the distances several times, but every hole drew a blank. After another half an hour, we gave up, tired of digging and worried that the soldiers might in the end take an interest in us.

In the car driving back to Bydgoszcz, Dr. Mierzwiński told me the story of the guns. Although after the defeat of the Warsaw uprising the Home Army which had fought the Germans throughout the war was disbanded, he and a group of friends defied orders and continued to fight in the underground, not against the Germans anymore but against the Communists. His unit attacked Party activists and Soviet NKVD units which had rounded up his comrades from the uprising. Their most daring undertaking, he said, was when they disrupted a May Day march in Bydgoszcz: they had managed to position a machine gun across the street from the honorary tribune and mowed down the assembled Communist dignitaries. But by 1948, three years after the war, they knew the game was up. Most of his colleagues escaped to the West via Czechoslovakia; he, being the youngest and least suspected, stayed. "If the Russians invade, I'll take you to another place, where we hid a sniper rifle and a mortar. Meanwhile, take this. Clean and conserve it. Pour new wax into the barrel, wrap it in oiled cloth, seal it in a plastic container, and hide it again." I took the gun from him as though it were a holy relic.

Over the next few days my parents wondered at my sudden passion for carpentry. It was out of character. The country was on the verge of a general strike, everybody was glued to the television sets for news of the unfolding crisis, while I spent the evenings in my father's workshop in the cellar. I cleaned and oiled the gun until the lock and the pin worked without a fault. I encased it as Dr. Mierzwiński instructed, and Stefan and I hid it in a wood a few hundred yards from my parents' house. If the Soviets invaded, we said, we would gain weapons from the enemy. We could start by holding up a guard with the gun to take away his Kalashnikov.

I wonder if I would have had the courage to use the gun had the Soviets invaded. When martial law was imposed by the Polish Army a few months later, the actual sight of tanks carrying Polish soldiers in the streets, martial music on the radio, uniformed speakers on the television, and news of thousands of arrests cooled heads hotter than mine. And yet, I regarded the Soviets as the ultimate cause of most things that were wrong with Poland: our system, our leaders, the humiliations of our daily lives. Their simplistic propaganda insulted my intelligence. I would have objected to their teenage soldiers, surveying *my* streets with that uncomprehending gaze of theirs, hardly understanding where they were, yet presuming to give us orders.

Fortunately it never came to that. On March 30, a Monday, all Poland watched the 7:30 evening news. Everyone I knew was somehow involved in the strike—my parents in their offices, most of their friends in theirs, an uncle in the workers' militia—and we all wanted to know whether to pack our sleeping bags or not. Even my grandmother had stocked up on bandages and offered her services and her apartment to take care of the wounded. The enthusiasm and the determination of ten million organized people is not something that can easily be broken, even by force. If the news bulletin spouted the usual propaganda, we would have known what to do. It meant that the strike was on. Instead, something extraordinary happened. The cameras trained on Andrzej Gwiazda, one of the top Solidarity leaders, with Wałęsa standing behind him, reading out a communiqué that the strike was suspended. There was no explanation, nothing about fulfilling the union's demands, no instructions, just the message that the action was off. In our apartment block you could almost hear the sigh from hundreds of throats. There was less relief in it than disappointment and anger.

We now know that Wałęsa had been under unbearable pressure to settle. The White House had warned him publicly that an invasion was imminent, and the Kremlin was doing nothing to disabuse him of the idea. His advisers told him the risk was too high. In the end, the church—at moments like this the final repository of the nation's soul—spoke. As has been revealed only in the 1990s, the Pope himself—after some hard bargaining with the Kremlin—gave Wałęsa an order to relent.

It is useless to speculate what might have been. The strike itself would certainly have crippled the country, but what then? Perhaps the regime would have lost its nerve and concessions could have been gained. But the truce could only have been temporary. A party whose ideology and very logic implied total control over society could not tolerate an organization which was a trade union in name but in reality the entire, alternative society. Totalitarianism, as represented by the Communist Party, and democracy, represented by Solidarity, could not exist within the same legal framework for long—as was eventually proved in 1990, when the Communist Party collapsed within a year of sharing power. If Poland had been an independent country, the Bydgoszcz events and the general strike would probably have destroyed the regime and marked the victory of democracy in Poland. It would have been a good, symbolic departure point. As it was, both Solidarity and the Party assumed that the threat of the Soviet invasion hung over us at all times. We could not go all the way, whereas the Communists could wait, wear us down, and regroup to strike later. Sooner or later some other incident would no doubt have been used as a pretext. In December, the regime thought it was sufficient to justify martial law by pointing to a sit-in at a firemen's school and a secret police tape of some wild remarks made by Solidarity activists at a conference.

What is certain is that the Bydgoszcz events were a turning point in the Solidarity revolution. People felt disoriented, betrayed, and appalled by the arbitrariness with which Wałęsa made the decision to suspend the strike. Never again was the union to muster similar enthusiasm and a sense of purpose. Harried by food shortages and more petty confrontations, lacking hope for an auspicious outcome, more and more people turned back to the increasingly difficult struggle to obtain the essentials of their daily lives. In the months to come, Communist intransigence was to drive the activists into militancy and many, perhaps most, ordinary people into apathy, so that when martial law was imposed many greeted it with relief.

The Communists, on the other hand, caught a second breath. The calling off of the strike showed that Solidarity could be beaten even at the peak of its power. We now know that it was at that time that preparations for the imposition of martial law intensified and arrest lists were drawn up. When they were eventually used they were somewhat outdated. When the police interned people in December 1981, they came for several who had died and who had changed their addresses since March.

In May, I passed my *matura,* receiving without examination the top score in English as a reward for reaching the national level of the English secondary school "Olympics." Probably undeservedly, I also received a five, the top mark in the Polish oral examination. I can only ascribe it to shock on the part of the teachers. After I had avoided buying myself a suit so as not to have to participate in all the Communist ceremonies, they suddenly saw me in a black woollen three-piece job made to measure by the best tailor in town.

Five days after the *matura* result came through, I went to London. I had hoped to practice my English and earn some money working in a pub, so as to study English literature in Poland the following year. While in Britain, I heard that some of my fellow conspirators had been arrested in Warsaw distributing our underground bulletin during the trial of Leszek Moczulski, a prominent political prisoner. When martial law was imposed Stefan was arrested, his house searched. The security police even dug up his garden, but Stefan never told them where to look for the gun. Nevertheless the authorities clearly knew what we had been up to. A friend passing through London told me to expect arrest on return. I asked Britain for political asylum, which after a couple of friendly interviews at the home office, was granted.

During the years of exile in Britain I kept in sporadic touch with Jan Rulewski. I publicized his cause as a political prisoner in an Oxford Union debate on the rights and wrongs of martial law. Wałęsa sent us a special address to the trade unionists of the world, read out in his absence by Lord Chapple, a prominent British former union leader.

It was with a sense of pleasant nostalgia that I met Rulewski for a longer chat in Warsaw in spring 1992, in a restaurant across the street from the U.S. embassy. His temperament was still the same but now mellowed by experience: the radical had now transmogrified into one of the more influential, centrist Solidarity MPs. Somewhat incongruously, given that he was older, I was senior in rank as deputy minister of defense. We discussed the possibility of quashing the sentence a military tribunal had imposed on him many years ago for an act of anti-Communist defiance. Some dissidents were now cashing in on the injustices they had suffered by getting compensation from the courts, but Rulewski merely wondered whether it was worth the bother to set the record straight.

Inevitably, we reminisced about the old days, the Bydgoszcz events, and the crisis which affected both our lives so decisively.

"You know that the whole thing was a bit of a misunderstanding, don't you?" he asked.

"Really?" I asked.

"Well, the way we were beaten and so on."

I did not know. What I vividly remembered was what all Poland still remembers: the pictures of Rulewski's bloodstained, toothless face, the video of the police charge, the scream "Women in the middle!" and what I saw myself: people carrying the unconscious Rulewski from the assembly building to the Solidarity headquarters. What had never been properly explained was what happened in the interval between the police forcing the activists out of the assembly room, and the activists appearing roughed up at the back of the building. Like everyone, I had always assumed that he and the others were deliberately beaten up by the police. I myself saw the police and plainclothesmen holding the activists by the arms and expelling them from the compound. Indeed, that was the logic behind calling the events a provocation and mobilizing the country to protest against it. I told him the perceived version I knew.

"It wasn't quite like that," he said, looking more sheepish as he went along. The staircase between the assembly room and the back exit was quite narrow, he explained, and the crowd stampeded, so that some people got injured by being squashed against rails and walls. And then, in the courtyard, Rulewski confronted the secret police major one-to-one.

"He hit me in the face only after I called him 'Ty pierdolony Ubeku' (you fucking secret policeman)," he said. "It was . . . you know . . . sort of . . . private between us." He looked at me to gauge my reaction. The pictures taken that night on the way to the hospital had looked so dramatic, he said, because he had removed his dentures, which made it seem as if all his teeth had been knocked out.

I was glad he still had a bad conscience about almost provoking an invasion of Poland.

PART
II

BYDGOSZCZ,
1939

IN MOST COUNTRIES, the fortunes of country houses rise and fall for a variety of reasons: grain prices and taxes go up or down, families degenerate, fashions change. In Poland, their curse has always been the same as the curse of the country as a whole—geography. If your distant ancestors unwisely chose a defenseless plain for your homeland, and you have belligerent neighbors, then you have three strategic choices: either you become a regional power capable of warding off aggressors, or you play along with one of them to keep out the other, or you get partitioned by both. Until the seventeenth century, the Polish-Lithuanian Commonwealth, which included today's Belarus and Ukraine, was a major regional power, well able to keep at bay a still-barbaric Muscovy and fragmented Germany. Taxes were easy, trade routes secure, and grain prices high, so the country, and country houses, flourished. It was from the mid-seventeenth century onward, when Poland weakened from misgovernment, that the interminable cycle of occupation, partition, and liberation began. Then, in the twentieth century, the wheel of fortune accelerated so much that within one lifetime, say my maternal grandfather's, you could be born in Germany, get married in Poland, bring children up under Germany again, age under Russian domination, and die in free Poland—never having left the same town. Each time a regime changed, troops were on the march, requisitioning, vandalizing, and burning private property. Each time, currencies, trade patterns, and property laws were thrown up in the air. Country houses suffered disproportionately.

It is thanks to a lucky turn of the wheel that I am able to restore Chobielin: I happen to have been born at the right time, a member of the Solidarity generation which saw Poland slip away from Russian domination, and worked to shelter it under the wing of Western institutions. But the awareness of living in a zone of heightened political risks, all of which might have an immediate bearing on my life, has been with me always. To my friends from more secure countries, it smacks of dangerous obsession but I could not help imbibing it from stories told in my childhood at the family table—and especially from stories about the Second World War.

My mother was only five, my father thirteen, when the war ended. Yet, they argued about it over dinner—the grand strategy, the stories of daily life passed on by older relatives—as if it had barely ended. Among family and closest friends, the people with whom one could speak freely, debates raged into the small hours of the morning. The unspoken assumption was that the war and its outcome continued to have a direct impact on our lives. If it had not happened, or if it had ended differently, Poland would not have ended up Communist—and there would not now be a queue at the meat shop, and we would not have to listen to lies on the television. That was why the arguments often had the vehemence of some bitter political dispute. Would the war have broken out had it not been for the Nazi-Soviet pact? Why didn't the French and the British attack Germany from the west in September 1939 as they were supposed to? Could Poland have been freed from the Nazis by the Allies instead of the Red Army if Churchill's plan for an invasion in the Balkans had been put into effect? Was Roosevelt or Churchill more to blame for selling us to Stalin at Yalta? To the lucky inhabitants of countries which have not, in living memory, had their fate determined by others, this sounds like scapegoating or self-pity. For us, it was logic anchored in the most concrete reality.

The war was always somehow present, even during vacations, which we often spent on our favorite Pomeranian lake called Dołgie (literally "Long" in Ukrainian). It was named thus by Ukrainians who lived in former German farms nearby, from which the German farmers had been expelled at the end of the war. Only later did I realize that the Ukrainians must have been expellees themselves, victims of another crime, after the war. Polish Communists had ethnically cleansed them in the 1940s from the southeastern corner of Poland, in an infamous operation, code-named "Vistula," carried out at about the same time that Poles were being expelled from western Ukraine.

My father indulged his obsession with fishing. I was fascinated by things that lurked in the woods along the lake. As far as you could walk, wild strawberries grew in profusion on the slopes of deep ditches that ran parallel to the shore. Every hundred meters the ditches were punctuated with a small concrete bunker, some of which still had heavy steel doors red with rust. Every few bunkers there was a command center with chambers on three or more levels. Some of the bunkers had a whole side missing, with chunks of concrete hanging on steel rods. All looked out of place, submerged in weeds, deep in the woods where once there must have been clear fields of fire. It was the remains of the German-built Pomeranian Wall, the eastern equivalent of the Atlantic Wall. Stalin sent several divisions to their deaths attacking it. The bunkers were superb for playing hide and seek in them and I dug in the ditches for spent cartridges.

My part of Poland is particularly suffused with mementos of the war. Wherever we went by car or on foot, we invariably passed little signs composed of two swords and a flame, which marked graves or execution spots. On the way to our favorite weekend spot, on the lake near Koronowo, thirty kilometers from Bydgoszcz, we passed several: one in Smukała, on the edge of the city, where over eight hundred people were killed in a labor camp. Halfway was Tryszczyn where the Germans shot and buried 1,500. Almost at our destination, another couple of signs marked a place where twelve people were summarily shot in the first weeks of the war in 1939 and where a labor camp was handily established in a former monastery. Most villages around Chobielin also have at least one such commemorative sign. Paterek, three kilometers from the manor, saw 250 people killed in October and November 1939; at Potulice, the prison whose chimneys we can see from the house, 1,200 people died in captivity; Szubin, the capital of our district, saw dozens of Poles and Jews shot.

In Bydgoszcz itself, the signs come so thick that their list looks like the city's street index, except that some streets have several entries. The main street, Gdańska, has three: No. 10, where thirty-three journalists, printers, and librarians were shot; No. 50, where several dozen were shot in the garden; and No. 147, the army barracks, where 204 teachers were kept, most of them later killed. On weekdays during the school term I walked the last few hundred yards to my secondary school through Kochanowski Park, with its bronze statue of a woman archer. On September 5, 1939, the first day of German occupation in Bydgoszcz, fifty secondary school students were shot there.

When I was growing up, I did not quite believe all the stories of German monstrosity. The stories we were fed were repeated so obsessively, on every official occasion, that one felt numbed. Weren't they propagated by the same people and the same media which kept telling us that the Soviet Union was our best ally and protector? If they said so, I thought dimly, perhaps the Germans hadn't been so bad.

But the truth was confirmed by my parents' friends and family. Everyone who lived through the war had a terrible story to tell. My parents' closest friends were the Króls, whose name means "king." I was later to get as far as kissing their daughter Kasia, but we quarreled when she would not go with me to the *studniówka,* the traditional ball which is held a hundred days before the final secondary school exams. Kasia's father, in keeping with his surname, had an air of Roman stoicism about him. A gaunt man, he was never quite well but rarely complained. He could not lift anything and had large off-color scars on his forearm. They were mementos of his stay in a German internment camp. His parents, Kasia's paternal grandparents, were well-off farmers in the village of Buszkowo, north of Bydgoszcz. The village was mixed and when the Germans arrived many of the Poles were executed by a local lake. Kasia's grandfather, who spoke good German and got on well with his German neighbor, was instead pressured into signing the application to become German. This was official policy, proclaimed by Albert Forster, Hitler's governor for our region. In a memo to his underlings he wrote:

As for the Poles of this area, most of whom have German blood in their veins, many will be suitable for Germanization. According to my estimates we are dealing with about 200,000 families. The order I received from the führer last year was to be able to report within ten years that this province is German. Accordingly, the 200,000 families must be Germanized within eight to nine years.

When the Króls demurred, the whole family, parents, two daughters, and three sons (Kasia's father, eleven years old, was the youngest), were locked up in a disused lard factory in Toruń. They camped on the floor of the production halls from which the machinery had been removed. There was overcrowding, dirt, and hunger. In the first week of their stay, a woman gave birth on the straw next to them. For six months, they ate only rutabaga. It was the lack of vitamins which produced the scars on Król's body. There were so many bugs in the place that they dimmed the light coming through the small windows. Young Król was assigned to work at carting corpses to the woods. With a few other children, he pulled wooden carts from the camp gate to a nearby wood where, under the watchful eye of a German guard, they dug a hole in the ground and buried them. Other times they went into the town sweeping streets—but those outings were regarded as special treats because people in the town would often toss a vegetable or another piece of food into the children's dust carts. He survived against high odds.

Measured against the stories of friends and acquaintances, my own family's war experiences were not untypical. On my mother's side they expected war well in advance. My maternal grandfather Kazimierz had come from a family of large leaseholders near the town of Kcynia and met my grandmother at the school in the village of Łochowo, halfway between Chobielin and the outskirts of Bydgoszcz, where he was director (and where his future son-in-law, my father, was something of a black sheep). The school was made of red brick, with large windows, typical of those built by the kaiser in what was then eastern Germany in the second half of the nineteenth century. The Łochowo village church, also red-brick, with its tall, copper-covered spire and a large rectory, was of a standard German Protestant design. Catholics had no church of their own so masses were held at the school by a priest friend of my grandfather's. On several occasions the priest brought along his younger sister Febronia, and the three of them would lunch together by the nearby Bromberger canal. The priest's sister and my grandfather got married in 1935.

It was the priest, my great-uncle Roman, who brought the news about impending war. He was three years older than my grandmother, one of eleven children of a master tailor from the town of Pleszew (in another part of Wielkopolska). They were poor but well brought up. They grew up in the pre–World War One atmosphere of resistance to *kulturkampf*—the German attempt to eradicate Polish aspirations. The soul of the Polish community was an energetic priest, a father Kazimierz Niesiołowski, who organized Polish scouting groups, Polish allotment associations, a Polish library, and Polish language and history classes at private homes. Nationalism—it is often now forgotten—was once a liberal, progressive idea. My great-uncle Roman's contemporaries in Pleszew included the patriotic Suchocki family, which, in 1992, was to give Poland its first woman prime minister.

Despite the Polish-German friction, however, intermarriage was common. One of great-uncle Roman's aunts married a German and moved to Berlin. In the 1930s, he visited them on his way to and from Louvain in Belgium, where he studied for a doctorate. On one occasion in the mid-1930s he stayed for a month and discovered that his relatives all sympathized with Hitler. The family were dining at home one evening when a cousin turned up late. He appeared in the doorway wearing an SS uniform, raised his arm and saluted *Heil Hitler* to the diners. The rest of the family, reasonable people until then, jumped up and shouted back the salute. From that moment on my great-uncle told everyone who would listen that war was inevitable.

Perhaps this was a contributory reason for my grandfather's circumspection at his school in Łochowo. The Poles and Germans were apportioned separate classrooms, and the Germans had full self-government in their part. One day in the 1930s a picture of Hitler went up in the main classroom of the German part. When she saw it, my grandmother—being a strong character and a fierce patriot—took it down. My grandfather, on the other hand, was not of a heroic disposition. Besides, the Germans were within their rights to decorate their classrooms any way they pleased. The same evening, when my grandmother was busy with something else, he put the portrait back up on the wall, so that nobody noticed that the picture was ever absent. This probably saved his life. A few years later, under the Nazi occupation, the report of such an incident would have sent them both to a concentration camp.

When the war broke out my father and his two brothers—pupils at my grandfather's school—taunted German boys in Łochowo, shouting that Poland would win. A week later, when the Wehrmacht was already in control, the German boys took their revenge. It was the worst drubbing my father received in his entire life but relations must have improved later. The German boys joined the Hitlerjugend and paraded in smart uniforms. My father envied them their military training and camps. Once, toward the end of the war, when the Hitlerjugend volunteers were learning to dig trenches and to fire machine guns, my father got up the courage to approach them. He already spoke German—it was forbidden to speak Polish—and he had a package of sausages and bacon pinched from his mother, which by then were scarce even for the Germans. In return for the gift, he was allowed to enter the trench and pull the trigger, sending a long series of tracers above the village.

Mere subsistence was a struggle too. Farmers were obliged to deliver most of their crops to the authorities and had barely enough to sow and to live on. Milk became a delicacy. Medicines were scarce and expensive. Because of the poor diet and lack of care, my father's father was to die in 1941. He was taken with sudden pains in his stomach and brought to the hospital in Bydgoszcz, where I was to be born twenty years later. During the war, inferior races such as ourselves were the last to be attended to, particularly at a time when the hospital was full of wounded soldiers from the Eastern Front. Three days later he was dead. The death certificate stated "cancer" as the cause but this was a lie. He had not even been diagnosed. It was probably just a burst appendix, which became fatal only for lack of treatment.

The war caught my maternal grandmother, Febronia, at a particularly vulnerable time. In September 1939 my mother was three weeks old, her brother one year. Like most Poles, my grandmother hoped that the war would be short and victorious. The Polish Army might have to retreat initially, but the Germans would stop when the French attacked in the west and the RAF gave the Polish Army air cover, as the government had said they would. My grandmother did not want to endure German occupation even for a few weeks. She feared that with her husband, a schoolmaster, at the front with the Polish Army, she would be singled out for reprisals. So she hid jewelry about her body and took to the road, walking east a day or two ahead of the Germans. Holding my mother on her arm, pushing the baby carriage with my uncle in it with the other, she was soon lost in the throngs of refugees which filled the roads. Cars honked trying to get ahead of the peasant carts. Every few hours, everyone had to stand aside to let an infantry unit or a troop of cavalry pass by. She attached herself to some neighbors who pulled their cow with them and let the children have some milk. Cattle, horses, and people shrieked in fear and ran across ditches into the fields on both sides of the road every time a German plane flew low and sprayed the column with machine gun fire. Cows which had been left in the fields by their owners, unmilked for days, wailed in pain. At night, they snatched a few hours of sleep in manor houses, peasant cottages and barns, the children constantly crying and wetting themselves. Before it became clear that the war was lost she walked over three hundred kilometers, beyond Kutno in central Poland.

When she returned to Łochowo, the school building in which they had lived was already occupied, all her personal belongings confiscated. She did not know what to do, where to turn. She just stood there in front of the school building, crying. She had run out of money and the children were hungry. Eventually German neighbors, with whom she had maintained correct relations before the war, emerged from an adjacent house and offered her accommodation. She stayed the night. The next day trouble erupted. Changes had occurred in the village during the few weeks of her absence. The Germans had appointed a new burgermeister, Mr. Bettin, a wealthy farmer, owner of the colonial store and a Nazi sympathizer. Our part of Poland—a borderland between Wielkopolska and Pomerania—was one of those now officially incorporated into the Reich, its Polish inhabitants to be Germanized, deported, or exterminated. The burgermeister's first act was to call an assembly of the entire village so as to divide the population into Poles and Germans. On a word of command everyone had to cross to the right or to the left, declaring whether from now on they wanted to be regarded as Poles or as Germans. Many of the families were mixed but, if in doubt, they were classified as Germans, particularly if the man was a Protestant. Those who were not deemed Germans were induced to become *Volksdeutsch,* candidate Germans. My father's parents refused, although they had been born subjects of the kaiser, and despite the fact that my grandfather had served in the Imperial German Army, which would have qualified them. Among the adults, relations in the village became tense. Germans and the *Volksdeutsch* acquired the power of life and death over the Poles and some used it. Several prewar disputes, typical rural vendettas over land demarcation or wounded pride which in normal times would have ended in litigation or a drunken brawl, now resulted in denunciations to the Gestapo, which was enough to have a whole family shot. The next day, my grandmother's German hosts told her she would have to leave—other Germans in the village were putting pressure on them.

She was back on the street but by this time word had spread and she was quickly approached by another neighbor. They were called Mill-brandt, a German name. Mr. Millbrandt was even a Protestant, but they spoke no word of German and regarded themselves as Poles. During the assembly when the population was divided up, the Germans had forcibly pulled him onto their side. Now, by granting shelter to my grandmother, they were showing their defiance.

My grandmother reciprocated their hospitality by doing shopping and helping Mrs. Millbrandt around the house. One day, she went into the colonial shop owned by Mr. Bettin, the Nazi burgermeister, in which his wife worked behind the counter. My grandmother purchased all she needed for the Millbrandts. As she was leaving, Mrs. Bettin asked her about the children. My grandmother was wary because the Bettins were clearly fanatical Nazis. Their son had joined the Waffen SS and hung around the village in a black uniform and a cap with skull and crossbones. But Mrs. Bettin was in earnest. She was a good woman, apparently ashamed of the antics of the men in her family. She insisted on giving my grandmother candy and vegetable oil.

My grandmother did not want to put her hosts in danger and after a few days she started planning to move somewhere safer and more permanent. Her parents-in-law lived in Kcynia, an ancient town on a hill about thirty kilometers away. She was still feeding my mother but she borrowed a bicycle and pedaled there quickly. She was back by the evening, in time to feed my mother again. Soon, they moved to Kcynia, where they spent the first two years of the war.

Meanwhile, her husband, my grandfather Kazimierz, had been wounded at the battle of Bzura, the largest battle in Poland's lonely

1939 war. The wound was not very serious—a bullet had damaged the palm of his right hand. As children, we teased him that it was not a bullet wound at all and that he probably never saw action. The scar from the bullet, we would pronounce gravely, looked suspiciously as if caused by a spoke from a bicycle wheel. In fact, his wound was serious enough for him to be taken to the hospital in Warsaw, and he stayed in Warsaw throughout the capital's defense, until the end of September. When Warsaw capitulated, he was discharged by the Germans and took a train back to Bydgoszcz.

It was a mistake. Bydgoszcz was living in terror. When the war broke out, a German fifth column in the city had attacked Polish units making their retreat. Small detachments made up of local Germans and reinforced by paratroopers attacked troops with machine guns and tried to capture bridges on the Vistula. The Poles were giving way to the main German offensive but found enough time to suppress the diversion. A few hundred Germans were killed, mostly armed ones, but, given the atmosphere, no doubt a few innocents as well.

When the Wehrmacht entered the city, the incident was proclaimed a "bloody Sunday" that the Poles had inflicted on the Germans. The reprisals were savage. Polish priests and teachers were specifically targeted for elimination and several dozen were executed. The documents of all passengers alighting at the Bydgoszcz railway station were being checked and all Polish members of the intelligentsia were arrested, my grandfather included. He was transported to a makeshift prison at the old Prussian barracks in Artyleryjska Street.

The conditions at the barracks were appalling. Priests were forced to tidy horse manure, the mayor of Bydgoszcz was savagely beaten, even the director of the botanical garden was singled out for execution. In all, historians estimate that about 120,000 people were exterminated during the war in the area between Bydgoszcz and Gdańsk, about fifty thousand of them in the first four months of the war. I had always assumed that ruthlessness became worse as the war went on and that genocide was at least partly the result of the progressive brutalization. Somehow, the impression has been created that massacres were usually carried out by specially trained fanatics from the dregs of German and Austrian societies. Around Bydgoszcz, the business started right away and the instigators were not *Sonderkomandos,* but neighbors. It was they who prepared the arrest and execution lists. Many local Germans had never accepted having lost mastery after the city became a part of Poland in 1920. Now they took their revenge, particularly on the veterans of the Wielkopolska uprising nineteen years earlier. Prisoners were herded into Bydgoszcz stadiums in September 1939 when the Prussian barracks filled up.

Word somehow got to my grandmother that my grandfather was at the barracks. She went to see him with a friend whose husband was also captured. The prisoners were separated from the street by the outer railings of the barracks and by a barbed-wire fence of the inner enclosure. The prisoners crowded against the fence from inside, while relatives rushed along the outer perimeter looking for faces in the crowd. My grandmother heard someone shout "Fenia," the short version of her first name. My grandfather looked miserable and needed fresh dressing for his festering wound. My grandmother's friend also found her husband. They came back with food and medicine and money for the two men. Their subsequent fates were very different. The other man, also a prisoner of war, traded the remains of his uniform for civilian clothes, perhaps thinking of an escape. My grandfather stuck to his uniform. Perversely, my grandfather's friend, a totally innocent civilian, was shot. His name today figures on a bronze plaque on the barrack wall. Probably by a quirk of German bureaucratic procedure, my grandfather, although belonging to the condemned category, was treated as a soldier and sent to a POW camp.

After a year or so, POWs like him were given the opportunity to become laborers in Germany. It was a big risk because some worked in conditions close to those of a concentration camp. On the other hand, if one managed to get assigned to an easygoing employer, one increased one's chances of survival through access to better food. My grandfather was lucky. He was assigned to Neustettin (today Szczecinek) in Pomerania, less than two hundred kilometers from his wife in Kcynia. His first job was scrubbing carpets in a laundry, but it was already an improvement on the POW camp. He spent an occasional weekend with my grandmother in Kcynia.

In another stroke of luck, the owner of the laundry where my grandfather worked was an exceptionally kind man, with a keen commercial eye. When he learned that my grandfather was an educated man and spoke German, he reassigned him to another of his businesses: an agricultural supply store cum warehouse, which had been commandeered by the state. My grandfather's job as an accountant consisted of cooking the books so as to hide massive filching of scarce supplies. Soon, my grandmother joined him, and they both became respected members of a Polish mafia which operated in Neustettin. Quarrelsome, envious, and often nasty to one another in ordinary times, Poles are capable of extraordinary selflessness in emergencies. These qualities came into their own in Neustettin. Moreover, as the fighting in the east intensified and more and more young Germans were called up, a labor shortage developed in Germany and Polish laborers filled low-level professions. Despite the racial divide, husky Poles became particularly popular with German widows with farms to run. The longer the war lasted, the less sure ordinary Germans were of victory and the better they treated their employees. The bigger the shortages of the war economy, the bigger the profits of those who had access to scarce goods. Butter, for example, became a delicacy, but my grandparents never lacked it. Poles under my grandfather scooped it out from the barrels in the warehouse and replaced the missing amount with margarine colored with carrot juice. "Grandfather never had so much as a gram missing in the books," my grandmother reminisces with pride. And even if he had, he could have covered it up in time because the owner always seemed to know in advance when an inspection was due. Stealing from the Germans was naturally regarded as the height of patriotism, as, in some quarters in Poland, it still is.

Their lives were in peril and, labor shortage or no labor shortage, they could have been shipped off to a concentration camp at the slightest pretext. But while they survived, my grandparents lived better than many local middle-class Germans. They had a small house in a back alley behind Neustettin's main thoroughfare. They ate well. When my mother became sick with scarlet fever, which left her permanently deaf in one ear, my grandmother fetched a German doctor. When it came to paying, the doctor asked for butter, which he had not eaten for some time.

The warehouse owner loved to celebrate his birthday together with all his employees. The Poles brought out of hiding their best supplies, including a profusion of flowers from greenhouses. While the house was locked up and someone posted on the gate to look out for strangers, real champagne and brandy flowed freely and rooms resounded with songs. Nevertheless, for all the fun he had in Neustettin, when I saw my grandfather for the last time forty-five years later, dying from Parkinson's, he handed me a souvenir. It was an official note in German, bearing a swastika—a receipt for a fine he had paid for not wearing a P badge on his coat to identify him as a Pole.

The good times ended in January 1945. Neustettin was just behind the Pomeranian Wall, which the Polish and Soviet armies took weeks to crack. The boom of artillery edged closer and closer, and streets blazed from bombs. My grandparents hid in the cellar of their little house together with another Polish family and the children. On one occasion, however, my grandmother was separated for some reason from the children and rushed into the street to look for them. Although the winter was exceptionally harsh and thick snow lay everywhere, the air was hot from burning houses. She climbed mounds of rubble trying to avoid bits of debris falling from the roofs and shouted, in German, "Where are my children, I've lost my children." A group of soldiers in black uniforms—the Waffen SS—lurked on the porch of one of the houses. They were Latvian, thought she was German, and shouted that she should hide because more planes were coming. But she was too distraught to think of her own safety. One of the SS men rushed out and pulled her inside the porch seconds before the street was strafed by bullets.

The day of liberation was an eventful one for my grandmother. Everybody woke up in the cellar at the sound of tanks in the street outside. My grandfather rushed to the house of his employer to protect him. Stories of what the Red Army was doing to Germans had been spreading by word of mouth, magnified by Nazi propaganda. If a Pole were on hand to testify to a particular German's good behavior, that might give him a chance. Soon after my grandfather left, the front door resounded with knocks. My grandmother, and the Polish couple who shared the house and who now hid with her in the cellar, conferred nervously whether or not to unbolt the front door. But before they came to a decision, a series of shots rang out and the door gave way.

Two soldiers burst in, Russian privates in long coats and leggings, waving machine guns. One dragged a German woman up to the bedroom. The other ordered the Polish couple and my grandmother to come out of the cellar. "He had the face of the devil," she told me. They spoke Polish to him, thinking that he was mistaking them for Germans, but this did not help. First, he demanded the man's watch, then eyed the two women. He first pointed his gun at the other woman but she crouched behind her husband. Then he swung the barrel of his gun at my grandmother and motioned her upstairs.

My grandmother escaped being raped by a lucky accident: the door rang out with loud bangs again—a second wave of Soviet soldiers was mopping up the last pockets of German resistance. Knowing what their fate might be, the two women rushed out into the courtyard while the first group of soldiers were distracted, determined to jump into the cesspool behind the outdoor latrine. They did not know how deep it was. Might they drown? The banging increased and they held hands ready to jump when my grandmother remembered a ladder lying against the high wall of a cigarette factory which overlooked the court-yard. With energy increased by frost and fear, they climbed up just as the back door cracked under the force of several shoulders. There were empty wooden crates stacked up below them against the wall on the other side. They could jump without breaking their legs. The only thing that could now betray them was the ladder. It was too long and heavy for them to pull it up. My grandmother crossed herself and pushed it as hard as she could. Her prayers were answered once again. The ladder fell alongside the wall of the courtyard and landed without falling flat on the ground. When the soldiers burst into the courtyard it lay against the wall as if it hadn't been touched. They went away.

A couple of hours later, my grandfather rushed in, distraught, to-gether with the other man. They could not find their women, and my grandmother and her friend could not reach from the highest crate to the edge of the wall. They heard the men despairing that their wives had probably drowned in the cesspool. The women shouted out their husbands' names, but the men at first thought it was their ghosts. "The ladder," my grandmother screamed, "put the ladder against the wall!" Wondering how my grandmother had managed to place the ladder so expertly, they eventually rescued them.

A few days later, when the front-line troops passed and Russian con-trol firmed up, abuses became rarer and they decided to set off for home. Regretfully, they had to leave behind a roasted calf which my grandmother had been keeping in the attic. In the last act of the Polish network in Neustettin, a Polish cobbler at a shoe factory gave them a new set of shoes and they set off for Bydgoszcz on foot. They walked for almost two weeks, sleeping in the open, hiding from the biting frost under filthy rags in villages and town squares. Eventually they got to a railway that was functioning again and made the last fifty kilometers by train, on top of an empty tank platform, their faces black from the soot. When they got to the Bydgoszcz railway station—the same one at which my grandfather Kazimierz was arrested in 1939—my grandmother remembered a distant relative who owned a house in the town. He was married to an American who, incredibly, had stayed and survived unmolested. Despite their rags and the dirt, their relatives recognized them. They were saved.

My grandmother kept herself going through the war, she told me, by putting her faith in a prophecy, written by a seer named Wernyhora, which she often recited to me when I was a child. Many people of her generation in Poland still believe in it, and some of its passages are indeed uncanny. Originally, an eighteenth-century Cossack fable, this text was apparently published for the first time in 1894, and opened with the lines:

> *In two decades the time will come*
> *When fire bursts out from the heavens*
> *Then will this song of Wernyhora prove itself true*
> *The whole world will be choking with blood*

This verse, my grandmother explained, predicted the outbreak of World War One in 1914.

> *From ruins everywhere, Poland shall arise*
> *Two eagles will crash*
> *But her fate is still wretched*
> *Her hopes still unfulfilled*

Poland was indeed resurrected after World War One, put together again after more than a century of partition; the eagles are the double-headed eagles on the coat of arms of czarist Russia and Austro-Hungary, two states which collapsed after the war.

When the black eagle blasphemes against the cross
And spreads its threatening wings
Two countries shall fall, which cannot be saved
Force is still stronger than righteousness

The black eagle was the emblem of Germany; the passage, my grand-mother explained, meant that the Nazis, misusing the swastika—an old Crusaders' sign—will succeed in taking Austria and Czechoslovakia (two countries) without resistance.

But soon Hitler shall launch the invasion of Russia, which will fail largely because of his mistreatment of the local populations:

But the black eagle comes to the crossroads
And when it turns its eyes east
Trampling everything with Teutonic customs
It shall come back with a broken wing

The account then becomes garbled but there are still intriguing phrases. "The Eagle and the Hammer" jointly take other people's fields—clearly a reference to the Nazi-Soviet pact. The lion—presum-ably England—joins with the cock—obviously France. Gdańsk and Mazuria (East Prussia) shall become Polish—which was hardly imagin-able in 1894, yet happened in 1945. And in the end, Wernyhora predicts, "the Hammer in the East"—the Soviet Union with its hammer and sickle, which hadn't even been conceived in 1894—"shall be broken."

Envisaging a return to a union of Poland with Belarus and Ukraine, the final outcome will be this:

A Poland from sea to sea shall arise
Wait for this half a century
God's grace shall protect us
So suffer and pray, O man

While this final phrase should disprove the prophecy: half a century from 1894 is 1944—the year of the Warsaw uprising and the Red Army's arrival in Poland, hardly triumphs. But in 1978, my grand-mother became convinced that the prophecy was right after all, and that it was our too literal interpretation of the timing that was at fault. She kept reciting:

> *Three rivers of the world shall bestow three crowns*
> *On the Anointed One from Kraków*
> *Four allies from the furthest lands*
> *Shall swear words of allegiance to him*

It was clear to her that this predicted the election of Karol Wojtyła, the archbishop of Kraków, as the Pope—the rivers symbolizing faith and the three crowns being the traditional papal headgear. The rest would come to pass too, the only question being from which date the fifty-year countdown should commence. She spoke of the prophecy often; later in her life, though, in her darker moments, she understood its final verses to mean that the war which had so disrupted her life as a young woman would return. *Będzie wojna,* she often told me when I came to visit her: "There will be war."

But in January 1945, while my grandparents were already safe in Bydgoszcz and preparing to return to my grandfather's school in Łochowo, my great-uncle Roman was still in a concentration camp.

In the summer of 1939, as usual, he had taken a train from Louvain in Belgium back to Poland, and saw Germany turning into an armed camp. The start of the war found him in his native Pleszew. His first sight of the Germans was on the outskirts of the town: they were shooting a group of youths. The main church was deserted, so he took charge of it as acting priest. Within days, he received a letter from the Gestapo, already established in the old police station, informing him that he was on the list of hostages who would be shot at the slightest sign of resistance. Other hostages were locked up in prison but he officiated at the funerals of those that were shot, so he remained at liberty. Provided he showed up at the police station every day at noon, he was allowed to hold mass on Sundays, strictly between 9:00 and 11:00. In the very first days, a friend of his in a nearby parish was murdered for taking a procession around the church without permission. Germans needed my great-uncle in yet another capacity: the parish was suddenly flooded with letters from Germans who had been born or lived in Pleszew before World War One and left when the town became a part of Poland. Now they needed proof of their Aryan pedigrees. My great-uncle issued confirmations of Catholic christenings and weddings.

The family spent the first months of the war brushing up on their German. Older members had learned it at school before World War One. It was now becoming a matter of life and death, so my great-uncle taught it to those brothers, sisters, and cousins who had been too young. By the spring, they were all reasonably fluent. But they knew that, as a Polish priest, he would be arrested sooner or later. About forty had already been picked off one by one in the surrounding area. Pleszew, like the rest of Wielkopolska, was being incorporated in the Reich and any trace of Polishness, and particularly of the Polish intelligentsia, was being liquidated. Friends from other dioceses suggested that he move to the General Government, a rump of Poland which the Germans were using as a pool of cheap labor before plans for a final solution could be put into effect. For the moment, Polish was still allowed and the Polish Catholic church continued to function. He refused. His duty was to remain and officiate to the remaining Poles.

So, on March 12, 1940, when he was thirty-three, his turn arrived. The police came in the morning. His mother packed his suitcase and they took him to Bruczków, twenty-five kilometers away. Bruczków was a monastery which had been emptied of monks and converted into a prison for several dozen priests. Roman expected to be interrogated but he never was. His file was marked simply "a Polish priest"; this sufficed for accusation, trial, and conviction. For the next five years of his captivity, nobody so much as pretended that he was guilty of anything, apart from the sheer fact of who he was.

Five months later, at night, after a twenty-four-hour rail journey locked in cattle cars, without food, water, or sanitary facilities, the priests disembarked inside a compound surrounded by watchtowers and electrified barbed wire. Lights were off because they arrived in the middle of an air-raid alert, but they made out rows of wooden barracks. It was Buchenwald, near the lovely historic city of Weimar. They stripped, went through showers, and exchanged their civilian clothes for ill-matched, torn, striped prison garb. My great-uncle was given a number, 21925, which was from now on his sole identity, to be recited at every encounter with authority. At the exit from the arrival compound they got their first inkling of what lay ahead: two men stood hidden behind the door with heavy whips and thrashed everyone who passed.

The wooden barracks were already full and the priests were put in tents in which Polish youths—scouts and members of sports and educational groups—had lived, until they had all been killed shortly before. At 4:00 A.M. they were called to stand to attention. Several hours later, the commandant greeted them with a short speech. It ended with the words: "You must all die like dogs here."

Buchenwald was infamous for its stone quarries, where prisoners worked with their bare hands and died off quickly. Despite the backbreaking labor, the food allowance was one loaf of bread for seven prisoners. My great-uncle Roman, a large man, soon weighed 90 pounds. Everybody had to run constantly, in fear of his life. There were no days off—no Sundays. One morning, on the way to the quarry, just past the gate with the slogan "To Each His Own," the prisoners saw the usual crop of dying bodies by the roadside. "Look, it's that famous lawyer from Poznań!" someone exclaimed. There was nothing anybody could do. My uncle was powerless as he saw his friend (a Monsignor Kupski, the vicar of a parish which my uncle was later to take over) beaten, kicked in the mud, and killed. In the six and a half years of its existence, according to the scrupulous Buchenwald books, a total 238,980 inmates were to enter it, of which 56,545 never left.

In December 1940, the Germans decided to concentrate priests from all over Europe in Dachau. More than 2,500 priests from twenty-four nations were herded together, 1,724 of them Poles, mostly Catholic, my great-uncle among them. Dachau was the oldest concentration camp in Nazi Germany, set up in March 1933 for Jews, Communists, Gypsies, and other undesirables. German Communists mostly served as *kapos*. It was they who did most of the screaming and beating.

The arrival procedure in Dachau was more elaborate than that in Buchenwald. The SS medical staff measured the prisoners' skulls to determine their anthropological type, and registered their previous diseases—this, as it turned out later, in order to make fake death certificates more credible. They lived in standard concentration camp barracks, designed for a few hundred people, which routinely housed a couple of thousand. Three prisoners lived in each bunk, the bunks stacked up on three levels. They worked in the surrounding factories, plantations, and building sites. Several died every week, their bodies taken to the crematorium with a piece of paper tied to their toes with their identification number.

For a time, my uncle worked at a giant sawmill making wooden ammunition crates. He worked indoors, which was considered lucky. Then he dug irrigation canals, where most of the Jews were said to have been worked to death. In the summer, he worked in the fields, harvesting wheat and herbs. Afterward, the fields were fertilized with the ashes of the dead brought from the crematorium. Then, for a year, he became a horse, working in a troika. A band of three priests, they pulled a two-wheel cart which carried cases filled with screws and aircraft parts. They marched about thirty kilometers every day, always guarded by a *kapo* and at least two armed guards. The dogs were Alsatians, trained to attack people dressed in the striped prison garb—they lunged for the throat. They passed peaceful German villages. Dachau itself was a pretty medieval town with a castle, a town hall, and a church. But the sight of normal life made little impression on them. They were so terrorized and humiliated that they regarded themselves as a world apart and thought nothing of urinating and defecating directly onto the neat streets. No wonder the German civilians thought that these dirty barbarians really were useless tissue. Even so, some of them must have had doubts, for once, when they waited with their cart at a railway crossing, a German girl came up to them and tried to ask who they were. When the dogs snarled at her and the guards motioned her away with their weapons, she ran.

Escape, even if an opportunity presented itself during work outside the compound, was almost impossible. A stripe of shaved hair from the forehead to the back of the head and prison garb immediately gave them away. Almost all escapees were caught. The beatings were savage. Barely alive, captured prisoners had to walk among the barracks with boards on the chest and the back which read: "I'm here again."

As more and more prisoners died, the camp crematorium could not cope with disposing the bodies. A second one was ordered and my great-uncle managed to join the construction team. The *kapo* was a German Communist, but a good sort, and they idled happily. Only when officers appeared did the *kapo* scream furiously and beat the prisoners. It was vital to work as little as possible so as to conserve energy. Thanks to the Communist *kapo* almost everyone in his construction team survived.

Apart from avoiding exertion whenever possible, one had to keep one's mind focused, my great-uncle told me. Many people died within a fortnight of arrival at the camp not of hunger, disease, or torture, but simply because they lost hope and broke down. My great-uncle adopted a private motto: *Cholery mnie nie dostaniecie,* "You won't get me, bastards," and it helped to keep his spirits up.

Their isolation from the rest of the world was alleviated somewhat by their priestly solidarity. My great-uncle never heard of an instance of priests cooperating with the authorities or betraying other inmates. Stronger characters helped to sustain vulnerable colleagues. The prisoners' spiritual leader, on the adjacent bunk, was Michał Kozal, bishop of Włocławek. German delegations inspecting the camp liked to call forward the taut figure in rags, make him stand to attention, and sneer at "our Polish bishop." He would not allow other prisoners to give him lighter work and shared his bread rations with others—the heroism of which perhaps cannot be appreciated by those who have never weighed 90 pounds as adults. Kozal ministered to the sick and the dying, heard confession, and used the shreds of his prestige to influence camp authorities to alleviate suffering. On June 14, 1942—my great-uncle remembers the date because it was the twelfth anniversary of his own ordination—he walked side by side with Kozal when he heard confession from a prisoner on the way to work. Marking the granting of absolution, the bishop made a discreet sign of the cross in the air. Unfortunately, it was spotted by one of the Communist *kapos.* The man went berserk with fury and both the bishop and the man who confessed were savagely beaten. When Kozal died in the agony of typhoid in January 1943, the authorities did not allow him to be buried in a cemetery—he was cremated with everyone else. Forty-four years later, during one of John Paul II's visits to Poland, my great-uncle stood witness as the Pope performed the rites of Kozal's beatification. Later, ninety-eight other priests who died in Dachau were pronounced as Martyrs.

Another reason my great-uncle survived was that there were moments of respite. From May till October 1941, probably as a result of Vatican diplomatic pressure, the priests were granted "privileges." Sunday was recognized, a chapel was allowed, the food improved, and, incredibly, compulsory work was discontinued. Delegation after delegation came to visit them from abroad. Then, in October, the commandant announced that the privileges would continue only for those who signed the *Volksliste,* the application for German nationality. The assembly was tense. Keeping the privileges meant a much higher chance of survival. Signing the *Volksliste* was treason to Poland. "If one of you Catholics steps forward," a Protestant pastor from Łódź whispered loudly, "I will smash his face." It was an unnecessary threat. The commandant repeated his blackmail. Nobody stepped forward. *Alles fanatische Hunde*—"Fanatical dogs, all of them," commented one of the SS men.

The Poles felt proud that their solidarity held, but their punishment was severe. The previous regime returned and now priests were put to the hardest tasks. Older men started dying faster and faster. They became so hungry that when on one occasion a prisoner managed to hit a stray crow with a stone, he and his two companions ate it raw. Their darkest moment was Easter Day 1943, when their barrack was ravaged by the guards and they were beaten and harassed so much they did not manage to eat. Nevertheless, thanks to the "privileges" of those few months, my great-uncle had regained some strength.

Conditions improved again after Stalingrad. Red Cross parcels reached them and, as young men were sent to the front, older, less brutal men took over as guards. The priests shared out parcels fairly—such acts of charity made them feel human again. Eventually, other prisoners could attend the masses held in the priests' barrack and even a sort of organization, the Fraternity of St. Joseph, began to be tolerated. Though heavily censored, mail began to get through. Hope returned. But as the Wehrmacht began to give way at the front, another threat haunted the prisoners: medical experiments. The Germans were short of quinine, the only malaria remedy at the time, and tried to find a substitute for it. Only healthier-looking prisoners such as my great-uncle were suitable as guinea pigs. More than once a *kapo*'s finger was pointed at him, but he somehow managed to wriggle away. The unlucky ones were tied to the beds in the camp hospital. Under a contract for I. G. Farben, a team of SS doctors under a Professor Schilling—later executed for war crimes—infected the prisoners with malaria and then tried various quinine substitutes on them. Other prisoners were dressed up in a pilot's uniform and thrown into freezing water, their body functions monitored until death. The worst were experiments with phlegmon, which caused high fever and patches of cheesy pus on their backs. While the prisoners writhed and their hearts raced, the staff took systematic samples of their urine and body temperature. Almost all the prisoners taken for experiments died.

With the end of the war, discipline at the camp relaxed, and, paradoxically, mortality increased further—from epidemics. The barracks were no longer kept clean and various strains of typhoid spread rapidly. The American army approached the camp on April 29, 1945. Just a few soldiers, apparently overreaching their orders, captured the main gate. The camp was now manned by anti-Soviet Russians from Vlasov's army who did not intend to fight. They dropped their weapons and put their hands up. But the Americans were so angered by what they saw that they shot several on the spot. My great-uncle saw one young soldier, crying, and mowing down a whole row of camp guards with his machine gun. There was a priest among the Americans and they all, the prisoners and the soldiers, fell to their knees in the mud and said "Our Father . . ." in their various languages. The Poles intoned *Te Deum Laudamus*.

Unknown to them all, some days before Heinrich Himmler had given an order that the camp was to be liquidated. All prisoners were to be shot. That night, a Viking SS unit, still in fighting order, tried to recapture the area and carry out the order. The handful of Americans would have been overwhelmed but they were fortunately able to call on their heavy artillery. From a distance of several kilometers away, the guns put a protective wall of fire and steel in front of the camp, and eventually the SS gave up. Finally, the camp was safe. Of the 1,724 Polish priests who had entered Dachau in December 1940, 798 were still alive.

Even though he knew Poland would be Communist and true liberation was still far away, my great-uncle Roman set off for Poland without hesitation. Whether Poland was ruled by the Nazis or by the Communists, he wanted to be with his flock.

ŁOCHOWO

WHEN I DRIVE FROM CHOBIELIN to Bydgoszcz, I pass Potulice, a large prison in which Edek, one of my father's brothers, spent several years. When I was a child, Edek was the black sheep of the family. He was one of only a couple Party members in our extended family. I hardly knew him because my mother discouraged social contact on account of his violent temper and prodigious drinking. I was seven or eight when a quarrel erupted between him and my mother in our small apartment. I remember coming to my mother's assistance armed with a slingshot.

Today, he is the relative with whom I most identify—who made me realize how little, particularly in our part of the world, distinguishes the road that leads to the manor house from the road that leads to prison.

Like my father, Edek spent his childhood in Łochowo, a few kilometers down the road from Potulice. The prewar village that had one school, one shop, and one church has now grown into a largish satellite of Bydgoszcz, and is in imminent danger of being swallowed up by the city. The red-brick school where my great-uncle Roman held mass, where my maternal grandfather met my grandmother, who as his wife, took Hitler's portrait off the wall, still stands. My paternal grandfather's home and workshop, on the other hand, has already given way to a modern post office.

When we drive past Łochowo, my father usually points out some detail of the landscape: the hill on which the Hitlerjugend had its trenches and allowed him to shoot from a machine gun, the barn in which he hid with his mother waiting for the front to pass in January 1945, a stretch of forest from which a band of defeated German soldiers emerged, only to be mowed down by the Russians. But my father was only seven when the war broke out—too young to be a reliable witness about what happened to our family. I only learned the full story from Edek's diaries. They are probably reliable because many participants, including his mother and brothers, were still alive when he wrote them and a lie would easily have been detected. He made appalling spelling mistakes but wrote neatly, and well, with hardly a correction, the work of a talented though untrained mind. Some of his passages are guarded, others perhaps written to please a censor or an interrogator—he wrote in prison.

Edek's father (who was my grandfather Franciszek Sikorski) had come from a family which owned land—in the only photograph in the family album we have of his father, we see him dressed in white tie with the dashing white mustache of a nobleman. World War One depressed land prices and most farms in Poland fell into debt in the 1930s depression. My grandfather was one of many children and he had to fend for himself. Being good with his hands, he taught himself to make and mend saddles and harnesses, eventually establishing a workshop which worked mainly for various cavalry regiments.

They were poor, but by virtue of having smarter relatives, Edek was spending his summer vacations in 1939 with his aunt at a beachfront villa in Gdynia-Orłowo, a fashionable Baltic seaside resort: the aunt kept an upmarket pension. Like my maternal relatives, he also soon realized that there would be war. A thirteen-year-old schoolboy at the time, Edek earned pocket money by fetching cigars and newspapers for his aunt's guests: colonels, diplomats, an aging countess or two. While the guests sat in wicker chairs on the veranda, he idled about in the garden just below, eavesdropping.

"German morale is low"—a colonel held forth. "They can only carry on for about a week before their fuel stocks run out. I doubt if they can penetrate more than about sixty kilometers into our territory. Thanks to our alliances with England and France, Germany will be squeezed economically. And then we can go on the offensive with our cavalry, attacking them where they least expect it."

"We Poles are united and ready," added a priest in the company. "Let us drink a toast for Poland's might and her future."

Edek's uncle, on the other hand, read German newspapers and his alarm grew. He neglected the administration of the guesthouse, drank, and quarreled with his wife: "There will be war one of these days. Everything we've worked for will go to the dogs. I shan't overwork myself. I'd rather be rested for the coming defense of Gdynia."

"You've gone mad," said his wife, clasping her hands as if in prayer.

Signs of crisis mounted every day. Hardly a train passed without being pelted with stones. By mid-August, the inhabitants of the little resort town were buying up flour, sugar, soap, and even bread, which the women made into dried crackers. Queues formed outside savings banks. Edek stood in one of them for his aunt, but the bank ran out of cash and deposits were frozen that day. Finally, mobilization was proclaimed and soldiers appeared, digging trenches, masking heavy guns, and spreading coils of barbed wire. Edek loved watching the navy exercise, the ships engaging in mock firefights in full view of the coast. He hoped the war would break out soon and anticipated the fun.

My aunt's villa was near Gdynia. Gdynia was a new port which Poland had had to build in the 1920s and 1930s, after the Versailles Treaty at the end of World War One turned the ancient Hanseatic port of Gdańsk into the Free City of Danzig, separate from both Poland and Germany. Nevertheless, railway lines to Gdynia crossed the Free City, whose largely German-speaking population was strongly pro-Nazi. So, on August 31, 1939, when Edek took the last train out of Gdynia into Poland proper, he traveled through Nazi-controlled territory. Before crossing into the Free City, the conductors locked the doors of the carriage in anticipation of trouble. Edek watched and listened at train stations as groups of German youths shouted anti-Polish slogans and shook their fists at the passengers. At one station a stone the size of an egg fell into the compartment, injuring a girl student from Poznań—they could do nothing for her until the train reached the Polish side again in Tczew. In Bydgoszcz there was already chaos, as refugees from border villages began streaming into the train station hoping to catch the last trains to central Poland. Edek walked twelve kilometers at night to his parents' home in Łochowo.

While he was walking the war broke out. Łochowo was on a line of Polish defense along the Bromberger canal; later that morning the order came for the entire population to move out. Peasants moved away on carts and on foot, filling the load with furniture and bedding, dragging their cows and goats. Edek saw a ten-year-old boy running after a wagon carrying a cage with two pigeons. *He probably didn't carry them far,* Edek speculated in his diary. *Probably he let them out soon after and they were the first to come back to the deserted house, perhaps already destroyed by war.* Another girl, sitting on the back of a cart, held a giant doll whose eyes blinked when the cart rumbled over the potholes.

Not being peasants, the Sikorskis did not own a cart. Now they were in a fix. Not knowing where to turn, the whole family just stood in the street in front of their house, small bundles in hand, hoping that someone would give them a lift. But everyone was too busy attending to their own families. Eventually, a corporal from an artillery unit came up to them and asked what the problem was.

"Where are your horses and cart?" asked the soldier.

"God did not grant us such luck," replied my grandfather. *It was strange of him to say that because he was an atheist and never used the word God,* commented Edek. The corporal stroked the children on the heads and said, "Just you wait, I will get you horses." He went to a German farmhouse nearby, and emerged with a horse and a cart. The Germans in the village were disobeying the evacuation order and hid in the woods or in attics and barns, hoping to wait it out until the Wehrmacht moved in. My grandfather took the reins and they were soon off. Unfortunately, the whole scene was witnessed by a pair of unfriendly eyes.

Off they went, to the southeast, into the heartlands of Wielkopolska, where they hoped the German offensive would not reach. Soon, they saw aircraft flying low over the ground. Optimists said that the planes must be French, and that the black crosses were painted to deceive the enemy during the flight across Germany. But soon the planes dropped bombs and then they shot up the road with machine guns. The planes were Stukas, and gave a terrible roar while diving. *The human mass panicked,* wrote Edek. *Mothers cried, terrified children screamed, the moans of the wounded, the dead, the road blocked by overturned carts and dead horses. People shouted names of relatives and children; orphans stood over the bodies of their mothers. When someone tried to take them away they wouldn't go; they kissed the corpse in despair and sorrow. Some people recognized corpses, loaded them up onto carts and carried them to the nearest cemetery.* A couple of days later, past Inowrocław, a message went around to prepare for a gas attack. *Again people panicked; they said farewell and prepared for death. Roadside ditches, dirty ponds, wells, and water pumps were besieged: we soaked rags and put them to our mouths, which was supposed to protect us instead of a gas mask. The more enterprising dug trenches and hid their families there, covering them with wet sacks and blankets. People sang religious songs, women prayed in unison. For three hours we lived in fear and uncertainty; then someone announced that the alarm was over.*

Nevertheless, morale was still good. That day they heard on the radio that England and France had declared war on Germany; the Polish air force was supposed to be bombing Berlin, and the cavalry reportedly destroyed a German tank division near Chojnice. Edek's father, my grandfather, being an old soldier from World War One, did not share the optimism. After speaking to several officers in charge of units that were withdrawing in disarray, he concluded that the war would be lost. He took the cart off the road, into the woods. That night they camped at a wealthy farm whose owner had stayed put, apparently optimistic that the enemy would not reach this far. The kind man let my grandmother use his kitchen, and the whole family dined properly for the first time in three days. *I remember well that wonderful moment of our family supper, in the open. We sat around our father, all of us quiet and pensive. He looked at each of us with his gentle gaze. That evening, far away from home, would be our last supper together in free Poland,* Edek reminisced in his diary.

Worn out by the hardships, everybody else slept soundly, except Edek, who, a precocious thirteen-year-old, set off investigating the barns and the manor house. He was intrigued by the fact that there were no dogs about, which is unusual at a Polish farm (even to this day). He entered the garden at the back of the house. Then, when he approached the windows, he heard whispers, in German! *I was very surprised because I had heard the farmer's conversation with my father in Polish, and he had said that Polish victory was guaranteed,* he wrote. The curtains were drawn but not very carefully. He peeped in: three young men were sitting around a transmitter; one wearing headphones, the others writing down his dictation. Then, someone opened the door into the garden, but Edek was faster and jumped out of the garden in time. He woke up his father, whose reaction was immediate: though it was past midnight, they ran to the main road. They accosted a passing cavalry squadron and Edek repeated what he saw to the commanding officer. After a brief discussion, the Sikorskis led a platoon back to the farm. *The attack was sudden. We liquidated the enemy and left the traitor's farm to join the refugee column on the road,* Edek wrote dispassionately.

They lived through more adventures that month, eventually ending up in a village so remote and so poor that neither army had bothered it. Then, after the whole country had been overrun for several weeks, my grandfather took the hard decision to go back to Łochowo. The village greeted them with a new road sign: *Lohau.* A Catholic shrine on the crossroads was wrecked, the figure of Christ in the ditch. The Germans had eradicated all signs of the Polish language or of Poland. Every house, even uninhabited ones, was draped in Nazi flags. German acquaintances from before the war now wore armbands with swastikas. His German friends from school greeted one another with a hearty *Heil Hitler.* It took Edek time to adjust to the new order in the village: *I would never have suspected Hans and Otto—with whom we organized sparring matches at school, went fishing, swam in the canal, and played football—would suddenly stop me in the street and beat me up because I had not taken my cap off to them and had not greeted them in German.*

Perhaps if they had been aware the Germans knew about my grandfather taking the horse and cart from a German farm on the first day of the war, the Sikorskis would not have come back to Łochowo. Now it was too late. Cursing the family, the Germans led them to their house and put them up against the front wall, with their hands up, as if for execution. My grandfather was beaten up. But an even heavier charge than taking the horse cart hung over the family's fate: my grandmother was on an arrest list prepared by the Germans well before the war. Her crime was simple: she was heard saying before the war that "if there's war it will be Hitler's fault." This qualified her as a "person hostile to the Third Reich."

There and then, my grandmother was arrested and locked up in the local guardhouse. At the guardhouse, *she was horribly beaten and then thrown unconscious into the adjacent stable, onto the horse manure,* wrote Edek.

The rest of the family eventually entered the house. It was in total disarray: furniture looted, mirrors smashed, broken utensils piled up on the floor. Overcoming his shock, my grandfather asked his friendly German neighbor, called Krynke, to intercede on his wife's behalf. Krynke inquired, but returned with bad news: my grandmother was on a list of Poles destined to be shot.

The four children—my uncles Edek and Roman, my father, and my aunt—huddled together in the empty house, praying for their mother. They were hungry, tired, and dirty. Outside, young Germans jeered and threw stones at them, first breaking the glass, and then threw rocks through holes in the windows. *Father didn't come back for a long time. We cried, pleading for mercy for our parents, and moaning "Mama, Tata,"* wrote Edek. The crowd looked at them as if they were a herd of animals. Another neighbor, once a perfectly civil woman, shouted at them: "Now you are crying, asking for help and mercy, but when your soldiers were murdering our people there was no one to show mercy to them. You are a bastardly nation and if you don't shut your ugly faces, you'll follow your dreadful mother." And the children cried louder than ever.

My grandfather went to see Herr Bettin, the German mayor. He begged and pleaded for my grandmother's life, falling on his knees before him. Eventually, the German relented. Fortunately, the farmer was stronger in him than the Nazi. He had a large farm, equipped with modern machinery which used leather belts for power transmission. Some of them had gone faulty in the last few months of chaos. If my grandfather would fix them, and all his bridles—free of charge, of course—Herr Bettin would see what he could do. He kept the bargain. My grandmother was released the very next day. She had to be carried home. She was supposed to be interrogated later on, but eventually the Germans let the matter drop.

A few days later, they saw what would have happened to my grandmother had it not been for my grandfather's craft. All Poles—except for my grandfather, who now had the mayor's dispensation—had to report at the guardhouse at 6:00 A.M. They were taken about the surrounding area, removing barbed wire and repairing war damage. They also had to dig up corpses of dead Germans, *probably shot by the Polish army for spying,* commented Edek knowingly. Other Poles—a woodsman, a railwayman, a farmer, and a few others whose names Edek forgot—those who, like my grandmother, were put on the arrest lists prepared before the war, were jailed in the guardhouse. They were beaten so savagely that relatives could barely recognize them. Eventually, while the village was watching, the prisoners were kicked and whipped toward a wood halfway to the canal. There, in bloodstained clothes, hardly able to stand, they were shot.

National characters are hard to suppress. Poles do not respond well to being humiliated or threatened. Something of the old gentry ethos has filtered down to the entire nation and one of the ways in which it manifests itself is the average Pole's stubborn personal dignity and defiance. It's not just that we call one another *Pan* and *Pani,* Sir and Madam, where Englishmen would use first names. Our behavior in everyday situations shows a spirit of independence which has been suppressed in lands further east. I have tested this repeatedly. You shout at a minor official in Russia, and you are almost invariably taken for an important person and are more likely to get your way. You raise your voice at a similarly lowly clerk in Poland, and he or she will argue back.

Such national characteristics must form early because young Edek reacted to the events in Łochowo in a typically Polish way. Undaunted by the beating he had already received, he vowed not to bow his head to his German peers, to his former friends who now wore Hitlerjugend uniforms. For several weeks he managed to avoid them, but one day three of them suddenly appeared on his path through the fields. They blocked his way with their bicycles, their pumps raised in their hands, waiting to see if he would take his cap off and greet them. He didn't. They were about to lunge at him but Edek reached for a stone, and threw it at the tallest, called Gunter. He fell and the bicycle collapsed on top of him. He kept the others at bay with another stone and hoped to go around them, when he realized that other Germans were approaching from the opposite direction. Another minute and he would have been surrounded. He hurled himself across the fields, toward the woods, seven Germans trailing him. He managed to shake them off. He headed for a remote village where he had friends. Going back to the house was out of the question. Only the next day did he send a ten-year-old boy with word to my grandfather. The news was that the Germans had the house surrounded all night, and searched it in the morning, thinking that he may have slipped in unnoticed. Edek was not to come back because he could put the whole family, particularly his mother, in jeopardy.

Not yet fourteen years old at that time—this was spring 1940—Edek was never really to return home. In retrospect, it was that encounter in the Łochowo field, when he would not take his cap off to the Germans, which robbed him of his chances for a normal family childhood, and for a normal life.

Edek found refuge in a nearby village with a German friend of his father's, a farmer called Neubauer. Neubauer treated him well, protecting him from other Germans and feeding him in return for Edek's help on the farm. In the spring, Neubauer transferred Edek to the farm of his mother, Emma. She was also a good woman, who told him to feel as if at home, because she could not tell the difference between a Pole and a German.

He was soon nicely set up. He worked in Bydgoszcz, carting building materials at the airport, where the Germans were constructing a concrete landing strip. He made money by selling food from the country. He became important among acquaintances as a source of news about the Polish government in exile and the progress of the war: he caught his landlady listening to BBC broadcasts in Polish—a crime punishable by death—and she had to let him in on the listening sessions in return for his silence. Their monitoring sessions were made easier by the fact that the landlady's other tenant—a jolly German engineer from Hamburg, who was unself-conscious as a member of the master race— tuned the radio for them and called them to it when the time came. In addition to political education, his year at the airfield also taught him the facts of life. He asked his landlady innocently why the pretty villa next door was so quiet during the day and so noisy at night, with lights blazing and music. She went red in the face and then explained to him what the Luftwaffe officers did before staggering out of it in the morning.

In 1941, when the airfield was completed, the Germans decided to build a chemical factory. It was named the Hermann Göering Werke and belonged to I.G. Farben Industrie, the same company which made Zyklon B such a familiar label. It was a huge project, employing POWs and forced laborers from all over Europe. For the first time, Edek met the British. They amazed him. *Their camp was very near my quarters so I followed what went on in the camp. They were young boys but kept neat; they were always in clean uniforms. They did not bear the scars of war, of terror and violence. After work they played soccer at a nearby pitch. They looked well fed and fit.* Their work consisted in digging trenches for the factory foundation and one day Edek contrived to take some boards into their compound and four Britons were assigned to unload his cart. They spoke German and as soon as they learned he was Polish, gave him a bar of chocolate and a pack of American cigarettes. Their biggest concern was girls. Disappointed that Edek did not have a sister, they demanded to see a photograph of Stefka, his girlfriend. *They liked it very much. It disappeared into the pocket of one of them and I never saw it again, the only memento I had of her,* Edek remembered. For the next few months Edek made friends with the English. He exchanged their chocolate and cigarettes for the moonshine produced by his landlord and acted as a courier between the POW camp and another part of the building site where Polish girls worked. He carried presents for the girls, letters, and the Britons' earnest invitations to the girls to come to a nearby clump of bushes. He was having a good time.

His mood changed abruptly in the summer of 1941, when the first Soviet POWs reached Bydgoszcz soon after Hitler's invasion that June. The Soviets were treated much worse than the English. They were tattered and hungry and looked like walking skeletons. Their faces and hands were running sores. They were fed a watery soup and bread mixed with wood shavings. They were expected to do the hardest work. Almost every day their work units carried back corpses, to be accounted for at the gate. *The Germans treated them worse than cattle,* wrote Edek. He brought them bread and cigarettes or picked up cigarette butts for them. It was then that I think he began identifying with the Soviets, underdogs like himself, and began mistrusting the pampered Westerners.

One day, he was driving his cart along a trench in which the Soviets were laying a cable. When he slowed down two of them walked beside the cart. He talked to them although barely turning to look so as not to arouse the suspicions of a guard. Two of them pleaded for civilian clothes and maps. If they couldn't escape, they would soon die, they said. Would he help them? Edek agreed.

That night he could not sleep, thinking over the details of an escape plan. He drafted the help of his landlord, an elderly Pole who had experience in such matters, having escaped from Russian captivity as a soldier in the German army in World War One. The attempt was to be made the very next day. It was a Saturday, the day on which Edek worked only a few hours and then went back to Łochowo to report to the owner of the cart, Emma. As part of the contract he was allowed to take away old timbering for her to use as firewood. This now came in handy. He told the Soviets the plan during another slow cart ride along the trench in which they worked. Then, when he finished his shift at 11:00 A.M. he asked the German foreman whether he could lend him a couple of prisoners to help him load the wood. The foreman had once beaten Edek up but later Edek arranged an affair between him and Emma's widowed daughter. Now, as an intermediary in passing letters and presents, he enjoyed special favor. So the foreman agreed at once. Edek rode to the pile of timbering, where the Soviets had built a tent-like structure, which they placed in the load of the cart, the two prisoners inside. Then they piled up the wood high and tight, so as to make any search as bothersome as possible. The cart full, Edek drove up to the foreman again, to get a stamp on his pass to confirm that he was entitled to take the wood out of the camp. Five minutes later Edek was smiling at the guardsman at the gate, praying that he would not pick on him for a spot check. Seeing his permanent pass and the stamp, the guard motioned him on with a bored wave of the hand.

Edek was elated. He gave his passengers the agreed signal that danger had passed; they laughed and sang school songs. Near the village of Białe Błota—literally, White Mud—he turned into the woods and stopped the cart in a thick coppice. He let the Soviets out. There was only time to give directions and for a quick cigarette together. One of them was an officer from Leningrad, the other a railwayman. Edek did not know—neither then, nor thirty years later when he wrote up his exploit in jail—that the men were probably doomed even if they made it across occupied Poland to Soviet territory. Stalin regarded all Soviet prisoners of war as traitors, and had most of them liquidated.

Edek was keen to go back to the camp to bask in hero's glory. It was not to be. That night he asked Emma for his monthly evening with his family—presumably to be able to boast of what he had done. On the way to Łochowo he saw eight young Nazis riding their bikes across the entire width of the road, singing drunkenly. He steered the cart out of their way but it didn't help: they beat him up, largely on the instigation of the one among them with a particularly Teutonic name and pedigree, a Kubinski, whom Edek remembered from a patriotic Polish organization before the war. Now Kubinski kicked the hardest. When a fortnight later he recovered sufficiently to go back to the building site, there was no more job for him and the Soviet soldiers had in any case been assigned somewhere else.

Soon he was on the run himself. The German labor office assigned him to work for a Gestapo guardsman, a German from the Baltic states who ran a greenhouse confiscated from a Pole. Edek disliked the family from the first. His wife was ugly and dirty, which did not stop her from having children—thirteen in all. For this feat she had received the Mother's Cross from the führer, which she wore proudly on her chest. It was a confrontation with one of the children which again altered the course of Edek's life.

When he came back from work one day, having ferried coal around the city, he found the boss's fourteen-year-old son, in a Hitlerjugend uniform, waiting for him and screaming that he had overworked the horses. Calling Edek a "Polish pig"—apparently a standard expression in those days of German victories—the boy lashed him across the face with a whip. *I lost my temper, grabbed a stick, and hit the brat in the back with all my might. He fell,* Edek recalled. He realized what the consequences might be. He had beaten up a German in uniform, the son of a Gestapo official, his father's favorite. After a moment's stupefaction, he ran out of the courtyard and into the hostile town. Like a rat—which apparently retraces its steps when panicked—Edek ran for cover to his previous landlord, the one who had helped him plan the Soviets' escape. But he could not stay more than a few days. He could not endanger his hosts for long. In those days in my home city, he said, *every Pole not yet expelled by the Germans was constantly watched.* He spent the next few weeks with a succession of acquaintances and relatives, then he decided to try his luck in the General Government, the rump Poland under German occupation, where he hoped he would find a more permanent hiding place. Today we tend to think that German-occupied Europe was a more or less homogeneous area in which German controls applied equally. The reality was different. He needed to smuggle himself into the General Government. He thought himself lucky when he found a goods train going that way and hid at night on a carriage underneath a pile of wooden boards. The next day, the train standing at a station across the border, a sharp voice ordered him to come out of hiding. Someone must have seen him finding his hiding place and passed the message along.

The Gestapo would not believe Edek's story—that he was from Warsaw and had simply escaped from a farmer in East Prussia who beat him up—which was hardly surprising since he suddenly forgot the *bauer*'s name and even the name of the village. He gave his real name, but it was a mistake—a warrant for his arrest had been issued in Bydgoszcz. On his return to Bydgoszcz—to the prison at the Wały Jagiellońskie—the Gestapo greeted him with a beating and three days in a bunker. Then he was thrown in a cell with two men. One was a priest from Chojnice who had dared to hear confession in Polish; already delirious from beatings, he died in the cell after another interrogation. The other was an English POW in tattered uniform, apparently on hunger strike, who did not move from his bunk. Edek pretended he could not understand a word of German—which he spoke quite well by now—and stuck to his unlikely story of having escaped a cruel farmer. But the Germans were having none of it. He was taken into the cellars, into a small room with walls and floor splattered with blood. Two men came in, whips in their hands. Playing with the whip, legs apart for better balance, one of them said: "In a moment, you will be talking, you Polish dog."

Edek gesticulated wildly, pointing to his ears and tongue, still pretending he could not understand. *At that moment, a miracle happened,* he wrote later. *The shorter German, who had been watching me closely said, "Let's leave him alone. Until tomorrow. Tomorrow we will confront him with the one he beat up."* Then, he clapped him on the back and led him back to his cell in a most friendly fashion. Even more strangely, the confrontation never happened. Perhaps his accuser had in the meantime moved somewhere else and it was too much bother to bring him over, or perhaps they judged that a young lad like Edek would be useful in supporting the war effort. A few days later Edek stood in front of a table draped in red cloth behind which, underneath Hitler's portrait, a tribunal heard his case. For work avoidance and an attempt to cross the border illegally, he was sentenced to two years in labor camp.

He was now transferred to a lower-security cell with others awaiting deportation to Germany. But one day just before departure, he was put to work shifting bundles of documents onto cars in the imposing red-brick railway headquarters. Now, perhaps Edek had heard the stories of what was happening in the concentration camps and did not want to risk being shipped to one. Or perhaps after imprisonment he just longed too much to be free. So, seeing his chance, he tossed a pack of documents on the back of the truck and simply ran for it, out of the gate and into the busy street. "Halt, halt," he heard behind him, and three shots rang out. He was already in a side street. He only stopped to collect his thoughts at a cemetery. He was again on his own—without identity papers or money. I often wonder how he managed to avoid arrest even for five minutes wandering about occupied Poland without an identity document—but obviously reality was different from films. Bydgoszcz tried to be a normal German city. A reasonably dressed boy keeping a low profile had a fair chance of crossing the city unmolested by the police.

Edek had no choice but to take the most dangerous course: he walked to Łochowo to try to contact his family. As he anticipated, the house was watched by the Germans, even after midnight when he made his approach. But he managed to sneak in through the open window of an old lodger—and a family friend. His father was already dead by then and it was to be the last time he would see his mother during the war. In darkness, he woke her gently, putting his finger to his lips and explaining what had happened. My grandmother said that the Gestapo had already been looking for him, threatening her with arrest unless she disclosed his hiding place. Then he washed and ate; his mother gave him all the money she had—and he sneaked back into the woods before dawn.

Aged sixteen, Edek was by now a seasoned conspirator. In order to deflect German attention from his mother, he staged a mock suicide. At a place on the Bromberger canal called Lisi Ogon, literally Fox's Tail—on top of one of the locks, the same one where I went fishing with my father as a child—he left his cap with a farewell letter inside, and a request to deliver it to his mother. As he was to learn later, the letter never reached its addressee. It landed in his Gestapo file. They believed it.

Edek made his way north, to Gdynia, where he hoped to touch base with relatives, those with whom he had spent the last days before the war. He followed the rail track across the forest, Bory Tucholskie, emerging into the cultivated areas to steal food and set fire to German barns. *The sight of the red glow against the autumn sky gave me great joy,* he wrote. He also piled tree trunks and stones on the rails in the hope of derailing trains; he enjoyed releasing locks on irrigation canals, so as to flood the fields and ruin the harvest. *If enough people carried out such sabotage, the occupier's economy would be disrupted,* he reasoned.

In Gdynia, his aunt's villa was now occupied by German officers, but the Poles ran an underground organization from the basement. Edek did not know its name, but took the oath with glee. Using forged papers, he escorted escapees from the nearby Stutthof concentration camp and monitored German naval traffic in the port, where he worked as a messenger for one of the managers. At night, they confiscated meat and other foodstuffs from the peasants and smuggled them into the town. After a while, he began suspecting it was a criminal scheme but his comrades told him it was a fund-raising operation for the underground. He never found out whether they were not simply doing a bit of business on the side. He was only convinced that the underground was for real when he saw one of the men that he helped to escape walking down the street in Gdynia in a German uniform. The operation must have been more important than he had realized.

It was in the underground that he met his second girlfriend, Magda. *She was sincere . . . and did everything to please me. One does not forget girls like that,* he reminisced. She was the romantic, dreamy type; she made plans for them after the war. She wanted to become a doctor. He confessed he wanted to be a tank commander. But it was not to be. After a few months of happy conspiratorial activity—thanks to his forged papers Edek could move freely about, even visiting cinemas—someone was caught, the cell's cover was blown, and arrests began.

Edek immediately moved out of his aunt's house. He was still free of suspicion at work and, by a lucky coincidence, his employer chose that moment to transfer him—deeper into Germany. This time, he ended up in a lovely old house in Frydland, a small town near the Baltic coast, where he again wormed his way into the confidence of his employer— a saddle and bridle maker, like his father. After a few weeks they trusted him so much that when the family went away to a wedding, they left Edek to guard the house and the workshop. The mistress gave him five marks for lemonade as an encouragement to be good. They were disappointed. *On returning from the railway station*—Edek recounted—*I plundered the apartment thoroughly.* He found sets of beautiful clothes, *obviously the property of their two sons, who were fighting for the führer and the Vaterland.* In the bread basket in the kitchen, he found food coupons for the whole family; in the master bedroom, in the drawer of a night table, 1,800 reichsmarks. The next morning he dutifully fed the farm animals and then fetched a French prisoner of war he had be-friended in the town who was going to help him to join a guerrilla unit in France. *Half an hour later, elegantly dressed in new suits, in Tyrol hats, neckties and briefcases under our arms, we left for the railway station.* The same day they were riding the S-bahn in Berlin. They walked up and down the Unter den Linden. In front of the Reich Chancellery, Edek wondered which window was Hitler's.

It was not just bravado that took them to Berlin: Edek had a family contact whose name and address he had learned by heart. They got there by a double-decker bus. The aunt was wary at first—as Poles they had been under Gestapo surveillance—but she soon invited them in. In the drawing room, her pretty daughter—Edek's cousin—was sitting on the lap of a young man in the uniform of a German tank officer. He proved to be a Pole by birth too, and perfectly friendly. The girl leaped at Edek and kissed him tenderly, as a long-lost relative.

Her father, a railwayman, supplied them with railway tickets all the way to Hannover. He also instructed them that beyond that point they should only buy tickets for stretches of less than a hundred kilometers. It was something to do with the way ticket offices reported sales to the security services. On the train, the only suspicions they raised were those of middle-aged German women in the carriage. They looked at them with hostility and envy—not because they were foreigners, but because they were assumed to be Germans. German boys their age, their sons, were all at the front.

Lulled into a false sense of security by the absence of any checks on the way to Hannover, Edek and the Frenchman bought tickets from Hannover to Osnabrück—longer than the hundred-kilometer limit. The train was almost empty, so Edek wedged himself into a corner and fell asleep. He was woken up by rude shaking on his jacket. There were two of them, a policeman and a civilian, and they demanded to see his identity documents. At Osnabrück he found himself locked up in a cell. Before he was handcuffed there was enough time to eat incriminating papers, such as food stamps marked with their place of issue. The Frenchman had evaporated.

This time, Edek knew better than to give his real name. He pre-tended not to speak German but when his Gestapo interrogator learned that he was Polish, he laughed and cursed him in Edek's native language: *Kurwa twoja mać,* an unsubtle allusion to his mother's morals. It didn't make any difference. The Gestapo man—though obviously a part-Pole by birth—forbade him to use the word "Poland" in his testimony, saying that such a country no longer existed and never would again. After a routine drubbing, he was again before a summary tribunal, which passed what was obviously the standard sentence for wandering *untermenschen:* two years' labor camp.

Three days later he was in a nearby mine, pushing carts filled with iron ore in sight of machine guns. It was a small camp, with only about four hundred prisoners, most of whom, like Edek, had short sentences. *But I doubt if anybody outlasted it because it was hell on earth,* he wrote. They worked fourteen-hour days and every day a few of the prisoners died. One day a Belgian boy who worked by his side fainted and never woke up again. On another, an escapee was captured and brought back. *They beat him up so savagely that his body was opened up with broad wounds oozing pus. Then they tied him up with ropes to a pole in the middle of the central square and hung a board on his neck saying "escapee." Clouds of mosquitoes and other insects ate at him and we had to walk around the pole and sing marches.*

Edek did not spend much time in the mine. One day he found himself among thirty of the prisoners selected for medical examination. They were attended to by a young doctor in the uniform of a Luftwaffe captain. Having sounded the prisoners' hearts and lungs, he selected two of them, another Pole from near Kraków, and Edek. Rumors said that they would be transferred to an ammunition factory, where they needed people in good health—but these proved false. A few days later the two boys were examined again in the presence of civilian Gestapo officials after which they were informed that they were both seriously ill. The illness is infectious, they were told, but fortunately it was diagnosed in time, so they would be taken to hospital for treatment. It is a strange strain, new in Germany, which is why they would be kept in isolation from other patients.

"Don't worry," said one of the civilians. "You'll be fine there. After the treatment you can choose the kind of job you want." *I suspected something,* wrote Edek, *got up my courage and said:*

"I am well. There is nothing wrong with me. I don't want to go to the hospital."

"What do you know, boy," said the civilian. "You've been diagnosed by a doctor who knows exactly what's wrong with you. You'll see for yourself in the hospital."

I was destined for death, wrote Edek, *but first my Polish blood was to enrich German science and that young Fascist doctor was to make some epoch-making discovery, earning a diploma or a cross.*

The hospital, probably a military one, was an imposing building with a lovely old park crossed by a stream. Edek and the other Pole were put in small rooms in the attic where he had a beautiful view of the countryside. They were washed, shaved, and well fed, attended by a nurse called Elizabeth, young and sympathetic but unforthcoming. After a fortnight, Edek gained weight and felt strong. Then, Elizabeth took a blood sample and, shortly afterward, jabbed him with an injection. *I felt my body temperature rise,* remembered Edek. *It surprised me because I hadn't caught a cold, I didn't even have a cough. I told the nurse about it and she said it was only the beginning. The sickness I have, she said, could only be destroyed with high fever.* He was injected every day for the next three weeks, the doses becoming greater and greater. *My appearance changed beyond recognition. My face was yellow, my lips were swollen and dry, my tongue covered with white slime. I could not walk or even raise myself on the bed. I just lay there like a log, shivering. I kept asking the nurse how long it would continue and begged her to hasten my death. But she always answered that it was not up to her, that she was only obeying her instructions.* He was conscious enough to notice that the door of the room next door, where the other Pole was kept, no longer creaked. Then, one evening, *a nun entered the room. She stood over me with hands clasped in prayer and asked me whether I was Catholic and whether I believed in God. At first I thought it was an apparition caused by fever. I looked at her uncomprehendingly and I could not speak because tears filled my eyes and I cried.* The nun asked Edek how old he was and where he was from. She prayed and then said, "So young and he has to go—what are they doing?" He thought that everything was lost when the nurse mentioned that a "second stage" of his treatment would begin. The doctor examined him again, and Edek heard him murmur to the nurse, "Look at what health those Poles have."

Edek was given pills which, to his surprise, made him better. He later speculated that he had probably been injected with malaria, and then with a new form of artificial quinine. The Germans must have been pretty desperate for the stuff: two members of my family—Edek and my great-uncle Roman, who was at about the same time wriggling out of the experiments at Dachau—had come in contact with similar tests. The injections stopped, he began to eat again, and within a few days he was well enough to walk. But he knew that he would not live through the "second stage," which would probably involve higher doses. He was shrewd enough to realize that, apart from anything else, the Germans would want to get rid of a witness.

Edek is not very good about giving dates in his diary, but this must have been 1944, for he describes his joy at seeing through his attic window waves of Allied bombers, with fighters above them, flying west toward Berlin. Because Osnabrück lay on the flight path from England, air raids were an almost daily event. During the raids, Edek remained locked up in the attic while his nurse ran for safety.

As he got better, he asked the nurse to take him for a walk round the park. With the doctor's approval, she agreed and Edek had a good look around. He was gratified to see that the hospital was not heavily guarded. He now pretended to be sicker than he was and three days later Elza took him out for a walk again. *The moment we entered the park, the air-raid alarm was sounded,* he recalled in his diary. *This was rare because normally there was always a* Vor-alarm, *an early warning, which gave people time to hide. But this time German anti-aircraft guns were caught by surprise. Sudden alarms like this created panic. Elza ordered me to go back to the hospital but I objected categorically, saying that it was dangerous in the attic. She screamed at me but I stood apart from her, in a threatening posture. When she heard the sound of approaching aircraft above our heads, she yelled at me not to wander off and ran for the shelter.*

My decision was immediate, Edek recounted. *I jumped over a low perimeter fence and into a hothouse. I grabbed some work clothes and, through the vegetable garden, ran into a field. Aircraft were flying low above my head and I ran with them, toward distant hills. Suddenly, I lost all my strength. I could not breathe, I felt gripping pains and nausea. I could not continue. With my last effort I lay in some bushes on the edge of the forest. I was totally ruined physically and further escape was out of the question. I prayed. I wanted to live, I was so young.*

Some hours later, he recovered and walked on but he had bad luck when he hit a barbed-wire fence with a plaque announcing a closed military area. He doubled back toward the town, and then walked all night trying to get away from it, falling asleep only the next day, in a cornfield.

He was woken up by the rattle of a cart and a conversation in mixed Polish and Ukrainian. The pair on the cart—he a Pole, she a Ukrainian—were forced laborers, and helped him immediately. A few days later, dressed as a peasant and with a pitchfork across his shoulder, fifty reichsmarks in his pocket, Edek sauntered into the historic town of Münster, untouched by bombs and pretty as a postcard. Thanks to the charming Nazi custom of making people carry badges stating their nationality, Edek could accost a stranger in the street with a letter P for Pole stitched to his chest knowing that he would be a friend. And so it proved. A man called Zbyszek, from Poznań, who worked as a messenger in a restaurant, happened to be cycling by. They were soon together in a workers' hotel run by German trade unions, unguarded and perfectly decent. The trouble was, how could they legalize Edek's status there, or get him legitimate documents for further travel?

After a few days' rest, Edek's new friends supplied him with tattered Ukrainian-looking clothes and led him to the hall at the railway station. He stood under a pillar and began to cry. As had been anticipated, a railway policeman soon came up to him and took him to the station. When questioned, Edek spun a story about his family being voluntary workers from the east. As their train stopped at the station Edek had been told to fetch some water. By the time he came back, the train was gone, separating him from his family and even from his identity documents. The Germans examined him. Almost the entire police station crowded into the interrogation room to have a look at him. *I did look pathetic,* remembered Edek. *My clothes were torn and dirty.*

"They all look like that, those people in the east. None of them has ever seen a suit," said one.

"Gentlemen, this is a savage; take him out of here or we'll never get rid of his lice," said another.

"They only wash once a year, on Stalin's birthday," the commandant pronounced gravely. "It's hard enough to have to look at them. Imagine having to rub shoulders against them, as our soldiers at the front sometimes have to!"

At every comment, the policemen boomed with laughter, and Edek could not stop himself laughing as well, but the Germans did not suspect that he could understand them. The ruse worked. The commandant told Edek through an interpreter—another Pole recognized by his badge with the letter P and grabbed from the street—"to stop crying like a lamb. You'll be all right. We won't look for your family, but we'll give you work here."

Half an hour later he was at a normal labor office, sitting across a desk from a young woman. Since he had stated truthfully that his father had a leather-working workshop and he himself was trained in the trade, he was assigned to a manufacturer of artificial limbs. The factory's owner and director, Dr. Robert Keller, drove him in his smart Opel and offered him cigarettes. Everything was turning out nicely for Edek except that he had to continue to pretend not to speak German. So, once at the factory, when he was ordered to strip naked for a bath, he could not react. Five Germans lunged at him and tore off all his clothes, which they disposed of in the oven. He was told to follow them to the bathroom. Again, no reaction. *And so it happened,* he wrote, *that the Germans carried me on their shoulders through the entire factory, in full view of the women employees, and dropped me into a bathtub, which gave me burns because the water was too hot.* When the Germans saw him close the hot water tap and open the cold, they pronounced that, for a savage, he showed promise.

Edek was assigned to a room with two Germans, a hunchback called Rott, with *a thin rat-like face,* and the other with an artificial leg, called Kirschmeyer. For living quarters he was assigned to the same workers' guesthouse, together again with Zbyszek and the Poles who had hatched the plan. Trading stolen food and cigarettes, they now obtained quinine for him from a pharmacy, which cured Edek's recurring attacks of fever. Even though he had to continue pretending that he could not speak German, his two work companions appreciated his aptitude with the needle and got to like him. The hunchback was a chatterbox. Edek soon realized that they both passionately disliked Hitler. They listened to the German service of the BBC, told rude jokes about Göering and his wife, and predicted that the war would be lost. Sometimes, Dr. Keller himself joined them in their discussions over a second breakfast.

At the same time they accepted stereotypes about Poland, a backward place for which, they thought, German occupation was a salvation. Most Poles, they said, were thieves and layabouts. The hunchback said he knew this for a fact because a cousin of his had come back recently from the Eastern Front through Kraków. He sat in a bar and went up to the counter to get a glass of beer. By the time he came back to his seat, his rifle and his rucksack were gone. And it wasn't the rifle he missed, stressed the hunchback, but there were two fat geese in the rucksack which he hoped to present to his family at home. Edek had to force himself, alternately, not to protest and not to laugh.

Life was good again, the only nuisance being the increasingly frequent air raids. But Edek did not particularly mind. The air-raid bunker was a multistory affair where segregation was enforced: Germans on the deeper floors, foreigners at the top. While the Germans prayed, wailed, and cursed after every bomb that hit the town, the foreigners cheered, sang, and laughed. *We didn't feel any pity for those underneath us*, remembered Edek.

Several months had passed. Edek would have seen out the end of the war if it hadn't been for bottlenecks in German steel production. Much of German industry lay in ruins. Because of the steel shortages, good-quality leather needles were in short supply. So, when he broke two in a row one day, Rott, the hunchback, cursed him. *He shook his fist at me and screamed that I was a savage and a Polish pig*, remembered Edek. *For a moment I stood there just looking at him, then I lost my temper. I said, very deliberately, in correct German, "What have I done to you Mr. Rott that you curse me so much?"* The Germans were struck dumb. *Rott took a step back and stood still as if glued to the ground. His mouth opened wide and he straightened out, his hunchback seemingly gone. Then, he suddenly turned and, screaming "informer," ran out. Kirschmeyer hobbled out behind him.*

Half an hour later, Edek was sitting in a leather armchair in Dr. Keller's study, the doctor visibly nervous. Knowing his anti-Nazi views, Edek risked it and told him his history, omitting only the theft in Frydland and the experiments in the hospital. When he finished, Keller said: "I need a man like you, Edward. As of today you will no longer work here and I will take you into my house, where you will have my sons' room."

Edek became the adopted son of a bourgeois family. He lived with the Kellers in their luxury apartment above the workshops, on the top floor. Mrs. Keller led him to her two sons' bedroom, opened their wardrobes and said to Edek, "Take anything you want. Gunter and

Hans will surely not be coming back, because few come back from this war." Three days later the news came that Gunter had indeed died. As Edek chose Gunter's bed to sleep in, Mrs. Keller said that he would now replace her dead son. She stroked Edek's hair, saying that he was similar to Gunter. But Edek gave his love to Anita, the red-haired maid. The race laws, which prohibited carnal relations between Germans and Poles, gave them both an added frisson of excitement. Their bliss was disturbed only by Mrs. Keller's depression. She developed stomach ulcers and shat herself, so wrote my uncle, at the sound of the air-raid siren.

One day, the bombers had a proper go at Münster. When Edek, Mrs. Keller, and Anita emerged from the shelter they saw the whole quarter in ruins. *Houses burned as far as the eye could see,* wrote Edek. *Even the asphalt on the streets burned. Charcoal corpses of women and children littered the rubble. Rows of trees blazed, looking like a torch parade. Screams and crying emitted from the cellars. For the first time, I was sad.*

The Kellers' house was also destroyed. Mrs. Keller stood in the ruins, looked around, and laughed. "Now I'm as rich as you, Edward," she said. "All that I have left is in those two suitcases you're carrying." Only later did he learn that the luggage contained gold and precious stones worth more than what had just been destroyed.

The two women now cried and Edek prospected in the ruins. He heard moans for help from the depths of a cellar. It was one of the employees. After an hour's work, he saw Mr. Rott, the hunchback, who as usual had been too lazy to run for the shelter. His legs were broken, so Edek and Anita carried him to the hospital on the back of a door. *Probably the same one which he slammed when he ran out after hearing me speak German,* wrote Edek.

To his own surprise, Edek worried about the Kellers' fate and speculated which of the machines in their factory might yet be salvageable. He heard himself giving advice to Mrs. Keller. *Why did I, an enemy of Germany and everything that was German, begin to care about their property?* he wondered later. *They were kind to me, as a Pole, which was one thing. And then, they were not one of those naive Germans who joined hysterical crowds at Hitler's rallies. Not all Germans were the same.*

Other Germans remained cocky until they heard guns in the west. A couple of weeks before liberation Edek spoke to the old gardener of the hospital in which he now worked. The man was still convinced that wonder weapons would turn the tide. He also hinted that a meeting of the city defense committee had decided that, as a precaution against sabotage, the SS would round up and murder all the foreign workers in the town. Edek and his friends armed themselves and prepared hiding places.

But the Americans surprised everyone with the speed of their advance. *The first tanks with a white star arrived at four in the morning. The roar of the engines lifted us up from our bunks,* Edek remembered. The boys on them were *tall and handsome, with teeth that shone white when they smiled, with camouflage on their helmets.* Edek was surprised that they were so clean and rested. A cheering crowd of liberated forced workers surrounded the tanks. Girls kissed the soldiers, Russians waved red flags, Italians shrieked, *the whole international crowd, brought by Fascism to poverty, hunger, and suffering, was giving vent to its feelings.* Edek waved his own red-and-white Polish flag. But his mood was not as high as he had hoped it would be. Alienated from the joyous crowd, he noticed that their liberators could hardly be bothered to acknowledge the enthusiasm. They seemed more like tourists than conquerors. Then one of the soldiers threw a cigarette butt on the ground. A Pole picked it up. The Americans laughed and snapped photographs. *I mulled over that scene for a long time afterward. I wondered why our liberators made a show of those poor people they were freeing. . . . I never liked them after that.*

With the war over, Edek said goodbye to the Kellers, who used the jewels to establish a new workshop in the country. Edek just wanted to go home—but it was not so simple. Even when the war ended a few days later, he had to wait for a train. Together with hundreds of other Poles he lived in a camp outside town. Couples of every conceivable nationality lived together. A jealous boyfriend knifed Edek in the back suspecting him correctly of an affair with his beautiful Yugoslav girlfriend, Lida.

The Americans were not arresting Nazis, Edek observed, so the foreigners took justice into their own hands. A policeman and several farmers who had mistreated their laborers were beaten to death. Food became scarce, so the foreigners looted. *You simply went to a German farmhouse a few miles outside the town, put the farmer and his family against the wall, and took what you wanted,* Edek related. It was worse if the house contained a picture of Hitler or photographs of family members in SS uniforms.

The looting became so bad the Americans surrounded the camp with tanks, barrels pointing inside. But some Poles got the guards drunk with camp-manufactured moonshine, and looting parties slipped out on wooden bridges cast over the perimeter fence. Once, the soldier on the main gate was so drunk he allowed himself to be put in a rocking chair. Some Poles kept rocking the chair while others used his rifle for a foray to get some sausage. The military authorities wondered how they managed to continue stealing while locked up. Another time, an elderly German woman was brought to the camp under American guard and allowed to inspect rows of Poles so as to finger the two who had raped her the night before. She had barely begun when a group of Polish girls lunged at her, stripped her of clothes, scratched her face, and tore out her hair. The Americans who guarded her were beaten up too.

Another German woman who came to the camp was a widow whose sons had died—she had to farm on her own. She demanded that a Pole and a Ukrainian girl who now lived in the camp come back to work. Edek explained to her that these people had been rounded up in the street and brought to Germany against their will and now wanted to go home. She would have none of it. They had been assigned to her by the labor office, she said, and if they didn't come back this instant, she would go to the police to complain. Edek laughed and ejected her into the street.

Perhaps in revenge for the reign of terror, someone—a German, it was assumed—shot a Polish couple walking in broad daylight in the Münster municipal park. Edek could not remember their names, but they were intelligentsia types, Warsaw uprising survivors who had just emerged from a concentration camp. Unlike Edek and his degenerate friends, they were most unlikely to have been looters. The funeral attracted several thousand Poles (and others) from all over northern Germany, including representatives of the Polish government in London and the chaplain of the Polish Army in the West. The procession stretched for miles. Edek and his friends from the camp waited for the mass and the speeches to end. They were prepared. *From mouth to mouth the word went to spare none. From the cradle upward, every German had to go,* Edek remembered. Everybody was armed—Edek had a

7mm Mauser. Others had machine guns, knives, or crowbars. As had been agreed, they struck when the first lumps of soil hit the coffins. *The streets of Münster on that day defied description. We beat up and shot every Gerry we met. Groups of a hundred waded the whole width of the street, smashing everything German. The Germans were so frightened, they knelt in the middle of the street, begging for forgiveness and mercy. Our hearts didn't have much.* Only when British and American troops entered the town in the evening, with machine guns and armored personnel carriers, did the pogrom stop. *The Germans later said that they would long remember the drubbing they got from us Poles,* Edek proudly noted.

Weeks passed and the transports were nowhere in sight, so Edek and four others decided to go it alone, on bikes stolen from Germans. Edek took particular pleasure in taking a nice new one from the old gardener who had been so arrogant on the dawn of defeat. He set off east into the hilly countryside with a Mauser in the tool box, five days' supply of food in the basket, and a little red-and-white Polish flag fluttering in the wind. They headed north for Meppen, at that time called Maczków by Poles because it was the headquarters of the Polish tank division, commanded by General Maczek, which had fought with the Allies in the west. The weather was perfect, the countryside beautiful, the roads good. Girls turned their heads when they passed by. Maczków greeted them with Polish flags on every house and streets resounding in Polish. The boys were elated. Edek in particular boasted of their plans to make it to Poland by bicycle, and encouraged others to join them. They decided to stay for a few days' rest and breathe Polishness for a change.

On the third day they were arrested by the Polish military police. *The interrogation started with a blow, from which I passed out,* Edek recalled. *Lying on the floor, bleeding, I felt kicks in my backside.* When he came to, a Polish sergeant was standing over him, screaming, "You Communist pig! You Bolshevik scum! You traitor!" Then a handsome major behind a desk told Edek that he was suspected of spreading Communist propaganda, and of fomenting Soviet-style agitation in favor of returning to Poland. Edek explained that he was no Communist, that he did not actually know what the word meant. He just wanted to go home because native poverty was better than exile. The major said that he wanted to help him and explained to him that Poland was going to be Communist and he should not go back. With luck, the West will eventually fight the Soviet Union and they could all go back to liberate Poland for real.

What Edek did not know at the time, and did not seem to appreciate even when he wrote his memoir twenty-five years later, was that many of General Maczek's soldiers were survivors of the Soviet gulag. They and their families were the remnants of over a million Poles whom the Soviets had deported from eastern Poland when they partitioned the country with Hitler in 1939. The same sort of horrors that Edek had seen in Germany they had seen in the Soviet Union. After the cold, the executions, and Siberian labor camps, they had been led out of the Soviet Union into British-occupied Persia. Having fought with the Allies, they now faced the prospect of going back to a Poland ruled by the Communists, their tormentors; they knew that there was no great difference between the Nazis and the Soviets. For Edek, on the other hand, the Russians were victims like himself. All the Russian characters which appear in his story are sympathetic; Kolyas, Volodyas, and Ilyushas who help him as much as he helps them. The one or two commissars among them—those who managed to avoid being executed by the Germans—also seemed good. The more Communist, the more anti-German, and the better Edek liked them.

The lectures about the dangers he would face if he went back continued for a few more days. Edek was not convinced. *It was in the cell there that my hatred rose up to those people, those bankrupt, quarrelsome band of émigré politicians,* he wrote. Eventually, he was made to sign an undertaking not to agitate anymore, and released. His bicycle was confiscated and they were ordered to stay put.

That night, together with a new friend, Janek, they skipped town. By dawn, they were riding west, to Hamburg in the cabin of an American truck driven by *a jolly Negro who gave us chocolate and cigarettes and patted us on the back saying* "gut kamerad." *Every fifty kilometers he stopped, went outside, and performed gymnastics with springs and weights, laughing all the time,* Edek remembered.

Hamburg was still smoldering from bombs, so their way was blocked. Only soldiers were allowed to cross the bridge onto the eastern bank of the Elbe. So Edek and Janek walked upstream along the river, to Magdeburg, where they were greeted by red flags, huge portraits of Marx, Lenin, and Stalin, and gigantic slogans facing west from the Soviet-occupied side of the river. The city had been captured by American troops and was still under their control, but under the terms agreed at Yalta was soon to pass into the Soviet occupation zone. Edek hoped that once the Soviet zone enveloped them, it would be easier to traverse it east into Poland. The looting in Magdeburg was good. Edek stole Nazi insignia, medals, and crosses. They fetched good prices with the Americans, who attached them to their belts as war trophies. In a warehouse he found packs of "führer gifts" for soldiers, each containing cigarettes, matches, a bar of chocolate, toilet paper, soap, and other necessities. Edek sorted them into separate piles and sold the goods on the black market.

At last, the morning came when Edek stood on a mound of rubble with a fine view of the pontoon bridge, watching the Soviet Army take possession of Magdeburg. A band of Allied officials, military, and journalists took positions on a makeshift podium. When everyone settled down, three Soviet soldiers crossed the bridge with a red flag in their arms. The orchestra played national anthems. Then an American soldier took down and folded the Stars and Stripes; on the same mast a Soviet soldier hoisted their flag. Then the Russian units marched across the bridge and passed the podium. Edek had been looking forward to seeing "the people who had liberated Poland" but the sight of them now disappointed him. After the sporting looks of Western soldiers, Edek was shocked by the Soviets' dirty, torn uniforms and unshaven faces. Nevertheless, they marched proudly, holding their heads high and smiling.

With a few more minor adventures, Edek eventually made it to Berlin where, after two days wandering in the ruins, he found the right railway station. He joined a mob which took possession of a military transport and, riding on top of a carriage, he found himself a few hours later in Piła—back in Poland. *I was beside myself with joy when I jumped off the roof of the train. Everything I saw was Polish: Polish uniforms, Polish flags, Polish speech. I could hardly speak with joy. I just stood there, looking about me, at all that I had dreamed of for years,* he wrote on the last pages of his memoir.

After taking a look at the new Poland, not only did he not escape back to the West, he joined the Communists. It happened at a military academy, which he attended together with Mieczysław Rakowski, a peasant boy from a village a dozen kilometers down the road from Ło-chowo. Rakowski was the future prime minister and last first secretary of the Polish Communist Party. Perhaps Edek still only wanted to be a tank commander. Instead, he became a political officer, a commissar. He probably took part in operations against the anti-Communist resistance. He said later that he only fought against the Ukrainians in the southeast of Poland, as if that made it any better. But he never became a Communist in the deepest, temperamental sense; he was never like the gray bureaucrats with dandruff on their shoulders, the figures I came to associate with the term.

Sometime in the 1950s, he took part in a bash for Polish and Soviet officers. Many of the top brass were Russians, albeit with adopted Polish names. He noticed that their Soviet comrades patronized and ordered the Poles about. Edek argued back. One of the Soviets, a general, astonished at his impudence, screamed and punched him in the face. It was well into the evening. Perhaps the memory of the Hitler youth in Bydgoszcz—the boy who had lashed him across the face with a whip—flooded his drunken mind. Or perhaps he remembered his German school friends in Łochowo, who would not let him pass unless he took his cap off. Or perhaps, as usual, he simply acted before he thought. Edek's palm made a wide arch in the air and its full force landed on the Soviet general's cheek.

It was a scandal. He was demoted, dishonorably discharged from the army, and expelled from the Communist Party. After that, he never settled down. An ill-matched marriage ended in divorce. He drank. He wrote the diary in prison, with a conviction for disorderly behavior. He went to prison again for looting shops in Szczecin during the anti-Communist riots in the city in 1970, when several people were shot. We don't know whether the looting was a political act, a throwback to his wild time in Germany, or perhaps an undercover operation instigated by his old chums in the Communist apparatus. After coming out of prison, he tried business ventures. With his customary enterprise, he ran a successful flower shop, then a leather workshop.

I wish I had read his diary earlier. I would have asked him what he now thought of his decision to defy General Maczek's Poles in the West and come back to Soviet-dominated Poland. I would have argued that he had got it wrong; that the Poles who told him in 1945 that Communism would be a disaster had gotten it right. Not in the sense that he should absolutely not have come back to Poland: he might have decided that even a Communist Poland was preferable to exile, or that he might better have served the national interest from outside. But Maczek's men had correctly predicted that all the promises of free elections, democracy, justice, and freedom given to Poland by Stalin and his Western allies were a sham. Poland would become Communist, and would bury two generations' lives in oppression, poverty, and hopelessness. Thirty-six years after him, in London in 1981, faced with a similar choice to the one he had faced in Magdeburg in 1945, I chose to stay in Britain as a political refugee. We both lived to see 1989, the collapse of Communism, the time Maczek's people had dreamed of as the true liberation. But for him, it came late. I last saw him in Bydgoszcz in 1992. His face was carved in deep bruises, his brow was sweating, and between bouts of lively conversation, he groaned in agony. A few weeks later cancer of the pancreas killed him.

The choice that Edek faced in 1945 and I in 1981—between living under Communism, or going into exile, either external or internal—still fundamentally divides us Poles several years after Communism's collapse. People will not shake hands with one another, not belong to the same political party—even though they agree on most things—not join the same trade union, or even send their children to the same scout camp, because they made a different political decision years before. To us anti-Communists, postwar Poland was an occupied country, and the Communist administration was illegitimate from the moment its founders received their instructions from Stalin. On this reading of history, official Poland was "their" Poland, the Poland of the Communist apparatus and, ultimately, of the Soviet system: collaboration with it was treason to Polish interests, ethically even worse than collaboration in the Vichy regime of France. The opposite view is that despite its limited sovereignty, Communist Poland was "our" Poland after all, imperfect to be sure, but the only one possible under the historical circumstances. Under that reading of history, it had been right to join its institutions.

When I was growing up in Communist Poland, our attitude to Communism dominated our lives. If my parents had joined the Party, they could have received faster promotion, better pay and perks, easier travel abroad, or vacations in special resorts. Actively resisting the system was by the 1970s and 1980s rarely a matter of life and death. More often it implied petty persecutions: perhaps one's passport would be withheld, perhaps one's children would have trouble getting a place at university, or perhaps one would just be stuck in a lowly job while the mediocre moved ahead. Being decent no longer required heroism—but it did require mental discipline. In countless daily decisions, one negotiated a line between compromise and collaboration. We took the need for such moral vigilance for granted.

Edek and his diary made me realize something that I had not conceded before: that a normal, intelligent man, good and sinful like all of us, could have slid into backing Communism without realizing that he was making a moral choice at all. If he had not—for noble motives—thrown a stone at the Hitler Youth in Łochowo, he might have seen the end of the war in his native village and would have stayed longer under his family's moderating influence. Had he not thrown that stone, he would never have gone to Germany and hence would never have been beaten up by General Maczek's Poles in the West. Had American soldiers not taken photographs of a Pole picking up their cigarette butt, Edek would have idealized Americans like everyone else in Poland. Had it not been for the unfortunate encounters with anti-Communist Poles and Americans, he might never have joined the Party. Had he not joined the Party, he would never have met and slapped the Soviet general. Had he not been punished for it and outcast, he would not have taken part in the riot and gone to jail again. This century's two totalitarianisms specialized in crushing impulsive and headstrong—typically Polish—characters such as Edek. Every time I pass the farm where he hid in the barn just after escaping from the Bydgoszcz Gestapo, I feel grateful that I was born late enough to be spared his choices.

POTULICE

WHAT MUST IT FEEL LIKE to live near Dachau or Auschwitz today, to farm the fields fertilized with human ash? Foreign tourists and journalists who come to Poland are invariably shocked by sights like Hotel Oświęcim, Auschwitz Hotel. The town had existed for centuries, and the hotel was there before the camp, but in the world's imagination Auschwitz means only one thing: extermination. To use the name for anything else seems like sacrilege.

I have a good idea of what it is like to live next to a concentration camp because, as I realized in the course of delving into Chobielin's history, we actually live next to one. You can see its chimney spewing black smoke, not two kilometers away from Chobielin: Potulice, the prison where Uncle Edek wrote his diary, used to be a concentration camp. As you enter the village, you drive past a huge oak tree, a housing estate, a soccer field, and a furniture factory with a gas station. On the other side of the road is a large compound dominated by watchtowers, walls with barbed wire, a large steel gate, and chimneys spitting black smoke. The road's asphalt covers cobblestones originally laid by the inmates. To most people around Potulice, as it would be to most people everywhere, this is all just a part of the landscape.

Until the 1930s, Potulice was an estate belonging to the Potulicki family, one of the wealthiest in Poland. It had a large neo-Gothic palace, a nineteenth-century church, and a deer park. It was surrounded by thousands of acres of land, carp ponds, and extensive manufactures. When the old Countess Potulicka, the last of her family, died in 1932, she bequeathed it to the Catholic University in Lublin. The palace became the seat of a theological seminary, training priests to minister to Poles abroad.

But when the Nazis arrived, they began to use the palace and its grounds as a transit camp: Poles were being expelled from the region to be replaced by Germans from Bessarabia and Romania. Its first prisoners were those few priests who stayed behind to protect the library after the seminary was evacuated. Prisoners began arriving in February 1941—over two thousand people from Bydgoszcz and the surrounding countryside in the first few days. The place was totally unprepared to handle such numbers. They slept in the palace rooms and in corridors subdivided into levels with rough boards. Like animals, they had hay for bedding. There was no heating, closets, or washing facilities.

Only later in the year did a proper camp come into existence, designed to hold ten thousand inmates, mainly Poles. Prisoners from the infamous camp at Stutthof near Gdańsk built thirty barracks as well as accommodation for sixty-five SS men and two hundred guards. The construction was personally supervised by Albert Forster, the gauleiter. Photographs show him during an inspection: a thin, handsome man in breeches with a swastika band on his left arm and a pistol in his belt. Fierce memos flew between the camp and his office. The building work was not proceeding on schedule and several hundred prisoners lived in so called "nigger barracks"—wooden boxes with dirt floors, where diseases spread.

Potulice became a classic camp compound with a barbed-wire perimeter fence and workshops. The organization was typical. Each barrack had its supervisor elevated from the ranks of prisoners, called an *Ordnungsfuhrer.* Work was overseen by *kapos,* answerable to a *Haupt kapo,* who reported directly to the Germans. Inside the compound prisoners made aircraft wings; in the palace a group of Jews from Gdańsk—the only ones in the camp—made furs for Schultz & Co.

New arrivals were examined by a specialist from the Chief Office for

Race and Colonization. Skulls and noses were carefully measured for Slavic and Germanic traits. Prisoners completed modern psychological tests. About ten percent of prisoners passed muster and were deemed suitable for Germanization. Others—633 in all—were deemed such interesting specimens that they were sent for further study in the office's headquarters in Łódź. Those pronounced deviant either in mind or in body were shipped off and never heard from again. A few weeks later the families received uniform notes stating the cause of death as "heart attack."

Apparently, the average Potulice food ration of 1,300 calories per day was low even by concentration camp standards. Food consisted of 250 grams of bread, weak coffee, and three quarters of a liter of thin soup. Work discipline was nevertheless good, maintained by the liberal use of punishments. Throughout its existence, between a third and half of Potulice's inmates were children, including several hundred Soviet children from near Witebsk—the children of captured or murdered partisans. Over five hundred Potulice children were later sent to Auschwitz and it is possible that they were among those whom the Red Army found there on the day of liberation. We see them occasionally on our television screens, rolling up their sleeves to show the camera their tattooed arms.

Polish testimonies of wartime Potulice are depressingly familiar. The road from Nakło to Bydgoszcz, the one on which I ride almost daily, was built by children, who carried stones from barges on the Bromberger canal. By comparison, it was considered a treat to be assigned to a group which picked berries in the woods for the SS men's kitchen. The work was easier but the mental anguish was greater. The children, shriveled from hunger, could not risk eating even a few berries. A German checked the children's mouths for blackness of the tongue at the end of the day. The SS men liked playing with the children: if one was found eating their berries they threw him into a pool, even in winter. When the child tried to come out, they kicked him back into the water.

The end came suddenly. In January 1945 the inmates were ordered to march west. Some guards were conscientious to the last—for example, those who shot twenty-one children between the ages of eight and thirteen near Więcbork—but most of them skulked away. In all, Potulice claimed 1,297 documented victims, who rest in the cemetery three hundred meters from the main road.

Today it's the largest prison in Poland. A boulder at the entrance to the palace avenue commemorates the camp's Polish victims; another one, a few hundred meters away, marks the spot where executions were carried out. German atrocities at Potulice are a part of local history that we were taught at school. In April 1995 I witnessed a ceremony at the camp cemetery in which our provincial governor—a former Communist—spoke to the survivors in the shade of a field altar.

I met an organizer of scholarly conferences about the camp. Out of curiosity, I asked whether she knew to what use the camp was put after the war, before it became a prison. "Oh yes, I know," she said. "Germans were kept here. Until 1990 there was a plaque which mentioned it but I intervened with the authorities and eventually it was removed."

Somehow, the story of an internment camp for Germans at Potulice doesn't feature in our local collective imagination. It features prominently, on the other hand, in the German government's collection of documents on "The Expulsion of the German Population from the Territories East of the Oder-Neisse Line." In fact, the Potulice camp seems to have been one of the biggest—it earned a separate chapter and references in dozens of accounts.

P.L., her name is kept secret in the documents, a German typist from Łódź, was engulfed by the Russian offensive in 1945 and had only the time to leave her child with another German woman before being locked up. In that year, the tables were turned on the Germans. Under the Yalta and Potsdam agreements between Britain, the United States, and Russia, Poland lost territories in the east and gained former German provinces in the west: Germans were to be expelled from east of the new border. Contrary to Nazi orders, millions of German civilians had already escaped before the advancing Soviet troops but in January 1945 millions more were trapped on the wrong side of the front line by the speed of the offensive. After the initial onslaught, when thousands were shot, raped, and deported, the expulsion became more orderly. The remaining German population from Poland proper, recent settlers from the Nazi period, and Germans from East Prussia, Pomerania, and Silesia—about five million in all—were gathered in internment camps all over western Poland to await trains west.

Little had changed in Potulice with the new regime. When P.L. arrived in the camp in January 1945 her belongings were immediately confiscated, including prayer books, savings account documents, and family photos, which were torn up and thrown at her feet. Next, the inmates had to paint large swastikas on the backs of one another's dresses, later changed to the letter N for *Niemka,* meaning German, and then to W for *więźniarka,* meaning prisoner. Fresh arrivals went into a fourteen-day quarantine, during which they were shut up in the wooden huts, sleeping in pairs or threes in narrow, three-story wooden beds which were called "bug cases." The quarantine was made particularly unpleasant, reported P.L., by the chief doctor of the camp, who insisted, for example, that the windows of the quarantine huts remain open day and night, even in winter. The penalties for closing a window were having to stand naked with a window open, or hop up and down in the hut passage, or mop up a bucket of water deliberately spilled on the hut floor. The doctor insisted on cutting off the women's hair all over their bodies, and took pleasure in watching it being done. "And we poor German women had to sit quite naked along the walls in the dressing room of the shower baths and were exposed to the lewd gazes and impertinent jokes of the spectators," complained P.L.

After the quarantine, the doctor organized "scabies examinations" which involved all the prisoners filing in front of him quite naked. "The women whom he selected," testified P.L., "mostly had no sign of scabies but had the bad luck to strike his eye, perhaps because as Germans they still had good figures." The chief doctor also picked pretty girls to do domestic work for him and "if they did not yield to him they were sent back to the camp under the pretense of having stolen cigarettes or other things. . . . They were then subjected to cross-examinations and shut up for as much as fourteen days in the air-raid shelter, that is to say a damp cellar without windows, where there was nothing to sit down upon except the damp floor," continued P.L. "After being discharged from the air-raid shelter the women had to do the hardest work, that is to say they had to drag the wagon which regularly fetched boards and other timber for building purposes from the sawmill, which was an hour away, to the carpenter's shop. This was terribly toilsome. In rainy weather, in the heat of the summer, or when it was frosty women dragged the wagon instead of horses. If there happened to be among the sentries guarding the wagon one who particularly hated the Germans, then they were also beaten." Subjected to the chief doctor's advances and persecution, one German girl hanged herself in the toilet.

Harassment was routine in the camp proper. Midnight searches of the huts, frequent beatings, forced vigils in the cold for hours on end were common. Prisoners were forced to sing incomprehensible Polish songs, or told fake rumors about imminent transfers to Germany, designed to rob prisoners of hope.

Naturally everyone had to work, typically from dawn to dusk, fed only on milk soup and potatoes. The women worked in the furniture factory, at a local sawmill a few kilometers down the road, and on farms both state-owned and private. Many were raped. Others submitted when threatened with being returned to the camp—Polish men could always invent the pretext that they had refused to work. If a woman became pregnant, she was sent back to the camp anyway. "The guilty Pole was called to account and had to pay a fine—but what is that in comparison with the beatings, and with the dirty and rough words which the German women had to suffer?" recalls P.L. "There were also cases," she says, "where the Germans worked for decent persons and received good food, necessary clothes, and even some money, but this was very seldom." Apparently, farmers did not obey orders to bring Germans back to the camp and bribed the administration in order to keep their workers as long as possible. Workers were put out to auction and farmers bid against one another to receive their allocation of labor. It cost them a tenth of what a Polish worker cost.

The Polish Communist security officers made the prisoners spy on one another and recruited those who might prove useful once in Germany. Bribes in the form of food, better treatment, or stamps for letters home; threats and persecutions such as being locked up in the air-raid shelter; beatings and assignment to the hardest jobs; interrogations, hard and soft ones in turn—all the classic recruitment methods were applied. Children were used to spy on adults and other children. The Polish officers were young, from the lowest social orders. One of them told an assembly of Germans: "You claim to belong to the intelligentsia, but do you know what you are? You are sows. In democratic Poland we don't require an intelligentsia."

Potulice clearly offended against every civilized standard, yet, as I continued reading P.L.'s account, my Polish mind became offended by something in her tone. "Feather beds," she complains, for example, "were not allowed in the camp and if anyone brought one, it was taken away." Did she imagine they would have been allowed in the same huts several months earlier, when the Germans were the guards and the

Poles the inmates? Somehow, I don't think it would have occurred to my uncle Roman, as innocent a victim as herself, to complain of the lack of feather beds at Dachau. The arrangement of the bunks seems to have been identical.

One of the camp officials was clearly a sadist who "took young women and beat them up on the smallest pretext." The next day he made each of them show their naked bottoms in order to see if there were traces of the truncheon blows. He then had the impudence, after having beaten the women, to offer them his hand with these words: "I bear you no grudge, and you bear me no grudge, but I had to beat you." He was a "Pole from Danzig." Had she really not heard what happened in the first weeks of the war, when thousands of the Free City's Polish inhabitants were summarily shot or expelled?

Once, when she was assigned to work outside the camp, P.L. managed to see her little son. He no longer spoke a word of German and did not recognize her—but the Polish farmers were good to him. "I found him well brought up and clothed, a good bit grown and well fed," she reported with relief. But many German women, and their children, had no such luck. "Children between four and fourteen years of age—those who were not subject to being put into a camp but came with their mothers—were simply taken away from them in May 1945, put into trucks and removed. I can still hear the weeping of the mothers and the screaming of the children when they were torn apart." Those who later rejoined their mothers often only spoke Polish. Some children were "adopted" by their Polish custodians, who refused to give them up. Some demanded money for the expenses they had incurred in keeping them. Still, P.L. talks as if she hadn't heard of the thousands of Polish children who, on account of their good Aryan looks, had been snatched away by the Nazis for Germanization.

She almost manages to make me sympathize with the chief doctor, clearly a monster. Not satisfied with molesting the women, he murdered a German prisoner of war. The German was caught trying to escape. His punishment was a vigil on the camp square, during bitter frost, where he stood motionless with his arms above him, until he collapsed. The chief doctor finished him off in the hospital in no time.

The chief doctor, scoffs P.L., "called himself a martyr of Auschwitz because he had been in the camp there."

P.L.'s tone of righteous indignation sounds genuine enough, yet she had come to Potulice in January 1945 from Łódź, where the second largest ghetto in Europe had existed until five months before, until the last of the 220,000 Jews in it were sent to the gas chambers. Could she really not have known what was happening in the middle of the city in which she lived? Did she not have an inkling about the fate of those who were packed into cattle trucks? Or did she think that it was all right because it had been ordained by the proper authorities? If she had known, then the treatment she was suffering could not have been so surprising. If she understood what had just happened, could she really not see why Poles who passed German work brigades would express satisfaction? Perhaps the Auschwitz survivor wanted revenge; or perhaps he merely wanted to show uncomprehending German women that total war is no fun; that nice German girls, and not just *Untermenschen,* might suffer. *Schadenfreude* is, after all, a German word.

On the other hand, if genocide is being committed all around you, and you do not know, doesn't such ignorance become culpable in itself? P.L.'s use of the phrase "called himself" a martyr of Auschwitz about the chief doctor suggests that she did not realize the evil of what had happened. If she had, and still wanted to attract sympathy, she would probably have suppressed this attitude in her testimony. But, in fact, she knew that there were concentration camps and that Potulice was one of them. "In German times," she says of Potulice, "the Poles in the camp were allowed to receive their guests in their huts where they were housed with their families. But the Poles kept married Germans and their children separated from one another. And yet in German times it was a punishment camp, but with Poles it was an internee one." So, she believed that you really must have been guilty to be sent to a concentration camp?

Her attitude fits in with our stereotype of the German as someone with a limited capacity for putting himself into other people's shoes, particularly those he despises. Or perhaps it just shows that we find it difficult to comprehend abominations which occur in our own time. Monstrosities which do not touch us personally seem bearable, even commonplace. Our imagination can't fully grasp their enormity. Only from a distance of time and space does it become credible. We react with revulsion only when the truth ceases to be just whispered rumor and is laid out bare and confirmed, best in print or on film, and the stories are colored with other people's moral reactions to them. How could they do it? we ask. How could people live side by side with it and do nothing? P.L.'s 1949 account shows that you may even go through a similar ordeal yourself and *still* not grasp what had been done in your nation's name.

Only when I discovered the lesser-known part of the history of the Potulice camp—in a London reading room—and started asking questions, did I discover that my own family had a connection to what went on there. My mother, it turned out, was brought up by nannies—German women from Potulice. After my grandparents had reestablished themselves at the school in Łochowo—ten kilometers from Potulice in the direction of Bydgoszcz—a fellow schoolmaster from Potulice offered to send them help from the camp. The first one was a middle-aged woman called Zelma, whom my grandmother called Marysia for her own safety because she spoke Polish and could thus keep out of trouble. In the first months after the war anti-German sentiment was still running high. Zelma was a railwayman's daughter, with a prosperous farm, married to a Pole before the war. But now everything had changed. The borderlands were being ethnically cleansed; she opted for Germany, while her husband wanted to stay in Poland. She was a hardworking, likable woman. She cleaned, cooked, and knitted. My mother remembers that for Christmas she made clothes for her rag doll, a new set each year to disguise the fact that she received the same doll as a present. She tried to teach the children German, but my grandmother banned it, which my mother now regrets.

The only tense moment came when Zelma's Polish husband turned up on my grandmother's doorstep. Zelma was convinced he had come to kill her—simply because he no longer wanted a German in the family. She hid in outbuildings at the back of the school and begged my grandmother to deny her presence. But my grandmother reasoned that the man knew about Zelma and might return unannounced. She allowed him to meet his wife but only in front of witnesses, herself and my grandfather. When the terrified Zelma came out of hiding, it turned out that her husband's concerns were more prosaic. In the interval between Zelma's internment and his own return from the war, some of the neighbors had helped themselves to cattle and machinery from the farm, which he now considered as his own. After Zelma had told him how to identify their property, he went peacefully away.

Some months later, Zelma finally received her call to leave for Germany. My grandmother claims to have fitted her out in warm clothes and food for the journey and Zelma must indeed have remembered her fondly because letters from her in West Germany used to arrive for many years afterward. There being little chance of travel to the West for the next twenty years, my grandmother did not keep up the contact. But, fifty years later, she is still using a pin cushion in the shape of a heart which Zelma made out of red cloth.

Within weeks, another German woman arrived in my grandmother's household, a petite blond girl whom my grandmother christened Zenia. She was illiterate, rough, and apparently did not know even her family name. All that was known about her was that she somehow became separated from a group of Black Sea Germans, who had lived in Russia since Catherine the Great's time, and which the Nazis settled in freshly conquered provinces closer to Germany proper. Zenia was more a farmhand than a nanny. In fact my grandmother nannied her. She panicked at the slightest mention of the Potulice camp, my grandmother recalled, cowering and begging not to be sent back there. After she had been around for a few weeks she described being raped by the guards. They would detach her from her work team and threaten that unless she yielded, they would shoot her and claim she had tried to escape. Once, she risked running anyway, and they did not shoot. Zenia did not want to go back to the camp, but neither did she have anyone to join in Germany. At her request, using the good offices of a relative who worked as a clerk to the court, my grandmother invented an identity for her, with a smart surname, a date and place of birth, and a brand-new Polish nationality. Eventually, she moved to a town in Pomerania, married a farmer's son, and had several children. She was last seen as a guest at my parents' wedding.

Today, Potulice, with 3,700 inmates, including on average about a hundred murderers, is among the largest prisons in Europe. Its dynamic warden wears a fashionable silk tie, consults a Filofax on his desk, and does good works for the local parish and primary school. The inmates have a soccer field, watch videos in their cells, and have better medical care than pensioners on the outside. Instead of making aircraft wings or furs, they can volunteer to make furniture. It is the furniture factory's smoking chimneys, spewing nothing more offensive than burning varnish, which give the compound its sinister appearance. The Nazi commandant's villa still stands in front of the entrance gate, its tiles and gutters worn and corroded. Today it is surrounded by modern blocks of apartments for the prison personnel. The barracks stand in the same neat rows but are now two stories high, made of bricks and mortar. The perimeter fence is also where the Nazis built it, although barbed wire has given way to reinforced concrete. Of the countess's palace—once a magnificent neo-Gothic monstrosity—only a corner tower remains. The building's main body, originally one story with a high pitched roof, is now a standard three-story block of apartments, with net curtains hanging in uniformly square windows. The adaptation was designed by an architect inmate who clearly drew his inspiration from the prison barracks. From the outside the only visible signs of the past—apart from the corner tower—are the foundations made of boulders and an oak tree to the side of the porch. High up on one of its branches bark has partly overgrown a rusty pulley block. The Germans used to hang people on ropes suspended from it.

Inside the palace, down a dingy flight of steps, the punishment cell—the same one to which P.L. referred as the air-raid shelter—is tended as a memorial. There is a plaque on the wall in remembrance of the Polish victims. Candles on the floor commemorate prisoners who used to stand there ankle-deep in water. The vaulted room is huge and beautiful, like a castle's refectory—except that the stones keep it damp and chilly even in midsummer. One night inside it without a sleeping bag would probably be enough to give a person rheumatism.

I saw only one other room in the palace. It is directly above the punishment cell and shares with it an entrance and a reception hall. It might once have been the countess's library. The windows are large and the beamed ceiling is decorated with stained wood. It is now fitted with a new parquet floor and a bar with stools, with halogen lights and taps for pouring draft beer. Every Saturday, the floor above the punishment cell shakes with the thumping of dozens of feet. Lights flash, the air vibrates from deafening music, and couples smooch in the corners. It's the local disco.

FREEDOM

CYCLES OF POLITICAL TURBULENCE which affect Poland—ultimately caused by our vulnerable geography—tend to produce similar biographies. I identified with Edek's wartime peregrinations. But Edek had never been to Chobielin, as far as I know. He might at best have seen it in the distance while working somewhere in the vicinity, dressed in his prison garb.

Maciej Wierzbiński, on the other hand, knew Chobielin well. I first heard his name thanks to a Mr. Sławiński from Gdynia, a distant relation of Chobielin's prewar owners who unexpectedly arrived for a look around the building site one day, not long after we had begun the reconstruction. Mr. Sławiński told my parents about a prewar author, Maciej Wierzbiński, who wrote a novel set in and around the manor house.

I looked Wierzbiński up in the dictionary of national biography. He sounded promising: perhaps his rediscovered literary works would make Chobielin famous. A dissident in the German partition before World War One, he won literary prizes after independence. The nearby town of Inowrocław named a street after him. The Prussians had imprisoned Wierzbiński for writing a subversive newspaper article. Intriguingly, he had earlier been an exile in London, writing for illustrated magazines and reportedly befriending Oscar Wilde. Literary cults have arisen around lesser men than that.

The novel was called *Freedom,* and it was set during the successful uprising at the end of World War One, which liberated western Poland from Germany, a dramatic time. In 1918 the Hohenzollern monarchy was imploding from defeat at the front and revolution at home. The Bolsheviks had triumphed in Russia, and were preparing to march west into Germany and Europe—passing by Chobielin on the way. After more than a century of German rule, authority in the region was collapsing and power lay in the streets; events were directed by revolutionary committees. Wierzbiński had found the raw material of an epic. Half a century after him, Günter Grass was to win literary prizes for stories from approximately the same area, about similar times.

I found *Freedom* in a public library in Warsaw and instantly warmed to the novel and its author. He described Chobielin as a "splendid" manor house, with a large hall adorned with rows of stuffed animal heads and antlers. I devoured his tale of the sack of Chobielin—apparently based on a true event—by a fifty-man band of Grenzschutz, the German border militia:

> *First they cut the telephone wire, then they smashed the desk in the landlord's study and stole several thousand marks. An iron safe gave them good resistance, which angered them, so they smashed everything, first in the room, then in the whole house. The sound of breaking glass pleased their ears, so they began with the mirrors and the chandeliers. Soon, the legs of chairs and sofas were flying about the drawing room like soccer balls. For good fun, the wing of the grand piano was broken, and bayonets tore into furniture upholstery.*
>
> *The party took a different direction when the meat was brought out of the pantry. The bandits forgot the upstairs rooms and took to the cellars instead. They could not drink all the wine so, carried by their Hunnish spirit, they smashed bottles on the steps, until a pool gathered on the floor. Thinking it was wine turned into vinegar, they left alone only bottles covered with moss.*
>
> *The more practical of them looted the sheets, silver cutlery, and anything shiny they could lay their hands on. Another group set four horses to a cart to try to carry away the pigs and the calves. . . .*

Fortunately, help was at hand. A troop of Polish cavalry under the gallant Pan Sobiesław comes to the rescue in the nick of time, so that the only harm that the inhabitants suffer occurs when Chobielin's owner, Pan Prusinowski, faints at the sight of a German militiaman lying in the middle of his drawing room with his throat cut and a "stream of blood spilled on the floor in ribbons of crimson."

I found *Freedom* gripping but it was not appreciated in its time. It was not a bestseller. In fact, the copy which I picked up in the Warsaw public library had lain undisturbed on a shelf since publication in 1927. It was still virginal, its pages not yet separated. Considering it dispassionately, it was not difficult to see why.

The sack of Chobielin is in fact the story's defining moment. The sight of his plundered house changes Pan Prusinowski, hitherto a German loyalist. Faced with the ghastly sight of his disemboweled sofas, his cutlery strewn about, and his expensive china smashed on the floor, he finally becomes a patriot and consents to his rescuer marrying his pretty daughter.

The girl in question, the blond Panna Aniela (Miss Angel), has "stars in her dark blue eyes," and "stands out with grace and the powerful spark of life." Wierzbiński tries to give her a sturdy aspect by making her work as a nurse in a Red Cross hospital. She drives into an ambush which German colonists stage in the woods near Chobielin. But, other than romantic rapture, she never shows emotions. The nineteenth-century Polish female stereotype was fatally flawed by the cult of the Virgin Mary. Every girl had to be a sinless angel devoted to a pure cause. Convent-educated Aniela does not stray from the path of virtue for a single instant.

Her other suitor is a perfidious German aristocrat uncannily called Kurt Waldheim, who pays Aniela insincere compliments. His baseness is finally exposed when he tries to carry Aniela off from her Szubin hospital in his automobile, supposedly to save her from the imminent danger of an assault on the town. In truth, Wierzbiński hints, it is to inflict on her a fate worse than death.

His rival for Aniela's hand, Sobiesław, is penniless but is a dashing Polish patriot: brave, proud, romantic, wise, and handsome, a male counterpart of the virginal Aniela, a knight without a blemish. They used to be childhood friends. *Freedom* opens with them meeting again after a few years' absence. It is autumn of 1918 when "the rusty leaves were torn away from trees by the wind, which swept the ground with them; the pale lapis lazuli of the skies was blurred with leaden masses of clouds." Aniela, chaperoned by her mother, visits Sobiesław in the Poznań prison, where the Germans had him locked up for his patriotic activities. Sobiesław is "tall, dressed in an officer's uniform, dark haired with a white forehead and a black beard cut into a wedge, which has grown in the three months of his imprisonment."

Aniela's meeting with Sobiesław in prison poses the obvious question of whether the boy will get the girl, but Wierzbiński leaves little room for suspense. Their interview ends with the girl "as if transposed beyond the earth and time," he writes. "With eyes shining with miraculous emotion, she looked at him as if at a messenger from heaven; despite herself she put her hand into his, trembling like a harp touched with a master player's fingers." Can we doubt for a moment that the master player will get the girl in the end?

Their love for each other is sublimated through the love of Poland. His love letters are at their most passionate when he speculates as to whether or not the statesmen conferring at Versailles would grant Poland the possession of Gdańsk. After their encounter at the Poznań prison they meet again in the park at Chobielin under a linden tree. He finds her lurking about the workshop where she'd been making charges for her father's hunting rifle which her brother was to take to the uprising.

> *"You have warlike intentions?" she asks breathlessly, with her heart pounding like a hammer.*
> *"For sure, I shall do what every young man of Wielkopolska should do. . . ."*
> *"I am sure. . . . You are such a Pole, such a whole Pole, such a . . . real Pole," she whispered.*
> *"You speak like a proper Polishwoman."*
> *"I am a real Polishwoman!"*

It is dark, and dogs are barking in the distance. Sobiesław ends their confessions "with the red seal of a kiss." In case we still didn't get the hint, Wierzbiński explains that Aniela's "strongly pulsating patriotic feelings were penetrating into the erotic sphere."

Politics permeates even Wierzbiński's descriptions:

In Szubin, as in Rynarzewo and a hundred other settlements in this land, the authorities took care that the Protestant church imposed its character. It was erected in the most pleasant, most modern part of town and in a style dripping of conceit. It pokes the eye with the loud redness of its brick, soars above the modest roofs, tramples the whole town under its Teuton foot, shoves everything into the dust of serfdom. And, gliding to the clouds with its sharply pointed tower, it proclaims, as far as the eye can see, bloated with arrogance: here I am, in this land—me, Germany!

And the Catholic church, mossed over with the patina of age, sits modestly, almost invisible in the corner of a square. It has hidden behind a row of houses, nestled into a quiet niche where market noise does not reach, surrounded itself with a circle of trees. It looks as if it has subsided into the ground and stooped amid a wreath of churchyard tombs. . . .

Instead of creating a genuine dramatic tension, Wierzbiński fakes it by pouring out a torrent of adventures: pursuits, ambushes, charges, spying missions, rapid marches, and miraculous escapes, which he probably thought were justified because many were apparently true events. As so often, the most improbable—Aniela and Sobiesław's escape from German-occupied Bydgoszcz by an airplane flown by a mechanic who had never flown before—was based on a real event. The story plods on toward its predictable end: Polish victory and the ceremonial entry, described in gloriously purple prose, of Polish cavalry units in Bydgoszcz's main square.

But, for all its faults, I grew to like *Freedom* and its characters. They may have been stereotypes in the 1920s but today they evoke nostalgia and yearning for what might have been. Pan Prusinowski, the money-pinching landowner, for example, is a stock Polish character who would disappear completely from the Polish landscape within a generation. Those landowners who hadn't been killed and exiled in the war were to see their farms confiscated and their family homes defiled. At Chobielin, as in thousands of other places across Poland, Pan Prusinowskis were replaced with collective farm managers—who were certainly no more enlightened, and rarely better managers. What Wierzbiński caricatured as penny-pinching—prudence, thrift, good accounting—was clearly more desirable than what followed: waste, economic idiocy, and sloth. Wouldn't Chobielin have fared better if a Pan Prusinowski had lived in it all along: fussing over his polished furniture, worrying about every leak in the roof, and scrounging to pay for it all?

Patriotic wives, daughters of Lwów professors, such as his wife, are also thin on the ground these days, and not just because Lwów no longer has a Polish university. How many of today's professors' daughters have the sense of duty and the leisure to organize public libraries for peasant women? Today, a professor's daughter living in the country would have trouble finding enough candidates for a single successful dinner party for many miles around. Few Polish women would now consent to live in the country, even in a mansion. Likewise, Miss Aniela may be laughable in her calf-like innocence, but what would a girl of her age be like today? Probably already practiced in exotic sexual techniques and au courant with designer drugs.

Sobiesław, a Polish officer of the old school, heel-clicking and honorable, is also gone. Sobiesławs went to war in 1939 and never came back. Thousands were to be slaughtered at Katyń, in the Warsaw uprising, in the concentration camps, or at Monte Cassino. Of those who survived the war, some stayed in England and ended their days in basement apartments in Earl's Court. Others fought on against the new regime and died in skirmishes. Many of those, like my uncle Klemens, who made their peace with the regime and served in the Communist army, were purged. Today, foreign dignitaries arriving in Warsaw see the Polish army's Guard of Honor march past them with the old dash, but it is an appearance which belies reality. When I lived at my parents' Bydgoszcz flat, which faces on to an army-owned block of flats, I saw the more typical specimens of Communist officer going to work every morning: overweight, in badly fitting uniforms, clutching fake-leather briefcases, clearly more worried about their pension rights than hungry for glory. The old panache—that indefinable quality which makes a young man want to be an officer—is just not there anymore. No wonder Polish youngsters dodge the draft but volunteer to join the Foreign Legion.

Needless to say, Franek, a faithful retainer who goes to war with young Staś Prusinowski, bettering himself through courage and wits, has also disappeared. The estate was collectivized, supposedly for the benefit of the Franeks. Expropriating the likes of the Prusinowskis was meant not only to lift up the likes of Franek economically, but above all to take away from them the stigma of servitude. With emancipation and equality, a new confidence would fire them and they would at last gain proper human dignity. In practice, at Chobielin at least, the opposite happened. True, in some respects, the last became the first under Communism. In accordance with the ruling dogma, farmhands, like the workers, were extolled as the society's leading class. Some of Chobielin's farmhands moved out of their cottages and into the manor house. But in the long run all that changed was that Mr. Prusinowski's neat house was itself turned into a hovel. Had the transition to a more egalitarian society happened more gradually, without fanaticism and brutality, the Franeks could have taken Mr. Prusinowski's place in a more orderly fashion, as they have been doing the world over. Fired by ambition and snobbery, Franek would eventually have risen to Pan Prusinowski's level, instead of bringing Pan Prusinowski down to his own. By conferring deference and respect, Franek or his descendants could one day deserve respect themselves. Instead, they were taught to hate and envy those more fortunate than themselves, so that today everybody envies and despises everybody else.

Nor did the confiscation benefit the likes of Franek economically, at least in Chobielin. Today the collective farm which was once the Chobielin estate has—after half a century's mismanagement—sacked all its workers. Most of the village's inhabitants are unemployed. I wonder whether it is more dignified to have been a retainer of Pan Prusinowski than a welfare junkie. Today's Franeks hang around in local *mordownie,* sleazy beer bars. You can recognize them by their unshaven faces, their lethargic manner, and their sour gazes.

The society of Wierzbiński's characters had its faults and its injustices. But it also had its firm standards and rules for respectable social advancement, which were hardly rigid. Mrs. Prusinowska favors the penniless Sobiesław over the rich German, trusting that the talented young man would be able to make himself respectable by buying a farm after some years' work as a lawyer in Poznań. Wierzbiński portrays a society which is civilized and normal by contemporary European standards, even while in crisis. It was war, and houses were looted and burned; brutalities were committed. But knocked-out teeth were more often the outcome than cold-blooded murder. When the Poles and

Germans took each other prisoner, hotel rooms rather than concentration camps were used as prisons. "Responsible citizens" from both sides met in the midst of hostilities and mediated the violence.

The turn in Poland's fortunes which Wierzbiński witnessed in 1918 was uncannily similar to our Solidarity revolution. Staś Prusinowski is on a blacklist at his German-language gymnasium in Nakło (the red-brick building is still the gymnasium today) for having lent Polish books to fellow students. A sleuth among the students reports him for his enthusiasm about the Polish capture of Poznań, which gets Staś expelled. Was that so very different from my parents being dragged before the director of my red-brick once-Prussian gymnasium to be told that reports had reached them of my dangerous anti-Soviet views? Our equivalent of Staś's Polish books were the smuggled copies of the émigré journal *Kultura*.

When Sobiesław goes back to the Poznań prison, this time as the representative of the new Polish authorities, he finds that a petty official, who during German times called himself Blum and pretended not to speak Polish, is now Pan Kwieciński. He protests that his erstwhile conversion to Protestantism was forced and fake. Today former party bigwigs, faithful Soviet stooges, speak as if they had been staunch anti-Communists all along.

Wierzbiński's account of children jumping over the fallen bronze statue of Germania in Nakło's main square in 1919 brought back the memory of an autumn day in Warsaw in 1989, when a small crowd of us cheered while a crane dislodged from its pedestal the huge statue of Feliks Dzierżyński, the founder of the NKVD.

In fact, Wierzbiński's very mediocrity as a writer is provocative because he probably reflects better the spirit of his time. A genius may use local stories and real-life characters to say something universal, eternal. Wierzbiński had no such ambitions. Some of his dialogues, and the views expressed in the little lectures he can't help himself from inflicting on the reader, are no doubt genuine—picked up at the dinner tables—and convey contemporary opinions and prejudices. And these are sometimes extraordinarily prescient.

For example, the basis for Sobiesław's imprisonment in Poznań is his diary, treacherously confiscated by German secret agents. The interrogation is set in the last week before the Armistice. The German prosecutor, furious, reads out from Sobiesław's diary:

"Prussia-Germany is an ulcer on the body of Europe, which must be radically operated on to cure the world morally and materially, and to build solid foundations for peace. German pride has no boundaries and is a constant danger to the world. . . . It should be broken for the sake of humanity and their own. . . . The Germans, like the Jews, regard themselves as a chosen nation and have their own, vengeful God. . . . In those foreign lands where there is one German, there is beer; where there are two, there is an organization; where there are ten, there is ancient German land. . . . The Germans, eminently sensible in small things, commit the stupidest blunders in large undertakings because of their dangerous madness of grandeur. . . . The Germans have developed a curious intellectual acrobatics which allows them to justify the greatest absurdity and the biggest evil. . . . There will be no peace in Europe until Europe dictates peace to Germany in the Berlin imperial palace. . . ."

"How dare you write such offensive sentences in your idiotic Slav language, you Slav-Slave!" the prosecutor explodes. "You are a German, even though of Polish language. You fought for our king and our fatherland, you became an officer!"

"An apple tree remains an apple tree even though you plant it in the cabbage patches," replies Sobiesław.

What is curious about their exchange is that, in the midst of their melodramatic clash, the Pole and the German in fact share common values, an assumption which would disappear within a couple of decades. Sobiesław keeps his cool because he trusts that the German court martial "is not composed of barbarians." He assumes that it will have to acquit him of the charge of treason on the grounds that the opinions were expressed in his private diary and thoughts are "free of censorship and customs duty."

Wierzbiński points to German mutability years before the idea was formulated in English. At their next interview a week later, after Germany has sued for peace, the German prosecutor is no longer threatening. Instead, he listens to Sobiesław with resignation. Wierzbiński asserts that "the mood of the German, whose kings have so thoroughly ripped out his individuality, depends exactly on the barometer of things German—on whether Berlin's stock is up or down. The German is a human automaton, wound up like a music box, to play this or that tune.

That's why the same German may lick your boots or brutally lord it over you." Accordingly, the prosecutor's voice now goes soft and he asks Sobiesław:

"Why are we Germans so generally disliked?"

"Because you don't let others live," answers Sobiesław.

"But haven't we raised up the Duchy of Pozen?"

"It seems to me," says Sobiesław, "that much has changed in the last hundred years in the world. You can't compare what was here a hundred years ago, with today. Had we Poles got on by ourselves, breathed our own air, had our freedom, we would be more worthy than those who were brought up in the clutches of foreign and doubtful culture."

It is as if I was listening today to diehard defenders and opponents of People's Poland. Didn't the Party rebuild Warsaw, didn't it eradicate illiteracy, didn't it build schools, roads, and factories? So argue those who *still* have not understood. Yes, you are right, today's Sobiesławs mock them. No schools, no roads, and no factories would have been built for half a century unless you had falsified elections, imprisoned innocent people, and imposed alien rule. To build public housing, health centers, and public libraries it was absolutely necessary to stifle the free press, debauch the courts, and pervert the economy. If the Soviet Union had not spread its protective mantle over us we would still all be illiterate.

In fact, it suffices to quote one statistic to show up the Communist achievement: Poland and Spain, countries of comparable size and comparably backward until recently, had very similar per capita income as late as 1950—despite the fact that half of Poland's national wealth went up in smoke during World War Two whereas Spain profited from the war. Poland's per capita income rose under Communism: from $775 in 1955 to $1,860 in 1988. Spain's rose too, from $561 to $7,740 in the same period.[3] All that heroic effort, all the sacrifice of innocents, so that Poland may, by comparison, become four times poorer. As the Russians say, it was all a *bolshaya oszibka*, a big mistake.

The confrontation between Sobiesław and his interrogator ends with the Pole giving the German the following advice: "You must now admit that your dogmas and philosophical theses are bankrupt. . . . You must beat your chest, confess your sins, look into yourselves, reform yourselves. . . . On this alone depends your future and the peace of Europe." Written in 1927, this has a certain poignancy. Middle Poland obviously had a better feel for contemporary Germany than many a great Western statesman. Being closer and more vulnerable, they picked up earlier the intimations of danger. Today we feel the same about Russia. A society which has wallowed in evil but is unwilling to face the truth about its own past, let alone confess and repent it, is condemned to offend again. Just as in the 1920s and 1930s, Western statesmen and intellectuals preferred to dismiss our warnings as typical Polish panic-mongering.

Wierzbiński's main fault as a writer—his hysterical patriotism—is more easily understandable today because the experience of peoples who came to the verge of extinction is more familiar now. To nations blessed with safer frontiers and less calamitous histories, such obsessions smack of tribalism; they seem simpleminded at best and possibly dangerous, as they often are. For Wierzbiński, "Polishness" was a besieged fortress liable to be taken by the enemy at any time. He almost succeeds in making me feel grateful for having been born in Communist Poland! Brought up as I was under what I regarded as Soviet occupation, I could hardly feel gratitude for the fact that the brainwashing and the propaganda at school, in newspapers, and on television was conducted in my native language. *Freedom*'s every page reminds me that there was a time within living memory when even this could not have been taken for granted. In fact, if it hadn't been for World War One, Polishness might have disappeared from the face of the earth. If two more generations had lived under German rule, we could by now have become little more than a quaint local memory, like the Bretons in France or the Cornish in England or, indeed, like the Slavic Serbs in today's eastern Germany. A few cranks would still be talking of "independence," but perhaps nobody would even bother to persecute them anymore. Like the Welsh nationalists, they might go as far as burning the weekend cottages belonging to rich Berliners. I might be a German, probably making up with patriotic zeal for my funny name.

Plowing through *Freedom* I began to feel that something in it still eluded me; that I still had not fully deciphered Wierzbiński. Something in the tone struck me as familiar all along: the occasional phrase which, I suspected, was archaic even in his own time. The naïveté of its philosophy touched a familiar note. Life, for Wierzbiński, was a game in which transgressions could always be made good; evil, when perpetrated by our side, seemed playful, and Poles, whatever inanities they might commit, always came out victorious in the end. The style, which tries to dazzle the reader with vast canvases of epic scenes—battles, ambushes and parades—that too had been copied from somewhere. The faults—like his inability to portray flesh-and-blood women—were also the same.

I smiled when Wierzbiński described a character behaving "like Zagłoba." Elementary. Wierzbiński obviously felt he did not need to explain who Zagłoba was or what Zagłoba-like behavior consisted in. Everyone in Poland knew it then and everyone in Poland knows it still. He is the outlandish nobleman in Sienkiewicz's *Trilogy*: a drunkard, a coward, and a braggart, but a good patriot and a wit, and therefore one of the most lovable characters in Polish literature. This was the key to understanding Wierzbiński's enterprise. He tried to do for Poland's western marches what Sienkiewicz had done for the eastern: anchor them in the Polish imagination by infusing them with a sense of romance. Like me, Wierzbiński had read Sienkiewicz in Poland's darkest hours to sustain himself in faith. After all, *The Trilogy* was written "to uplift the hearts." Like *The Trilogy, Freedom* was not literature but nation building; that's why Wierzbiński, pathetic scribbler that he was, received prewar literary prizes.

Though separated by a century (Wierzbiński was born in 1862, I in 1963) I had found a soul brother. Chobielin inspired us to a similar task. Where he piled an unnecessary adverb upon a redundant adjective, I pile up plaster on concrete. Where he reenacted his battles with German prosecutors, I wage battles against obtuse bureaucrats to persuade them to sell me adjacent plots of land I need to relandscape the garden. Where he created literary characters as role models for his contemporaries to follow, I try to make my contemporaries understand that it is natural for a man to hold and to cherish his own place on earth. He and I really tried to achieve a similar goal—a Poland at peace with itself. I just hope I am a better restorer than he was a writer.

RITES OF
PROPERTY

WE STARTED THE RESTORATION with the keeper's lodge, a hand-some cottage by the entrance gate. My parents moved in so as to be able to oversee work on the main house. Now that we'd established resi-dence on the old estate, I felt confident enough to attend the meetings, on the last Thursday of every month, of the Listed Buildings Owners Club, held in a dilapidated palace in Warsaw's old town. In threadbare tweeds and imported English shoes, with recycled signet rings flashing on their fingers, members reported on the progress of the restoration work of their beloved palace, castle, or manor house. Until 1990, a spirit of neofeudalist bonhomie reigned. Good-natured arguments raged over the relative merits of wooden as opposed to ceramic roof tile: the former is more classically Polish, the latter more practical. Then, as Communism became history in autumn 1989 and spring 1990, a feeling of unease crept into the discussions. By the summer, anyone who had acquired property at any time in the past fifty years began to worry that his right to it might now fall into question.

By the anger on their faces and the defensiveness in their arguments one could tell which members of the Listed Buildings Owners Club possessed questionable property deeds. "These people could have done what we've been doing for fifteen years now," a bald plastics manufacturer who had rebuilt an eighteenth-century mansion railed at our rivals, the Landholders Association. The Landholders did not have any land but they often had good prewar claims to some of our members' properties. "If they really loved their family house as much as they now say, why have they only taken any interest in the place recently, when there might be a financial gain from it? I've spent fifty thousand dollars on the place, not counting the effort and the worry. They are welcome to it if they refund me the money, and with interest," he ended in a huff.

The chairman was a bearded architect who had spent his professional life reintroducing traditional materials and Polish features into modern designs. He had channeled all his fees into rebuilding a lovely little castle in the south. He used to boast that he lived in harmony with the family of the old owner. The son of the prewar owner had encouraged him to buy and restore the place, and came to stay for weekends and praise the restoration work. Now the family wanted their castle back.

In theory, once a notary act was signed and sealed, and the name of the buyer entered in the land register, the right of ownership was virtually unassailable, even in Communist Poland. A court challenge could only be mounted if there was something technically wrong with the notary act itself. Regarding compensation for the prewar owners, the legal position was also clear. State authorities had accepted the money paid by new purchasers, and it was up to the state to make amends if the original confiscation was now deemed illegal or unjust. Yet nervousness prevailed. Some members were worried because instead of property deeds they only had long leases. Others were upset because they had invested time and money on the basis of a local authority administrative decision, which was once deemed perfectly sufficient but was now open to challenge. Most were merely irritated. Before, we had basked in the glory of being the vanguard of forward-looking neofeudalism. Suddenly, we felt like thieves.

The arguments were complicated by the fact that many of the members had their own family claims on landed properties. Most had bought ruins in good faith, out of sentiment for tradition, or because their own houses had been leveled, or were not for sale, or stood in Poland's eastern territories which had been absorbed into the Soviet

Union after the war. In principle, the members sympathized with claims for restitution, even though it was going to be a legal nightmare. Warsaw's old town, for example, had been razed to the ground in the Warsaw uprising in 1944. The Communist authorities confiscated the land and rebuilt the old quarter to look exactly as it had done before. Behind the facades, however, houses did not match the prewar land plots. Sometimes, three fake medieval facades would contain one house with one modern staircase, with apartments and corridors crisscrossing the old boundaries. Elsewhere, parts of several new houses covered a single prewar plot. How do you decide who owns what? Despite all this, we were the one group of people in Poland most conscious of tradition, most fanatical about old houses, most keenly aware of the injustice of the earlier Communist confiscations—yet now it looked as if we were profiting from them.

However much we reassured ourselves that our intentions had been pure, the mood was spoiled. It was as if during a *stypa,* a funeral banquet, someone shouted that the family had falsified the will. The only ones who kept smiling were those who had bought in the formerly German districts of Silesia and Pomerania. No government was going to reinstate expelled Germans, so none of the angst concerned them. But Chobielin was not in this category. Not coincidentally, a new sort of tourist began arriving at Chobielin that summer.

We had become used to uninvited visitors. Almost every weekend for months on end, curious strangers came by the dozen. If they called at the gate lodge and asked for permission to look around, we invariably gave it. If they were polite or interesting, one of us would usually give a small guided tour of the building site. Usually, they just marched in as if they had a right to do so. Alerted by the dog's barking or by a glimpse of color on the balcony, my father would go out and challenge them.

"Good morning. What are you doing here?" my father would engage, politely.

"Oh, we are just looking. What's it going to be: a restaurant or a hotel? We hear an Englishman's bought it."

"Have you asked the owner's permission to be here?"

"And who are you?"

"I'm the caretaker."

"It says 'listed building' on the gate."

"It also says 'private property.'"

"So, you mean," they would say, genuinely puzzled, "we can't walk around here?" The idea that anything bigger than a small farm might not be state-owned and therefore open to all was new to them.

"How would you like it if I wandered into your backyard?"

"But I was born here. My parents lived here in the fifties and sixties." We had heard that up to seven families had lived in the manor at that time, all rural workers who were placed there by the local collective farm. But was it possible that they had reared literally scores of children?

"Yes, I can believe your family lived here. I can see how well they cared for the house," my father would reply, pointing to the holes in the roof and the peeling plaster. The intruders invariably went away in a huff, complaining of our lack of hospitality. *Prywaciarze,* some hissed contemptuously on walking away, using the derogatory Communist word to describe a private entrepreneur. The closest English equivalent is "privateers," but without the swashbuckling connotation. They would then stand on the road and gape for several minutes at one of us working in the garden. "Look," my mother once overheard someone saying, as she pruned the cabbage patches, "they've already brought a serf to do their dirty work for them."

But in the summer of 1990 a new sort of visitor began to arrive. We would hear the sound of a car engine and a couple would appear, tastefully dressed. Some came and talked to us in the lodge, reminiscing about a great-uncle who had lived in the manor, or a distant cousin who had allegedly been married in the garden. One or two produced photographs. Such people usually prefaced any conversation by assuring us that they had no claims on the property, they were merely there for the sake of nostalgia.

Others were less forthcoming. For a while, there was a regular flood of visitors who would leave their car beyond the park, out of sight, and then talk surreptitiously to Mr. Erlich in his cottage or demand access to the mill in order to assess its value. It was after the latter sort of visit, of which we invariably learned within hours, that threatening letters arrived at the local authority office, demanding restitution and compensation.

Only one of the letters came from a genuine claimant. It was from Mr. Andrzej Sławiński, the prewar owner's grandson, who remembered being expelled from the manor house as a teenager in 1946.

This was at a time when the work on the restoration of the lodge and general tidying up of the manor itself was in full swing. Several men worked at stripping the old plaster and asbestos, laying new floors and roof tiles, installing electricity and central heating. Should I have stopped everything and handed it over to the rightful claimant? Or at least wait for a restitution law to clear the legal position? I did not feel I deserved the stigma of enjoying the fruits of someone else's misfortune. Should I at least make contact and explain my good intentions?

I would have loved to talk to him about Chobielin, learn the story of his family and tell him about my plans for a place with which we were both now bound. On the other hand, I feared that my gesture could be misinterpreted. The confiscation was probably the greatest tragedy in Mr. Sławiński's life. Had it not happened, he would have grown up in prosperity and prestige. Like other children of gentry farmers, he would have gone to a good school and maybe to a university abroad. Instead, he was uprooted and cast away. In the 1950s and 1960s, when Communist zealotry was still strong, children of landowners were virtually barred from universities. Without a university education, or membership of the Party, and with the stigma of the wrong class background hanging over one's neck, one had a hard time in People's Poland. He probably ended up a minor clerk or technician, and eked out a living keeping a low profile. By now he was probably a pensioner, living on the subsidies from relatives abroad. The wound, dealt in youth, festering for forty years, had just been reopened by the prospect of restitution and it must have been hurting.

Moreover, he was unlikely to see justice done. In the public debate about reinstating prewar owners to confiscated property, no one, not even the landowners' associations, suggested reversing the land reform decree itself. However dubious legally, and however absurd economically, the land reform had benefited millions of peasants, who would have risen up in revolt at the merest suggestion. All that could be hoped for was that restitution would be made in those frequent cases where the Communists had broken their own law. When farms owned by politically inconvenient landlords measured less than fifty hectares of arable land, and should therefore have been left with their owners, the meadows and fallow land were counted in and the confiscation carried out regardless. Or, as often as not, the expulsion of anyone who seemed too prosperous was carried out first, and the legal position ignored. All that those who lost their property in the confiscation could hope for was the compensation which the decree promised but the authorities never delivered. In any case, the new owners were protected, and any claims could only be addressed to the handler of stolen goods—the state. Personally, I would gladly have helped him in the battle to regain the valuable parts of the old estate: the mill, the land, and the farm buildings. I would have preferred to have a private owner as a neighbor than the boors from the collective farm. But by making contact in 1990, I could have given the impression of being afraid, or wanting something. Perhaps cheating them of their last hopes for justice? The wound was fresh and no doubt sore. I decided to wait until the restitution law has been passed and get in touch when the legal position has been clarified beyond any doubts or hopes. My intentions would then be *seen* to be pure.

But three years went by, and no restitution law was passed. Our democratically elected parliament found time to debate the precise shape of the crown on the head of the eagle on our national crest, but its schedule did not fit the compensation bill. In the summer of 1993, the bill was still nowhere in sight and, when the fourth government since Communism lost a confidence vote, and the prospect for the bill receded by another year, I decided to wait no longer. I wrote on Chobielin stationery to the address that Sławiński had given on his letter to the local authority, enclosing a photograph showing the progress of the restoration: red tiles in the morning light and the handsome porch. I invited him to come and see the progress for himself.

What would the old man reply? Would he be pleased to see his birthplace restored, or would he feel the injustice of it all even more keenly? Would he see my good intentions, or would he vent his anger at me? The letter said I would telephone soon to confirm my invitation and to ask when he might like to come. I ordered the call to Piła and waited for the operator to connect, battling with conflicting emotions. Would he treat me like a kindred soul, or like a thief?

When the telephone rang and the operator put the call through, a female voice replied.

"May I talk to Mr. Andrzej Sławiński. My name is Sikorski. I'm calling from Chobielin. I wrote to him last week."

There was a long silence.

"My husband died last year," she finally said. "If you want to talk about Chobielin you will have to talk to"——and here she gave the name of a member of the family delegated to deal with the matter. I was so surprised that I forgot to write it down, made my apologies, and hung up.

The last man who could plausibly claim Chobielin as his birthright was dead. It looked as if I was never to hear what it was like to be expelled from Chobielin.

It took a year before I gathered the courage to call the number in Piła again. Now that the grief has subsided, I thought, maybe the family will look at it more calmly. Perhaps they will want to tell me their story after all. I was passed on to a Mrs. Hanna Mieszała, also in Piła.

We immediately hit it off. She was of professional background, middle-aged, bright, and energetic. A few weeks later we were standing together in front of the porch:

"What does your wife think of this project?" she asked.

"Widziały gały co brały," I answered colloquially. "She knew what she was letting herself in for."

"Men." She sighed.

For Mrs. Mieszała, Chobielin was a foreign place. She had seen it for the first time a few years before. She was one of the mysterious visitors who hovered about the gate in 1990. But there was, in fact, one more person alive in Poland who remembered Chobielin from before the confiscation—her mother, who now lived in Poznań. She did not want to come to Chobielin. It was too far, there were too many memories, and, in any case, her recollections of it were not all fond. It had been a lonely childhood in the manor in the middle of nowhere. But Mrs. Mieszała knew her family's story. To the Polish ear, it sounds ordinary.

They were not aristocratic. Julian Reysowski, Chobielin's prewar owner and Mrs. Mieszała's great-grandfather, started in life as a restaurant owner in a small town nearby. He moved into the vicinity of Chobielin just before World War One, and ran the sawmill in Gorzeń on the vast Potulicki estate. It was really by chance that they acquired the estate.

During the Wielkopolska uprising in 1918, Bydgoszcz remained a German bastion while Chobielin stood on the very front line. The river Noteć divided Poles on the southern bank, who held the manor, from the Germans in the mill on the northern side. For months, local laborers, farmers, and squires sniped at one another from the thickets on opposite banks.

The Germans lost both militarily and diplomatically, and the area fell to resurrected Poland. Just as the last Polish owner before the partition, Józef Hulewicz, was selling the estate in the time of turmoil in 1791, so now it was the Germans' turn. Two million German farmers, landlords, and town dwellers all over Pomerania and Wielkopolska were selling up and leaving for Germany proper.

Reysowski took his chance. With the money made in an obscure business deal involving grain supplies and Bromberger canal barges, he made his bid. There being so many farms of fleeing Germans on the market, the price he negotiated was low. He had another stroke of good luck. The sale price was fixed in German marks and, as was the custom in those days, the payment was spread over several years. Shortly afterward, hyperinflation exploded in Germany and the mark rapidly lost most of its value. As the local peasants remember to this day with undisguised envy, Reysowski became the landlord of hundreds of acres, the mill, the manor house, shares in the Nakło sugar refinery, and considerable capital in machinery, buildings, and livestock, all for the equivalent of a few sacks of grain.

Reysowski was already married and had five children, two sons and three daughters. The daughters all married military men. The wedding receptions at Chobielin were splendid affairs, with half the district joining in the festivities. The youngest, Maria, married in July 1939. A photograph exists of the young couple standing between the two huge elms, with lancers in attendance, the buttons of their uniforms shining, their faces full of youthful swagger.

The management of the estate gradually passed to one of the sons-in-law, Jan Sławiński, Mr. Mieszała's grandfather—he was a convivial character, a good talker and soldier, but uninterested in business. Documents confirm this. The amount of the mortgage charged to the estate kept increasing even though no major investments were undertaken: a loan of 12,000 zlotys was registered in 1927, a further 15,000 zlotys in February 1932, and then, in December later that year, a neat sum of 100,000 zlotys—a huge amount of money at a time when my grandfather's monthly salary as a school headmaster was 300 zlotys. There is no mention in the documents that the mortgages were ever paid back.

In 1937, a new threat appeared—land reform—but the prewar version was to be a civilized affair. The land register stipulates that under the terms of the 1925 act, 180 hectares of arable land and 249 hectares of other land were to be excluded from "compulsory purchases."

The reform was never carried out in Chobielin. The destruction of the Polish gentry was to be much more brutal.

The newlyweds, Maria and Wacław Stankiewicz, whose wedding Chobielin had witnessed only a month before, were immediately separated at the end of August 1939. Wacław led his cavalry regiment into eastern Poland where they were captured by the invading Soviets. He never saw Maria again. Interned in the Kozielsk camp, he was to be shot in the Katyń Forest on April 11, 1940.

His wife, meanwhile, also traveled East, together with the rest of the family. When the first refugees arrived in Nakło and told stories of the speed of the German advance, panic broke out on the estate. The entire family, twenty people, were still together at Chobielin for the summer. They were at a loss but were swayed by a troop of sappers who mined the wooden bridge between the manor and the mill. While peasants begged for carts and horses for their own escape, servants packed incongruous luggage into three motor cars. They set off on roads thronged with refugees, with children sitting atop the load. Attacked by German aircraft from the air, they drove past Warsaw, toward Lwów. On September 17, Soviet tanks appeared in the vicinity, and they were again at a loss. Should they continue into the Soviet occupation, or should they return and submit to German rule? Within a couple of days the cars and their personal possessions were quickly seized by marauding bands of Ukrainian peasants. Maria realized she was pregnant. One of the sisters, Helena, was sick.

Helena—she had been the prototype for Wierzbiński's Miss Angel in *Freedom*—with her children would make her way back to Chobielin; the others would push on to Lwów. It was a fateful decision.

When Helena finally reached Chobielin—sick, dirty, hungry, and penniless—the German who had taken over the house gave her just one night's rest and turned her out. She found refuge with another German, a neighbor with a large house in nearby Jarużyn. The brave man was risking his life sheltering Poles, particularly on account of Helena's husband, Jan Sławiński. He had commanded a unit which defended Bydgoszcz during the German subversion behind Polish lines in September 1939 and was now high on the Gestapo wanted list, destined for certain execution. Fortunately, Nazi bureaucracy was not as good as is commonly thought. While the local Gestapo spied on his family to try to find out where he was, Helena received postcards sent by him from a succession of prisoner-of-war camps.

The rest of the family, who crossed to the Soviet side, were less lucky. In April 1940, Maria gave birth to a son. By September they had all been deported six hundred kilometers east of Moscow and put to hard labor in the forest. The work was backbreaking, the food was scarce, and disease flourished. Within the year, all the men, including old Julian Reysowski, and the little Krzysztof, were dead. The women survived until Hitler's attack on the Soviet Union in July 1941; they joined the Polish Army under General Anders. Via Persia and Palestine, they finally reached London. One of the sisters, whose husband was captured by the Germans and liberated from a POW camp by the Americans, left with him for Canada, eventually to end up in the United States, where they are still alive at the time of writing.

The only man of the family who could claim the family inheritance when the war ended was Major Jan Sławiński, who turned up at Chobielin in 1945 wearing an English uniform. He spent a few days in the manor. At first, the omens were good. A note has been preserved in the archives, dated May 14, 1945, annulling the German expropriation and restoring the property to Julian Reysowski (who was presumed still to be alive). Then, when the news spread that he was back, three heavies from the Szubin Urząd Bezpieczeństwa, the Communist security police, handed Sławiński an order to get out.

Fortunately they had another property, a mill with a house in nearby Białośliwie. Helena and her children had managed to hang on to two rooms after Russians moved into the mill and the People's Militia took over most of the house. Apparently impressed by Sławiński's English uniform (the Cold War had not started yet), the Russians and the Communists moved out. The mill was only confiscated in the 1950s.

The 1945 *Guidelines for Workers' Teams Parceling Out Estates* urged the activists:

> *If an owner still resides in the manor, he should be sent out of the commune within three days. He may only take with him his personal items. Employees such as administrators, stewards, or overseers should also leave. There may be cases in which the heir or his*

underling manages the property. They should likewise be thrown out. It is unacceptable for an owner or any of his appointees to remain at the manor and affect the parceling out of the land.

Chobielin's turn came on August 12, 1946. The last page of the land registry is a curious sight. Under the German headings—prewar authorities continued to use solid, German nineteenth-century volumes—the last transaction is recorded in German on January 8, 1920—Chobielin's sale by Friedrich von Falkenberg to Julian Reysowski. Underneath, a Polish bureaucrat's hand wrote that under the terms of the September 6, 1944, land decree (issued by a group of Stalin's Communist puppets in Lublin) the estate was being confiscated. The "Polish State" was entered as the new owner.

But this was not the end of the matter. The confiscation was insufficient to satisfy the new regime. The zealots wanted to indicate that the very concept of property was being abolished. History was to have come to an end. From now on, the land would be in social, i.e. state hands, forever. There was no need for a land registry anymore. Another hand wrote in underneath: "This land registry was closed on January 23, 1947." And then, so as to underline the finality of the verdict, the same pen made a huge cross over the entire text above it, across both German and Polish entries. The verdict on the past was supposed to be irrevocable.

BYDGOSZCZ,
1346

OUR BEST WORKER on the building site has been Pan Stasiu, the village drunkard. He is middle-aged, with a good-natured face wrinkled by hangovers. He always wears worn overalls. He is bright, hardworking, and strong as a bull. Curiously, he is also a perfectionist. When Pan Stasiu stacks up pieces of wood in a basket you can barely put a needle between the planks. When he advises my mother which trees to plant and when—he used to work in greenhouses—she invariably benefits. We like him, particularly because he has his pride. Knowing that he lives off his brother's family and eats badly, my mother sometimes cooks him breakfast. He eats only when he thinks nobody else is in sight.

Unfortunately, the demon drink always gets the better of Pan Stasiu. He lost the farm he had inherited a long time ago. He spends all his wages on drink. My mother tried to help him by paying him into a savings account, but he would not have it. I sometimes see his money sleeping in the middle of the day under an apple tree behind the village shop. The drinking makes him unhappy. "If I was decent," he once sighed to my mother, "you could take me for a caretaker; I could get married and be someone. But I know I'm no good." He has tried several jobs but he never keeps them for long. We always take him back. Given his hard work when he does turn up, he is really quite a cost-efficient worker. And it is a mark of his honesty that, when he saw something white gleaming in the sand while digging a trench, he immediately called for my father.

It was a silver coin, half an inch in diameter, with a royal profile. By its uneven edge I guessed it was pre–eighteenth century but only the museum in Bydgoszcz identified it precisely, as a half grosz, dating from the reign of Aleksander Jagiellon, king of Poland from 1501 to 1506. It is of course possible that someone dropped the coin just wandering in the woods or on a riverbank. But it is just as likely that the Chobielin mill was already there. In the early 1500s the Jagiellon dynasty was at the height of its power and prestige, occupying the thrones of Poland, Bohemia, and Hungary, as well as ruling the vast Grand Duchy of Lithuania. In other words, the dynasty ruled virtually all of Central Europe, from Prague in the west to Smolensk and the borders of Crimea in the east, and from the Adriatic and Black Seas in the south to the Baltic Sea in the north. At the time the coin was minted, the country was in the middle of two centuries of unprecedented economic growth—and the river Noteć was prospering. Since water power was in those days almost the only alternative to animal and human muscle, it seems probable that in this flat part of the country every spot on a river which offered the opportunity of building a waterwheel would have been used. Documents provide circumstantial evidence. An obscure guidebook to the antiquities of the area, published in the 1960s and long out of print, lists Chobielin as belonging to the castle-keeper of Nakło in the Middle Ages; it would probably have helped supply agricultural produce and crafts for the upkeep of the castle.

In 1569 an Anne of Chabielin (the slight misspelling is not unusual—the place has sometimes been called Kobielin as well), the widow of a castle-keeper, owned property in Bydgoszcz. The land register still lists Chobielin as a knightly *dominium,* perhaps granted to Anne's husband for martial valor. The Chobielin *dominium* had feudal obligations and privileges such as the right to keep the mill and an inn. So, it is reasonable to suppose that the mill already existed in the sixteenth century. Perhaps the half grosz dropped, rolled, and fell between its floorboards while a merchant was paying the miller his dues.

But the coin also made me think. It is easy enough, in Poland, to assume that the upheavals everyone remembers—the German and Russian invasions of the past century—are of utmost importance. But in fact, the cycle of invasion and counterinvasion is older than that in my part of the world—and much more complicated than we often care to remember. In the sixteenth century, Chobielin stood in the heart of a prosperous Poland. Another two centuries later, and that was no longer the case. Nor had it been true two centuries earlier.

When I was a child, my hometown was simply my hometown. My kindergarten, my school, the park where we went picnicking, seemed not so much human creations as geographical formations. They belonged to the landscape as if they had been there since time immemorial, like mountains. If buildings were made of the same, high-fired red brick, well, that must have been how our ancestors made them. Posters and calendars of our city always showed the picturesque old silos on the riverbank; the most popular postcard portrayed the bare-breasted woman archer whose statue stood in one of the city parks. Give or take a few concrete blocks built since the war, almost the entire furniture of a civilized nineteenth-century city—the trolley depot, the post office, the gas works, the army barracks, the county council, the town houses along the high street, the slaughterhouse—were in one style.

There were variations: the austere utility of the army barracks, made of unplastered red brick, differs from the neo-Gothic post office, which differs from the Secessionist facades of the town houses and department stores. But some common thread bound them together. They were of the same culture and sensibility—but it was the culture and sensibility of Königsberg and Berlin, not of Warsaw or Kraków. The secret of Bydgoszcz, the unspoken truth about our city—never mentioned at school—was that its architecture was German. Germany and Germans were always portrayed as our enemies, evil occupiers. At school, we were taught about the age-long *Drang Nach Osten* (Push to the East) and scouts kept the guard of honor in the Old Square, where scores of Bydgoszcz citizens were shot just after the Nazis marched in in 1939. We tended the graves in "Death Valley," the hills where they were buried. We held rallies against German revanchists who, in league with the Americans, wanted to come back and do it again. I never even suspected that Germans might have made a contribution to the city.

In the turn of the century English Baedeker guide to "Northern Germany," on the other hand, Bydgoszcz, Bromberg in German, earns the following note:

> *Bromberg (hotels: Adler, Moritz, room 2½–4 Marks; Lengning, room 1¼–4 Marks; Railway Restaurant), on the Brahe, with 47,200 inhabitants, the seat of the government of this district, owes its commercial importance to a canal constructed by Frederick the Great, which connects the Vistula and the Oder, two of the greatest rivers in Europe. A monument to Frederick adorns the market place. The Wissmannshöhe, to the S. of the town, affords a fine view. There is another pleasant promenade near the locks on the canal.—From Bromberg to Dirschau (p. 214), 79 M., railway in 3 hrs.*

Not a mention of any non-German element or past, even if there was room. And the 1914 Polish guidebook[4] hardly challenges that view:

> *The external aspect of the city is purely German. A very few Polish shop fronts may be found only in the back streets.*

As a child, I knew that Bydgoszcz's main street, the May Day Avenue, was before the war called Gdanska, meaning Gdańsk Street. Now I know that it was also known for a few years as the Adolf Hitler Strasse, and in the nineteenth century it was called Danziger Strasse. Jagiellonska, the Jagiellon Street, where I often visited my mother at her architectural design office, across the street from the local Communist Party headquarters, was once the Generalissimo Joseph Stalin Street, had also been Wilhelmstrasse and, briefly, Hermann Göring Strasse. Only now did I find out that the Old Town Square used to be Friedrichs Platz. Other street names seem to have been picked with deliberate spite. Or was it irony? Nineteenth-century Bülowplatz became the Weysenhoff Square, after the Polish inventor of Esperanto. Blücher, the scourge of Napoleon, alternated with Stefan Czarniecki, the scourge of the Swedes.

In any case, it is undeniable that Bydgoszcz entered the modern age under German rule. It was taken over by Prussia in the very first partition of Poland, in 1772, a process which would lead to the annihilation of the Polish state in the 1790s. With foresight and good planning, Frederick II's spies and engineers had had the land surveyed well before the partition was effected so that by the time the troops moved in, administration began instantly. By the spring of the following year, work began on the Bromberger canal to join the Oder with the Vistula. Eighteen thousand workers brought in from Germany lived in shacks. Although a quarter of them died of fever and dysentery, the vast project was finished in record time—the first barge passed through the canal's ten locks and twenty-six kilometers of waterway by September 1774. The king was said to be pleased. Nevertheless, the wooden locks were hardly usable and had to be completely rebuilt in brick and stone later on.

German control did not firm up for some time. The city fell back into Polish hands during the Kościuszko uprising, swore allegiance to Poland and then to Prussia. During the Napoleonic wars, Napoleon's marshals, Ney and Augereau, entered with their Polish guards, but the city became Russian and then Prussian again over the next seven years. Every time the city changed hands, administration suffered badly as the local government was ethnically cleansed and countercleansed.

Yet despite the turmoil the town grew. Bolstered by the authorities' policy of improving the eastern provinces, and partly financed with France's reparations to Germany after the 1870 defeat, the city surged. Financed with municipal bonds, gas works, electric power plant, trains, slaughterhouse, water works, municipal theater, sewers were built in quick succession. All along, local authority was based on suffrage sensibly limited to the payers of taxes. The boom years at the turn of the century unfortunately coincided with the fashion for imitating Teutonic Knights castles. Then, the new Secessionist style set in just before the outbreak of World War One. The high street was completely rebuilt and splendid patrician houses rose up along the tree-lined Bülowstrasse next to a park; it was the neighborhood of lawyers, doctors, and bankers.

All along, the Germans improved their city aesthetically as well as economically. The Society for the Beautification of Bydgoszcz initiated the planting of trees, cobbling of streets, and the laying out of parks and promenades. A botanical garden was founded next to the agricultural institute, or rather the Königliches Kaiser Wilhelm Institut für Landwirtschaft. Freethinkers had been congregating since 1784 at the Janus im Orient masonic lodge; the more politically inclined belonged to the German Colonial Society; patriotic women to the Fatherland Women's

Society. The bare-breasted woman archer who graces Bydgoszcz post-cards to this day was actually donated by a Jewish banker, Louis Avon-sohn. The building of my secondary school was finished in 1890. It was a Prussian lycée.

Yet when I was growing up, the city bore no trace of its nineteenth-century German patrons. Our Polish chronicles did not mention, let alone praise, the city's nineteenth-century mayors. Under Communism, Polish guidebooks to Bydgoszcz did not even mention the fact that Schinkel, Germany's foremost nineteenth-century architect, helped to design the county council building—surprising, given that Bydgoszcz is hardly a Florence of the north. A backwater in the last years of the Polish Commonwealth became a major industrial center in the last years of the German Empire. But Communist historiography could not acknowledge this because praising Bydgoszcz's amazing nineteenth-century progress would not only have acknowledged the German contribution but might come dangerously close to praising the economic system which made it possible: capitalism. At school we were taught that the nineteenth century, particularly late nineteenth century, was a history of class struggle which led inexorably to humanity's most glorious achievement: the Great October Socialist Revolution. In fact, nothing could be further from the truth, at least in Bydgoszcz.

The main dividing line in *fin de siècle* Bromberg was not class but tribe. Here, in the borderlands, the theory of workers' transnational solidarity broke down completely. Both communities were overwhelmingly conservative. It appears that the German Social Democratic Party was almost as chauvinist toward the Poles as the German right-wingers, an attitude in which the Bromberg German socialists differed little from German socialists elsewhere: the great Max Weber, a socialist and a member of the Pan German League, was once heard to say that "only we Germans could have made human beings out of these Poles." At the Frankfurt parliament, left-wing Liberals such as Wilhelm Jordan argued that "the preponderance of the German race over most Slav races, possibly with the sole exception of the Russians, is a fact . . . and against history and nature, decrees of political justice are of no avail." (This was hardly a shocking statement at the time: even Goethe had written pamphlets advocating the teaching of German to Poles as a means of uplifting us.) Predictably, few Polish workers joined the Bromberg Social Democratic Electoral Union, which numbered 183 members at its peak. In elections, socialist candidates received about two thousand votes—no more than 12 to 13 percent—even when the candidate was as famous a figure as August Bebel, and even after Rosa Luxemburg came to Bromberg to rally the ranks. Bromberg never returned an SPD member even to the city council, let alone to the Reichstag.

Western accounts sometimes portray nationalism as if it were a nineteenth-century invention. But Prussian authorities had adopted a nationalist policy in the lands acquired in the first partition of Poland already in the 1770s, and the policy only intensified as the nineteenth century went by. The workers who toiled on the Bromberger canal in the late eighteenth century—convicts and vagrants from Germany proper—were encouraged to settle down so as to permeate the new province with a German-speaking element. The state paid the moving expenses and half the cost of building a house to merchants and officials from the hinterland who settled there. Even a pro-German schism in the Catholic church was tried. The followers of Jan Czerski split away as a "Catholic Apostolic" parish which later merged with the German Evangelical church, its members Germanizing completely. Jews could be emancipated provided they adopted German surnames and undertook to speak German in public.

Things became even nastier for the Bydgoszcz Poles after the proclamation of the German Empire in 1871. The autonomy of the Duchy of Poznań, of which Bydgoszcz had been a part, had been abolished in 1848. Now the Polish language was finally banned from schools, eventually even from religious instruction. Priests who would not teach religion in German were expelled. Polish was banned even as a foreign language, and could not be used for teaching German to Polish children as it had been previously. Officials Germanized Polish names at secular registries; place names were changed to sound German. Letters addressed with their old Polish names were sent back to the sender. The law on association banned public debates in Polish unless over 60 percent of inhabitants of the district were Polish—in practice this meant an almost total ban. In 1873 the recalcitrant primate of Prussian Poland, Archbishop Mieczysław Ledóchowski, along with ninety other priests, was first imprisoned and then exiled. Many of the new municipal buildings applied a policy of national segregation. The splendid agricultural institute, for example, barred Poles completely.

As so often in human affairs, the policy produced results directly opposite to those intended. Nineteenth-century Germany was a civilized state and its policies took the form of laws and orderly procedures. As such, they were powerless to prevent a Polish revival. No amount of subsidy to Germans and restrictions on the Poles could outweigh the impact of rural Polish Catholic fertility. It was the very civilizational improvements which were supposed to benefit Germans that made Poles live longer and helped more of their numerous children survive. Eventually, the countryside's surplus population began flocking into the cities. So, despite the authorities' best efforts, the Polish minority grew in numbers, while Germans, sensing trouble, sold up and flew west, three million of them in the twenty years before World War One. Even the Colonization Commission helped the Polish cause. By buying land in order to try to keep it in German hands, it merely helped to inflate prices, thus encouraging German landowners to sell, often as not to Poles.

Weighed down by the official nationalism of Imperial Germany, the Poles also responded with a *kulturkampf* of their own. To the chagrin of Communist historians, the patriots were mostly bourgeois and gentry. They founded housing societies, cooperatives, itinerant and stationary libraries, banks, a gymnastic club, choral and trade associations, an Industrial Society. Polish banks such as the Discount, the Bydgoski, and the People's were so profitable and reputable that Germans opened accounts and bought shares in them, so much so that a secret decree had to be issued to ban public employees from associating with them. Only now do I appreciate the irony: the streets named after Bydgoszcz patriots such as Emil Warmiński and Teofil Magdziński, which remained on the city maps in the Communist years, were those of bankers, industrialists, and priests, the very people whom the Communist authorities would have persecuted had they lived a few decades longer. It was also such people who sustained the city's Polish press, which again was hardly left-wing. The main Polish language newspaper, the *Bydgoszcz Daily,* supported the right-wing "national democracy."

Only fear of Russia, its border fifty kilometers away, brought the Germans and the Poles together during the First World War. Bromberg's Germans were some of the most generous in the empire in supporting the war effort, subscribing 47.5 million marks to the war loans. The Poles contributed 586,300 marks to the German Red Cross and to war loans, eight times what they gave toward helping fellow Poles in the Russian partition.

But with stalemate at the front and hyperinflation at home, war enthusiasm had passed by 1917. "Times are sad and it is useless to describe them," was how Bromberg's German mayor closed his diary on November 26, 1917. Within a year, authority collapsed. Revolution in Germany echoed in Bromberg, but here it again took on a tribal rather than class garb. The disturbances were directed by two rival organizations. The German Worker-Soldier Council had no intention of supporting Polish demands, while the Polish People's Council was, despite its name, conservative, its main aim being to try to join Bydgoszcz to the newly resurrected Poland.

On December 27, 1918, Poles in the German partition staged an uprising—the one which Wierzbiński described in *Freedom*. The February 1919 Treviso armistice with Germany approved a demarcation line which gave Bydgoszcz to Poland. By June, the *Bydgoszcz Daily* noted gleefully that large numbers of furniture vans were being loaded up in the streets for despatch to Germany. At 10:40 A.M. on January 20, 1920, units of Polish cavalry, infantry, and artillery entered the city in triumph, greeted by an ecstatic population. In the Old Square, the newly installed Polish authorities welcomed the troops from the pedestal of the overthrown statue of Frederick II. Departing German soldiers promised to be back, but amid the jubilation, no one paid them much attention.

I now realize why the park where we used to go picnicking was known as the Stiffs' Park—it was a leveled German cemetery. My school, built at the turn of the century, once resounded with the language of Kant and Schiller. When I now walk in Bydgoszcz's streets I survey the buildings with an amateur archaeologist's eye, but it's hard to unearth layers of our Polish, pre-German past: there are too many nineteenth-century accretions. Like a Ukrainian in Lwów or a Lithuanian in Vilnius, I know I am not securely at home here. I try to like the German buildings as well, telling myself that after all they were built by natives out of affection and that we are all good Europeans now. But my heart is not in it. The Secession is too sugary, the Teutonic revival too heavy, the red brick too gloomy. My Polish eye always searches for a Renaissance portico, a Baroque flourish, or a neoclassical triangle, and these are few and far between in Bydgoszcz. If I have business at the county council, I'm reminded of Schinkel and wonder why he didn't do a better job here. If I take a train, the German-built station reminds me of a World War One film set, with huge pipes that can swing over the rails, originally built to deliver water to steam engines. If I go to the city library, the courts, the city museum, take a stroll along the canal or down the high street, go to church, take a room in the best hotel—every time I am reminded that a different speech once echoed in them. Every shopping trip questions my sense of belonging.

But when Pan Stasiu found the coin, I decided to look further back in time: perhaps I would be able to reassure myself of Bydgoszcz's identity if I dug deeper than the nineteenth-century German accretions. They are the most visible today because the nineteenth century happened to have been Bydgoszcz's boom time but, surely, the city's Polish soul dwells underneath them.

Yet in the seventeenth and eighteenth centuries, Bydgoszcz's history was possibly even more gloomy than the history of the rest of Poland. The turning point had been the "deluge" of 1655, during which the Swedes occupied the whole country, Bydgoszcz included. Like a cloud of locusts, they stripped it clean. Poles recaptured the city the following year but not before barges filled with loot had floated down the Brda and Vistula to Gdańsk on their way to Sweden. The rapacious northerners took books from the Jesuit college and even court records—the National Museum in Stockholm still displays some of the captured booty. The old castle and the mint were destroyed.

The city's fortunes never picked up after the Swedish deluge. The invasions and sackings became so frequent that one wonders how anything survived at all. While in 1596 there had been 300 tax-paying households within the walls, in 1659 there were only 183, dropping to 94 later, with 130 empty houses and plots. And the bad luck continued. The Saxons sacked Bydgoszcz in 1702, followed by the Swedes, twice. Then the Russians ruled for two years, to be replaced by Swedes again. The plague of 1709 left Bydgoszcz with only forty inhabitants, but the following year the Russians marched into the ghost town anyway. In 1759 the Prussians burned the granaries during their short stay; the Russians settled in for three years just after them, to be pushed out by the Prussians again later. The agony was cut short in 1770 when the Prussians came for good, their presence to be sanctioned two years later by the partition treaty. England protested, weakly as ever, on the grounds that the partition might disturb its profitable trade with Gdańsk.

One has to reach further back than the eighteenth and second half of the seventeenth century to begin appreciating what Bydgoszcz, and Poland, were once like. Indeed, during the clearing of the rubble in 1772, three layers of cobblestones were found in a Bydgoszcz street, each separated by three feet of soil and rubble, each a distant reminder of a former era of prosperity. Like the rest of Poland, Bydgoszcz prospered during the two centuries between the final Polish peace treaty with the Teutonic Knights in 1466 and the Swedish wars of the 1650s. In the sixteenth century the medieval walls defended about ten thousand inhabitants—ten times more than the Prussians would take over in 1770—which ranked Bydgoszcz among twenty of the largest towns in the kingdom. It had four monasteries and convents: the Bernardine, the Carmelite, the Jesuit, and the Poor Clares. The Bernardines copied manuscripts and kept an astronomical observatory. The city's salt yard was one of the biggest in Poland. Poems were written about huge pots made in the local potteries. Of the barges which shipped grain and produce down the Vistula to the international markets in Gdańsk and then on to Amsterdam and London, every sixth was from Bydgoszcz. The city had eleven guilds: barge skippers, merchants, and archers among them.

The town's prosperity attracted immigrants. The influx of Scots must have been large because in 1568 King Sigismund Augustus banned new ones from buying houses within the walls. They persisted as a separate community at least as long as 1651, when nine families are documented, namely: Wilhelm Wallace, Henry Wolson, Jan Barthon, Henry Meller, Michael Barthon, Wilhelm Stanebs, Peter Wolson, George Watson, and Samuel Watson. (Bydgoszcz's last Scot, one Konstanty Wilson, was to prove a good patriot and emigrated to Warsaw shortly before the Prussians arrived for good, not wanting to live under occupation.) Protestants and Jews were banned from full citizenship, but their trade was unaffected. The majority of the citizens had Polish names, and the town was indisputably a part of the Polish crown; if I wanted to prove that Bydgoszcz was an indisputably Polish city, I could rest my case here.

But then—when I dig deeper still—tribal realities become confused again. The landscape of my childhood contained huge, forbidding Teutonic Knights castles. There is one in almost every town in the area. Built of the same large medieval brick, they come in different shapes and sizes, each a wonder of medieval military technology. At Kwidzyń, the castle forms a whole with the cathedral. At Gniew and Świecie, the castles tower above the high escarpment of the Vistula. We went on school trips to the Teutonic Knights' capital, Malbork, which is by some measures the largest castle in Europe—a mountain of walls, towers, and gates. Communist authorities enhanced it aesthetically with a row of prefabricated concrete blocks nestling beside its perimeter. Lesser castles are no more than a defensive tower on a hill, but they are never further apart from one another than a day's march, making a web in which small numbers of troops could control a huge territory.

Sometime in the 1970s I became intrigued by the mark on my father's road atlas which indicated a castle in the middle of the countryside; I persuaded my grandfather Kazimierz to come with me by bicycle. We rode thirty kilometers across rolling, empty countryside to Zamek Bierzgłowski, halfway between Bydgoszcz and Toruń. At last, a tall square tower rose up on a hill. We approached the gate across a spit of level rubble which filled part of the moat. The gate was surmounted by a Gothic arch with a life-size figure of a mounted knight in worn terra-cotta. Made, as it should be, of heavy oak boards with large nails, the gate proper was shut, but we entered through a small door in it. Inside, there was a modern extension with square windows and a flat roof. A few old people played chess or read newspapers sitting on benches along the wall. Others walked round the courtyard as if in a prison exercise yard. Most just sat and stared into space. Suddenly, two of them noticed us and rushed up. Their white hair was badly cut and disheveled and they looked at us with unsettling intensity.

"Have you brought the mail?" one of them asked intently. He suddenly changed his tone to menacing: "You're not stealing it, are you? I haven't had any mail from my son for a year now." He now sounded plaintive.

"I'm not the postman," I replied. With sudden twists of mood like that, I thought he might be mad, but no, the plaque on the extension proclaimed that it was a normal old people's home. The mood of discovery left us. We barely glanced at the chapel before pedaling home in silence.

In medieval Bydgoszcz, the castle remained in royal hands, but the city itself seems to have been predominantly German: most of the inhabitants and the majority of the city council had German names. This is hardly surprising at a time when even the Polish capital, Kraków, had a majority of German inhabitants. From here it is not far to the moment of truth, the year 1346, when the city was officially founded.

One would imagine that a city's founding would determine, once and for all, which tribe can truly claim it as its own. And it is true that it was Casimir the Great, king of Poland from 1333 to 1370, who as every Polish child knows, "found Poland made of wood and left it made of brick," who granted Bydgoszcz its charter. The name of his dynasty—Piast—is synonymous with Polishness. When, in later centuries, the gentry wanted to elect a native as king, they would talk of offering the throne to a "Piast." So Bydgoszcz's founding should prove its Polishness beyond doubts except that the incorporation charter also mentions the town's two *zasadźcy* (founders): Jan and Konrad Kiesselhuth, Germans.

In the king's honor the new town was to be known as Königsberg[5]—but it didn't stick. Locals kept calling it by the older Slav name: Bidgoszcza, from which the later German Bromberg no doubt takes its root. My sense of belonging is as confused as ever.

Like the history of Bydgoszcz, the history of Chobielin also cannot be told without acknowledging a German contribution. But the search to uncover this truth was frustrating. In the last three hundred years, the language of public administration has changed several times: Latin in the Old Commonwealth, German after the 1772 partition, Polish from 1920 until 1939, and German again during the Second World War. The area's administrative allocation has changed even more often. We belonged originally to the Nakło starosty; then the Bromberg department in the Duchy of Posen; then the Wyrzysk district of the Pomeranian voivodship, with the capital in Toruń; then the Reichsgau Danzig-Westpreussen; and finally, the Szubin commune of the Bydgoszcz voivodship. Under the government's brave new plans for territorial reorganization, we will be reassigned again. Bureaucrats are beating themselves into a lather over whether we should be ruled from Nakło, Szubin, or Żnin—three equally neglected little towns.

With each change of government, documents were destroyed or filed away into oblivion. The wars, naturally, have done their bit too. The court records of the Old Commonwealth, which might have yielded the property deeds over the centuries, were stored at the Poznań castle during World War One; these were burned during the Polish uprising in 1918. Most of the records from the German period were likewise removed when the German administration receded west. But I was fortunate in one way: whereas overzealous Communist bureaucrats had destroyed land registers all over Poland and Eastern Europe in the 1940s, ours survived.

After Pan Stasiu's sixteenth-century coin, the first hint in the written record appears only at the beginning of the eighteenth century when the landlord granted a new lease to the miller. I found a mention of it in the Bydgoszcz municipal archive, which is located in a turn-of-the-century German building, once grand, now dilapidated. As with so many such institutions in the Poland of my youth, the archive ultimately depended on some anonymous, underpaid, tyrannized little slave who made the place work despite all the odds. There may have been no proper index, to say nothing of a computer, but there was a Pan Henryk or Pani Helena, who remembered by heart where each book or file could be found. The place faced complete chaos when Pan Henryk or Pani Helena retired or died of overwork. In the Bydgoszcz archive such a man was Roman Mikczyński, rotund and talkative, wearing a gray polyester overcoat stained with chalk marks, a man only in his thirties but seeming as old as the archive itself. For a small fee, he turned the place upside down on my behalf, searching through hundreds of German and Polish files across three centuries.

Some weeks later, Mr. Mikczyński put a gray old file on the rickety table in the archive's dark corridor. The look of triumph in Mr. Mikczyński's eyes told me that he had found a trophy. I made out the date written by quill pen in the splendid script of an eighteenth-century court clerk: August 12, 1791. It was a contract of Chobielin's sale, made between a Pole, Joseph Hulewicz, and a German, August Falkenberg.

By the fact that he spelled his name the German way, "Joseph," rather than Polish "Józef," we may deduce that Chobielin's owner had already adapted himself to the Prussian status quo, nineteen years old in this part of Poland. But his name might also have been a cover: like many Poles, he may just as well have used the money from his estate to

help fund the Polish war effort—or perhaps he had properties in unoc-
cupied parts of Poland and needed the cash to pay war taxes.

There is also another possibility. The area around Chobielin and
along the Bromberger canal was being vigorously Germanized at that
time. Perhaps Hulewicz had had enough of petty harassment from the
authorities, and sold up when offered a good price for his land by the
Falkenbergs—a military family from dependable Prussian stock.

The Falkenbergs proved to be good managers. In 1886, when the old
mill on the river burned down, Friedrich Falkenberg, August's son,
now styling himself "von Falkenberg," built a modern one. An artificial
riverbed several hundred yards long was dug and a new dam constructed across it with several sluices. Upstream from the dam, thousands of acres of meadows were irrigated. The new flour mill consisted
of two identical red-brick buildings; another, smaller building housed
the sawmill.

Like the rest of the Prussian partition, it could not have been a very
harmonious community. An 1870s census in a contemporary geographical dictionary notes that 176 souls lived at Chobielin, 104 Protestants
and 72 Catholics, half of them illiterate (the dictionary does not say
who). Most Catholics were Poles and most Protestants were certainly
Germans. Each Sunday, the religious split must have been accentuated.
The Poles went to hear a Latin mass and listen to a sermon in their language at their church, the Germans at theirs. They married, christened
their children, and buried their dead separately. They lived together but
there was probably little love lost between them. Echoes of national
tensions—school strikes and shop boycotts—no doubt reached even
here.

But materially the manor prospered. The property surveys Mr.
Mikczyński dug up from the archive get longer and longer as the nineteenth century progressed. By 1912, the last year for which German
records exist, there were, in addition to the manor and the mills, an
eiskeller—ice house, a wagenremise—coach house, and a treibhaus—
greenhouse or orangery. The manor still retained rights over the mill,
which was obliged to grind manorial grain for free, to cut up to
four hundred trees a year, and, on St. Martin's, to pay a rent of twelve
reichsmarks and fifteen pfennigs. Given that little survived from
the Old Commonwealth days, and that Chobielin's Polish owners did
not change the manor much between the wars, the conclusion was

inescapable: what remained of the manor's historic substance that I took over in 1989 was mainly German.

Today, Polish resounds in churches built by Germans. German tombs are untended. At Chobielin, the looted Falkenberg graveyard has overgrown with weeds. No trace remains of the statue of Frederick the Great in the Bydgoszcz Old Square. Instead, an overbearing statue to Nazi atrocities dominates it. On the green in front of my school a bronze Wilhelm I, with bushy whiskers and a spiky helmet, once confidently surveyed the city from the saddle. It is now covered with granite slabs covering Soviet soldiers who died liberating Bydgoszcz in 1945. Bydgoszcz is no longer a border town, either with Russia or with Germany. Whereas in the nineteenth century the Russian frontier was fifty kilometers away and between the wars the German frontier was forty kilometers away, today it takes four hours' hard driving to get to either of them.

But Germany remains a presence. In the 1970s and 1980s many of my schoolmates became German. They were mostly as Polish as I was and spoke not a word of German. But with the Communist economy in a nosedive and what seemed like no prospect for political change, they took their one opportunity to escape to the West. What used to be a skeleton in the family cupboard, the fact that a father or grandfather had signed up to be a *Volksdeutsch,* a candidate German during the war, suddenly became a prized asset. We called them "Volkswagen Deutsch." Having made some money and learned the ways of the world, many are now returning to set up businesses back in Poland, to the sullen annoyance of those who stayed behind.

Every few months I learn of another strand that links us with Germany. The Erlichs, the family who lived in the ruin of the manor when my parents bought it, have probably lived in the area since the time of the building of the Bromberger canal in the eighteenth century, or at least since the nineteenth-century colonization efforts. Mr. Erlich's father's generation was unsure of its ethnic allegiances. Typically in my part of Poland, the family split on the issue during the war. Mr. Erlich's father quarreled with his brother. The brother, Mr. Erlich's uncle, took what seemed like the easier option and allowed his name to go on the

Volkslist. Mr. Erlich's father stuck to his Polishness knowing full well that it might mean deportation. The uncle, as a prospective German, was called upon to fulfill his duty toward the fatherland by being drafted into the *Wehrmacht*—and died on the Eastern Front. Mr. Erlich's father, the stubborn Pole, survived.

Even my own family could have German links. By an unprovable family legend we are supposed to seal ourselves with the coat of arms called *Cietrzew,* literally pheasant, showing a black bird on a red shield. If true, then our Polish credentials reach back to the fifteenth century, when the *Cietrzew* shows up in battles. But before the fifteenth century, the *Cietrzew* coat of arms was called *Abdank,* German. Most likely, it is nevertheless an original Polish coat of arms—they are unique in Europe in having remained unchanged in their simplicity since pre-Christian times; it was simply Germanized in the two centuries when my part of Poland belonged to the Teutonic Knights. But I can't prove this, so I could be racially impure.

Germany's attitude to Poland now seems to be that of the Kiessel-huths, the first mayors of Bydgoszcz, rather than the Teutonic Knights. In the fourteenth century, Germans came east and gave to the locals their superior know-how and civic culture. They made their fortunes and eventually went native, possibly changing their names to something like Kieślowski.

Today, much of our local industry is already in German hands, with even more work under contract for German companies. Economically, Bydgoszcz looks to Berlin as much as to Warsaw, to everybody's benefit. Perhaps for this reason, tribal defensiveness is on the wane. Unthinkable even a few years ago, the bookshops in Bydgoszcz now sell albums of nineteenth-century photographs of Bromberg—showing clearly German street names and shop fronts—with captions in both languages. The publication of such an album would have been a criminal offense under Communism—in the unlikely event that it had ever made it past the Communist censors in the first place. They are now sold by the Bydgoszcz Friendship Society, a font of local patriotism. We are at last free to love our city while acknowledging another tribe's contribution to it. Members from a German organization of Bydgoszcz expellees are frequent visitors at municipal ceremonies and a bronze plaque was recently unveiled to a German patron of a nineteenth-century orphanage, even though he was a known Polonophobe. At this rate, we might one day have enough confidence even to name a street after our city's founders.[6]

But at Chobielin, we still fear the return of German soldiers. Or rather, we worry about a particular German soldier, a captain in the *Bundeswehr*. He will come to Chobielin one of these summers and we will be in trouble. In the 1980s, in the dark days of martial law, he and his family had kindly sent my parents parcels with food, clothes, and cosmetics, as millions of Germans then did. One day, they will want to see that their aid went to the deserving poor. When they see Chobielin, looking more prosperous every year, will they understand that it is simply Poland that has changed?

Perhaps we worry in vain. We have already had one German visitor who might have been awkward. One day, Mrs. Else Borowski stopped her car at a respectful distance from the gate, timidly knocked, and was overcome with joy when my mother showed her around and served tea. She had been born von Falkenberg, she explained, and just wanted to see the place about which her grandmother kept talking even on her deathbed. When she left, we found a fifty-deutschmark note in the visitors' book.

PART III

MY HUNDRED DAYS

THE WINTER OF 1992 was exceptionally mild, so the work on the house continued. The roof skeleton had been erected the previous summer using technology that differed little from a century and a half before: using an ax and a handsaw, Mr. Primaka, a retired Belorussian, planed cavities in the middle of each rafter, so that it could rest on support beams. When Chobielin's original roof was constructed, iron must still have been expensive because nails—square, handmade, each one a little different—were sparsely used. Wooden stakes held the timber together instead. We did not have to economize: during that winter we used eight hundred kilos of nails in the roof alone.

When the skeleton was finally complete, Mr. Erlich hung a traditional *wiecha*—a wreath of green branches—from the top of the middle section. When he finished, he told me gravely that I would have the honor of driving in the last nail. Work stopped and everybody crowded around to see how I would cope. The nail was as thick as a small finger and half a foot long; the hammer merely bounced off its head. I asked for a heavier hammer but all the large ones had mysteriously disappeared. I noticed that Mr. Erlich's son, Jacek, was beginning to smirk.

They counted my strokes out loud. I began to sweat. The nail had barely moved. Eventually, they took pity on me and handed me a proper hammer, which lay hidden behind a beam. It still took me several blows to drive the nail in and only then did I learn what the purpose of the exercise had been. By an ancient tradition, Mr. Erlich informed me, I was obliged to stand them a bottle of vodka for each stroke of the hammer. It appeared that I owed them several cases, which would have killed all of them many times over.

We spent the autumn covering the roof with insulation. We were cannibalizing the house's own body: Mr. Erlich and Jacek used an old rotary saw to cut up the old beams into planks. The wood inside was orange, rich with resin, with studs of raw iron where the saw had cut through a nail. Once the planks covered the empty spaces between the beams, it was time to call on Mr. Jeske, our local roofer, who had already replaced the asbestos roof with ceramic tile on the keeper's lodge. He was short and wiry and a compulsive angler, like my father. Sometimes, when my father was out of luck, he brought a carp or a pike from the river. He had a job with a local construction company but agreed to put a new roof on Chobielin after hours.

As he worked, I pondered: ever since discovering how badly damaged the structure of the house was, and how much of it would have to be replaced from scratch, I had wrestled with a philosophical dilemma. Was I restoring an old house, or was I building a new one? Certainly the first floor and the roof were brand-new. The old plaster had to be stripped and new electricity cables laid before it was replaced. Sewers, central heating, water pipes, ventilation ducts, and chimneys would all have to be new.

I decided that the house would preserve its character only on one condition: that we re-cover the roof with the original nineteenth-century tile. The trouble was that many had broken when we took them down; there would not now be enough to cover the whole roof. Fortunately, the German name of the factory which made them was stamped on the back. I traced it to Ostromecko, a large estate on the other side of Bydgoszcz, whose huge barns and outbuildings were covered with the same tile. Only a chimney remained of the old brickworks but I chatted up a farmer whose house and pigsties were also covered with the tile. As it happened, he was keen to replace the old stuff and I bought two hundred lovely old tiles for the price of a few sheets of asbestos.

By February 1992, the house was wreathed in scaffolding. Mr. Jeske ran about like a monkey on top of it. Several tiles in both hands, he could run up to the top of the roof in just a couple of paces. I climbed on all fours and watched him disappear in clouds of dust as he cut tiles on the old rotary saw.

One day I was sitting on top of the roof breathing in moist air and taking in the view over the river and the carp ponds beyond, when Pan Stasiu appeared, galloping from the lodge. There was a phone call for me, he shouted, *from Warsaw.*

Polish telephone charges being extortionate, I ran down to get it and picked up the receiver, panting. "The minister of defense would like to speak to you," a secretary said. I heard a click followed by the voice of Jan Parys, the first civilian minister of defense since Communism's collapse. He had only been appointed a couple of months previously but had already made a name for himself. He had forced his Communist predecessor to retire and called for faster withdrawal of Soviet troops from Poland.

I knew him well. Barely in his forties, he had dealt with Western embassies on behalf of a part of the underground opposition in the 1980s. I liked his clear language, the legacy of his philosophy studies. His girlfriend and future wife for a couple of years, Małgosia, ran a salon in her Warsaw villa. Our first fully democratic elections had been held a few months previously and it was in her salon that the first coalition government of that parliament was formed. The new prime minister, Jan Olszewski, with the key members of his administration, had been meeting at Małgosia's for months, planning future strategy. I knew Parys liked my articles, and he had read my book about the war in Afghanistan. We had spent hours discussing how our army could draw lessons from a war in which a poor, small country defended itself against the might of the Soviet Army. Parys had been a senior official in the Central Planning Office, in charge of contingency war preparations, so he was an obvious choice to be a new minister. I had advised him on contacts with the West.

He wanted me to come to Warsaw immediately—and that's what I should have done. Instead, I asked what it was about. He said he wanted me to consider becoming his deputy, in charge of security policy and the army's international relations, which meant contacts with NATO. I said I would think about it and ring him back. A deputy minister's pay was at the time $266 dollars per month. Resigning from my job as the representative for Rupert Murdoch's News Corporation meant a 95 percent pay cut, so the restoration of Chobielin was bound to slow down.

What Parys wanted was no less than to overhaul our entire Soviet-style defense establishment, including personnel, equipment, defense posture, army intelligence, and the ministry's own structures. Our top brass had been trained at Soviet military academies for the task of invading northern Germany and Denmark. Now the only possible danger came from the east. Poland had specialized in aggressive types of weapons: aircraft and tanks. What we needed for self-defense were anti-tank and anti-aircraft weapons. Our Ministry of Defense did not have a single department devoted to strategy: all the plans and orders had always come from Moscow in the past. Seventy percent of our troops and equipment were stationed west of the Vistula, poised to attack NATO. In the east, we were completely exposed. Only a few battalions stood between Warsaw and Kaliningrad, the rump of East Prussia, now a part of the Russian federation, which contained a garrison of 200,000. Our air defenses were so antiquated that if hostile aircraft were to fly over our territory, we would learn about it only when they had appeared on the radar of Warsaw's Okęcie international airport. Our military intelligence had for decades been subordinate to Soviet military intelligence, targeting Western technologies and plans. As to the personnel, a U.S. congressional report acknowledged four years later what we knew then: "Communist political-military officials permeated the apparatus from top to bottom."[7]

In fact, I needed about thirty seconds to make up my mind. I spoke the West's language, both literally and metaphorically, and had contacts in the British and American military establishments from the time when I had lectured about the Afghan war. Unlike the great majority of our officers, I had seen a war, and a victorious one at that. I could be useful. If we managed to inch closer to NATO, our cycles of war and occupation might at last be broken. To serve a free Poland was exactly what I had dreamed of for years of exile. Besides, my twenty-ninth birthday was in a fortnight. Not every day do you get the opportunity to join a government before reaching the age of puberty.

After a brief consultation with my wife-to-be, I rang back and accepted. The next morning I got into my car and drove to Warsaw.

My conversations with Parys had lasted all of two minutes, but they were a crucial early mistake. They were picked up by the military intelligence, called WSI in Polish, who bugged the minister's own phone, "for his protection," as they later claimed. Parys's desire to reform the Polish army to conform to Western standards may have been greeted with enthusiasm by people like me, but this was hardly shared by all of the officer corps. This was particularly true of the military intelligence. In the past, the politically reliable, those who toed the Soviet line, had been rewarded with promotions and foreign postings. Now, their future looked uncertain: NATO, if we were to join it or even begin to negotiate with it, could not trust people who had been spying for the Warsaw Pact. They had to go.

And military intelligence let us know very quickly how they intended to treat us. In the old days, when Communists wanted to give credibility to a piece of information, they customarily bounced it off foreign sources, even if it had to be a far-left publication such as the British *Morning Star.* I remembered American documentaries about Poland, no doubt heavily edited, being shown on our television screens in the 1970s, apparently praising the great achievements of Edward Gierek. So it happened this time. I talked to Parys on a Thursday—and to no one else. By Saturday, the information had been passed on to the London *Observer,* which ran a little diary item about it on Sunday.

What happened afterward has always reminded me of a scene in *War and Peace* in which one of the heroes, Nikolai Rostov, goes into battle for the first time and hears bullets whizzing past his ears. He thinks, "Are they shooting at me, *me* whom everybody likes so much?"

My appointment was bound to raise an eyebrow or two. I was young for the job and I held a second passport, British, which I had acquired a few years before when, with everybody else, I had assumed that Communism was eternal and I would live in exile for the rest of my life. But then, I was not the youngest member of the government—a deputy minister of privatization held that honor. My immediate predecessor was a dissident mathematician whose closest brush with danger had been as a speleologist, and the media had proclaimed him perfect for the job. Second passports held by politicians are not so unusual in countries with convoluted histories. Two prewar Polish presidents had held Swiss passports and even in 1992 several freshly appointed Polish ambassadors had come from the Polish Diaspora in the West; some held a second citizenship. Émigrés held senior positions in the governments of Estonia, Lithuania, and Ukraine. There were historical precedents. Kościuszko, our national hero, had been an American general. Our own general, Józef Bem, had commanded the Hungarian Army in the 1840s. Józef Piłsudski, our prewar leader, had been an Austrian officer. No law barred it in Poland in 1992. Surely, I thought, the press would judge me on my record and not on what papers I held. As a journalist, I flattered myself, I would be able to handle it better than most. I imagined that the media would like three things about my record: that I had been educated in the West, that I had helped the anti-Soviet resistance in Afghanistan, and that I was restoring Chobielin. I was wrong on all counts.

The *Observer* story helped set the tone. "Why," asked Polish newspapers in hostile tones, "are the British media first to know about appointments in Poland?" "Rambo Has Landed!" "God Save Poland!" screamed the headlines. I must be a CIA agent, one newspaper argued. After all I had written a paper for a London defense institute which had a former CIA director on its board. No, I was a British agent, suggested another. Who but the Secret Intelligence Service could have paid for me to go to Oxford? Now "as a reward for successfully carrying out an assignment in one half-colony [Afghanistan] London has moved him to another," commented a weekly. Communist deputies protested in parliament against the appointment of an "agent of international capital."

Either way, I was an imposter. On the day that the official announcement was made, I attended a lunch with the Canadian ambassador, from which I had to excuse myself halfway through to check over the text of the CV which was due to be released to the press in an hour. It stated that I had delivered lectures on the war in Afghanistan and irregular warfare to such bodies as the Institute for European Defence and Strategic Studies, Cambridge University, and the Soviet Studies Research Centre at Sandhurst. In the rush, I failed to notice the omission of a comma in the sentence. There is no Institute for European Defence and Strategic Studies at Cambridge University! the newspapers thundered. They had me nailed.

For several days, a dispute raged in the national press about whether the lectures I had delivered at a couple of military academies and several foreign policy think tanks could be called lectures at all. (The Polish word, *wykład*, has a more nineteenth-century weight to it, hint-ing at a professor in a bow tie.) Would I agree that I had the psychology of a terrorist? one charming radio interviewer asked. Would I like to impose martial law? asked another. Is it true that I wanted to declare war on Russia? wondered a third.

Reporters did not stalk me on the doorstep as they would have done in England. In fact, nobody ever asked me any factual questions—investigative reporting was still in its infancy in Poland at that time. The rumor mill just fed on itself. Someone had heard some snippet from an acquaintance of an acquaintance and rushed it into print. Once in print, it was treated as fact, which gave grounds for ever wilder conjectures. What was frightening was the speed with which the stories multiplied. You try to cooperate with the media and prove that one allegation is incorrect, say the one that MI6 paid for my studies. It takes a while, particularly in those days, when international dialing was still a problem, before you get through to the Inner London Education Authority, which was the source of my very ordinary grant. It takes them a couple of days before they find the documentation and fax it over. But by the time you have the proof, the media are on to something else.

Most Polish journalists were only superficially familiar with the West at that time and some Communist propaganda had brushed off on them. So many thousands of Poles had emigrated over the decades and most of them had ended up washing dishes or laying bricks in Chicago and London, they mused—so how did he manage to go to a prestigious university? He must have had a leg up from a murky source. Their ignorance led to comic results. A friend of mine from the university, the proud owner of a tile factory employing fifteen people near Winchester, had long arranged an engagement party for me. Not to attend would have seemed like the arrogance of my newly elevated position, so I kept the date. Two dozen friends and acquaintances gathered for a couple of hours in a pleasant mews house in London belonging to another friend. Among the guests was another contemporary from the university, then working as a gossip columnist at the *Evening Standard*. The account in next morning's *Londoner's Diary* was lurid and funny, describing my host as a "millionaire secondhand car dealer"—an evident leg-pull. But our media and politicians completely missed the English sense of humor. "What is our minister doing hobnobbing with British plutocrats?" MPs asked angrily in parliament the following week. "Is he going to award them arms contracts?"

Needless to say, Chobielin grew in size and opulence in reports. My parents' New Year's Eve party for a dozen close friends at the keeper's lodge became a Roman orgy for five hundred. The brass door handles which my father and I had personally installed on the doors turned out to be made of "pure gold." Simultaneously, a journalist who bothered to look the house over dismissed it as a pathetic ruin and expected that the dam on the river might burst and flood it any minute. But whether a rich man's toy, or the venture of a hopeless romantic, the restoration of Chobielin clearly disqualified its author from any position of responsibility.

Even my travels with the Afghan resistance counted against me. Was I in favor of those guerrillas who produced drugs, or did I favor those who specialized in throwing acid in women's faces? wondered one journalist. And again, he could not have just gone to Afghanistan as a reporter, just like that, on his own initiative, speculated another. Which Western intelligence service put him up to it? In any case, a supposedly sober news magazine pronounced gravely, I should go to jail for serving in Afghanistan without the permission of Polish authorities.

This last comment stands out in my memory as a summing up of the intellectual and moral confusion that reigned in Poland in those days. To quote it in full: "Radek Sikorski, according to experts on military law, should serve five years in jail for his service in Afghanistan without the permission of Polish authorities," wrote the weekly *Wprost*. In other words, when I was planning my trip to Afghanistan in 1986—whose purpose was to bring back news and photographs of the war so as to shore up the West's support for the resistance—I should first have applied for permission to the Polish authorities at the time, that is the Communist government in Warsaw. I tried to imagine the letter that I should have written to the co-author of martial law and interior minister, General Czesław Kiszczak.

> *Dear General,*
>
> *As a political refugee from Communism in general and your regime in particular, I was thinking of going to fight the Soviet Army in Afghanistan. But, on second thoughts, I decided that I would be more useful to the anti-Soviet resistance if I were to report on what your friends from the Red Army are up to there. I intend to focus in particular on the scorched-earth policy which has*

to date laid waste to half of the country's villages, killed over a million people, and sent a third of the population into exile.

I hope, General, I may count on your sympathy and encouragement in this project.

I remain, sir, your obedient servant, etc. etc.

It was, of course, absurd. But since I had not sent such a letter, I should now, in a free Poland in which General Kiszczak was being investigated for a massacre of striking miners, keep my toothbrush and underwear packed.

On the first day after my appointment, my ministerial car drew up in front of my flat. It was an old Polonez, Communist Poland's 1970s answer to the Volvo, its normal sluggishness compensated somewhat by a specially modified engine. I opened the door and the driver, a young recruit in soldier's uniform, saluted me, introduced himself, and made a brief report. I made a joke, trying to put him at his ease, but he only stiffened. "Let's go," I said and noticed with appreciation that the morning's papers were already lying on the back seat. The soldier clicked his heels and rushed to the car. He had locked the car doors—thievery was so bad in Warsaw, you could not leave anything open even for one minute—and now he couldn't open the door. He kept fiddling with the lock, but it wouldn't give. Ten minutes had passed and I was beginning to feel silly. I was standing on the doorstep, a briefcase in hand, and noticed that passers-by began recognizing the face they had seen on the previous night's news. Finally, I took the keys out of the hands of the driver and opened the door myself. It proved easy. As I worked the lock and the soldier leaned forward to look at it closely I saw large drops of sweat going down his neck. His hands were shaking. The army was obviously as nervous of me as I was myself.

It was a ten-minute drive from the vicinity of the old town where I kept an apartment (one room an office, the other the bedroom—gratifyingly described by the media as "luxurious") to the Ministry of Defense building across the street from the then presidential palace at the Belvedere. An iron gate swung open as we approached and two soldiers inside the guardhouse saluted.

My office was in a small villa at the back of the main compound. There was a garden sloping down toward a fence and behind it, no further than two hundred yards, a pile of stone slabs with porticoes and window frames in the heavy neoclassicism so beloved by dictators—the Russian embassy. I never bothered to have the villa swept for bugs. At this distance, the Russians could listen to us with direction microphones. It was a ludicrous site for the Defense Ministry—that is if you wanted to conduct a policy independent of Russia. There was a gate in the fence between the two compounds and legend had it that it was installed there in the 1940s for a minister of defense of Communist Poland in the 1950s, a Russian. I went down on my first day to have a look. I was relieved to see that the gate was locked, with old rust in the hinges.

The office itself was a long room with large windows, facing the Russian embassy. Reputedly, it had been used by General Jaruzelski to record the speech which announced the imposition of martial law in December 1981. Now it was drab and looked empty, as if someone had left in a hurry. I asked for a telephone connection to Brussels. "Three hours wait, two with luck, minister," replied Pani Halina, my secretary. Ordinary Warsaw phones already connected within a couple of tries. But I could not dial direct to anywhere outside Warsaw. Those trying to reach me were often connected to the teachers' common room of a primary school in another part of town. Yet I was responsible for the foreign relations of a 220,000 man army.

True, an official, ministerial telephone stood by the side of my desk. It was a large chest covered with inscrutable dials and buttons, just like a time machine from a 1930s science fiction movie. I told the staff to take it away and give me an ordinary Panasonic. They were surprised: "But minister, you are *entitled* to a telephone as large as this." Apparently, the size of one's telephone used to be a phallic symbol, a sign of political potency. But of all my office appliances only the shredder worked tolerably. So much for the myth much peddled in the West that, whatever their sins, the Communists were at least professionals, expert at running the machinery of government. My office was a 1950s time warp, and I know for a fact that the first fax machine in the Polish government appeared at the Cabinet Office in 1989, brought personally by Professor Jeffrey Sachs from Harvard. Just like the country at large, we inherited the structures of a government in terminal decline.

Later that day, I took part in the first military council, the meeting of the joint leadership of the army command and us, the civilians. Several faces were openly hostile. There were among them the last generals who had been members of the WRON, the military junta which ran Poland under martial law. They knew that this was likely to be one of their last military councils. They were right. Parys had them sacked within a fortnight.

The chief of military intelligence, Admiral Wawrzyniak, briefed us. Menacing NATO aircraft had been probing our air space, he said, and NATO ships were skirting our territorial waters. As he spoke, I felt transported back to the era of the Warsaw Pact. This was how they must have gotten themselves into an anti-Western frenzy in the old days. Parys did not want to embarrass the old spy in front of his colleagues and had a quiet word with him on the side. NATO, he explained, were now our friends and potential allies. By the next meeting of the military council the following week, our strategic situation had been totally transformed. The admiral now warned that Russian aircraft were menacing our airspace and Russian ships were skirting our territorial waters. I was more depressed than gratified by the military intelligence's sudden change of mind. They had obviously tailored their message to what the politicians wanted to hear. If so, their information was worse than useless.

A few days later Parys invited me for supper at Helenów, a closed military compound a dozen kilometers from Warsaw. It was an eighteenth-century mansion surrounded by a park with several large ponds, confiscated from a charitable foundation set up by a prewar aristocrat. General Jaruzelski agreed to the details of his attack on Solidarity in 1981 there with Soviet generals. He had finished writing his memoirs at Helenów only a couple of months before. After supper, we took a walk around the biggest pond, which stretched for a kilometer into the night. Parys's two bodyguards hovered behind us, just out of hearing.

"Now you have to know something," Parys said.

"Yes?"

"What do you think would happen if Poland acquired nuclear weapons?"

I looked at him, but his face was tense, expectant. He wasn't joking. I thought rapidly. Poland was signatory to the nuclear nonproliferation treaty. There was no point in having nuclear weapons if the potential adversary does not know about it—the point is that he should know, and be deterred. But if the adversary knows, then everybody else is likely to know too. In the wake of the discovery of Saddam Hussein's secret nuclear program the year before, the West was understandably concerned about nuclear proliferation. Nuclear proliferation was the worst offense a country could commit.

"You mean, our own industry has developed them?"

"No, not our industry. We can buy them."

"Who from?"

"The former KGB. They are selling everything. First they offered us American Stinger missiles they had captured in Afghanistan and now we can have five tactical nuclear warheads for a million dollars."

"I think we should decline. If they find out, the Americans will classify us as another Libya or Iraq. And if they are kept under wraps, then what's the point?"

"I'm glad you think so. I'm also resisting it."

It hadn't been his idea. The head of military intelligence, the same admiral who had given us the briefing, had made a top secret appointment with him, laid some papers on a table, and said: "By order of President Wałęsa, please sign this authorization."

It was an order to proceed with the purchase of the warheads. The added twist was that the sellers were to be cheated out of their payment. The swap was to happen on Polish territory. Our troops would stand by and take the money back soon after the transaction. The operation was practically "without risk," the admiral had said. Wałęsa was pressing Parys about it at their formal meetings. Wałęsa's former chauffeur, a murky figure called Mieczysław Wachowski, now chief of staff, approached Parys at a reception and hinted darkly: "You do what we tell you and you'll be minister forever." Fortunately, Parys's signature was necessary for the disbursement of cash from the secret intelligence fund.

Was it possible that Wałęsa would be so reckless? I had met him for the first time since March 1981 a couple of months before, when I conducted a formal interview with him for Polish state television to mark the first anniversary of his elevation to the presidency.

I went to the presidential palace a Wałęsa supporter. In 1991, when most of Warsaw's establishment had been denouncing him, I wrote articles with titles such as "Why I Shall Vote for Lech Wałęsa." So now, in front of the cameras, I was respectful and sympathetic. After all, "our" Lech was president at last and with a bit more time he would surely sort things out. But Wałęsa interpreted my sympathy as weakness, failed to answer any questions, and simply ranted incoherently. Only ten minutes of the forty-minute tape were remotely usable.

It was a strange experience: I had interviewed Gulbuddin Hekmatyar, the murderous leader of Afghan fundamentalists, and clashed with Jonas Savimbi, the Angolan guerrilla leader accused of burning his enemies at the stake. Both were psychopathic liars. But I still rate my interview with Wałęsa as the worst experience of my journalistic career. He exuded strength, but it was untempered by civility or even a trace of modesty. More alarmingly, I was appalled by the atmosphere around him in the presidential palace. The language was that of the beer hall; the ambience that of a gang of racketeers in a third-rate thriller. The yes-men in his entourage pandered to him as if to some African tribal chief. I left the presidential palace humiliated, ashamed, and saddened. Humiliated by his rudeness, ashamed of having been blind enough to support him for so long, and saddened that a man who had achieved immortality was in the process of destroying his greatness with his own hands.

Since that time, news had seeped out that during the anti-Gorbachev coup in Moscow the previous year, Wałęsa had written a letter of congratulation to the hard-line plotters which was intercepted only at the last minute by the then prime minister. Now Wałęsa was doing the rounds of European capitals peddling an idea of NATO-bis, a second NATO, a plan for some kind of East European military alliance which might include Russia and to which Russia would cede its nuclear arsenal. It was either naive or crazy, and the vehemence with which he argued for it stupefied prime ministers and presidents, particularly as he had failed to consult even with his own chancellery, let alone the Foreign Ministry or us, at Defense. I had to face the fact that my former hero was half Mahatma Gandhi, half village yokel, and you could never be sure which side of his personality would predominate. He seemed capable of anything.

But his attempt to acquire nuclear weapons could have proven a disaster in a league of its own. It was hard to decide which prospect was more frightening: if the operation was successful, then Wałęsa, his chauffeur, and their friends in the unreconstructed military intelligence would obtain access to the nuclear button. A few tactical warheads were unlikely to increase Poland's security. These were battlefield weapons that might destroy a tank division or two, but would not win us a war. Their use would, on the other hand, certainly rob us of any international sympathy.

On the other hand, if news of the operation leaked out, with or without us getting the warheads, then Poland could become a pariah state. Our credibility as a new democracy and our chances of joining the institutions of the West would disappear. Perhaps, I thought, that was indeed the object of the exercise. Perhaps the Russians were trying to draw us deeper into the intrigue and then blow the whistle. The whole world would learn how irresponsible the Poles were. Much better that they were kept under the thumb of a more reliable power.

Either way, it was better to stay away from the affair, and that is what we did. Parys refused to sign the authorization. Wałęsa and his people now stepped up pressure, but Parys stood firm.

Instead of toying with nuclear weapons, we decided to sack the people who had devised the plan, first of all, Admiral Wawrzyniak. It was ludicrous for him to pretend that such an operation carried "no risk." It meant that he was either a bad intelligence officer, or was manipulated politically.

It was not just that military intelligence had proven itself hostile and irresponsible. This was the spring of 1992, only a few months after the failed coup against Gorbachev in Moscow and literally weeks after the collapse of the Soviet Union. Tens of thousands of Soviet troops still occupied dozens of bases all over Poland. Meanwhile, the WSI was the last institution in Poland that had not been touched by reform. In Communist times, particularly the 1980s, it had been much more than just the eyes and ears of the army. Under martial law, the army ran the country. Generals took over the civilian secret police and ruled as provincial governors and even company directors. The military intelligence, with a secret budget and cells in every military unit, independent of nominal commanders, kept an eye on the army itself. It was therefore General Jaruzelski's ultimate instrument of control. Had the coup in Moscow turned out differently and the Soviet Union and the old guard reasserted its control, they could have been insane enough to try to reestablish their stranglehold over Poland. If they had, the WSI was still there to be used.

A month later, Parys summoned the admiral to his office without warning. "We have a paramilitary unit in reserve if they resist," said Parys.

His replacement—a general from outside WSI—was already waiting. We drove to the military intelligence headquarters—a grim office
block unwashed for decades—in a convoy: Parys in an armor-plated car
in the front, his bodyguards in another. I took his chef de cabinet in my
Polonez. He was a likable colonel, but very fat. I don't know whether it
was his weight, or his nervousness at our mission, but the front seat in
which he sat just would not move back and so he drove to witness the
most dramatic episode of our time in government with his head
strangely bent over the driver's gear stick.

In the event, the handover went without a hitch. We introduced the
new chief of intelligence to the department chiefs and he took over on
the spot. It was the right thing to do but President Wałęsa was furious.
He liked having as cronies men who were in some sense compromised:
they were more malleable. He did not mind old Communist spies, as
long as they were useful in hatching his intrigues. Three years later,
when he fought an unsuccessful reelection campaign as a champion of
anti-Communism, I could only laugh. Now, the breach between Parys
and the president became unbridgeable.

But my job was to explore ways in which we could approach NATO.
My predecessor in the job had still argued that the Warsaw Pact was a
very good alliance if only Russia would respect the excellent provisions
in the original treaty. We did not want an alliance with Russia, however
"good," but simply for Poland to rejoin the mainstream of Western civilization. It takes two to tango, though, and the West was far from en-
thusiastic. Only a few months before, in August 1991, President
George Bush had made a ludicrous speech warning the Ukrainians
against the dangers of separatism and intoning "Long Live the Soviet
Union!" It has been called the "chicken Kiev" speech. Three months
later, Ukraine opted for sovereignty. Western policy toward Central Europe was similarly shortsighted and I came up against it again and
again. The West had ossified in Cold War attitudes as much as the
gerontocrats at the Kremlin had done. Its leaders were completely at a
loss as to what to do with the newly liberated East. We got the impression that they would have preferred it if we had stayed on the other side
of the barricade and not upset their cozy world. Indeed, most of the
diplomatic exchanges and conferences in which I took part were a
waste of time.

One was a grandly proclaimed North Atlantic Cooperation Council, which gathered the top security officials from all the former Warsaw Pact and NATO countries in Brussels. Security was supposed to be enhanced if we "talked" about our concerns like psychiatric patients. The only trouble was that Russia, whom half the delegations regarded as a potential aggressor, had a veto power over the proposed solutions. The Ukrainians proposed that the nuclear weapons they were giving up and which they were handing over to Russia to disappear God knows where, should be dismantled under international supervision. Estonia proposed a resolution which called on countries to remove their armies from the territories whose governments objected to their stationing. Both were perfectly sensible proposals. But Russia objected and the West acquiesced. We hardly felt reassured.

Another occasion was a conference in London to which the Foreign Office flew me club class along with several dozen officials from other post-Communist states. The British put the Czechs and the Hungarians, representatives of countries on the borders of the European Union, into the same grouping with Tajiks and Uzbeks, whose countries bordered on China and Afghanistan. I observed how highbrow Czech dissidents tried to network with fat Soviet generals, their mouths shining with gold teeth. The Foreign Office clearly thought that we should build our security together with the very people from whose grip we had just managed to slip away.

Of all the Western diplomats and politicians I met in my time in office, only the Germans, the Japanese, and individually Mrs. Thatcher made any sense. The Japanese ambassador called on me soon after my appointment and conveyed the message that, unlike the West, his government did not intend to pour billions of dollars in aid to Russia while Russia was still finding the money to stoke up colonial wars on its periphery. The Germans backed our inclusion in the European Union from the start and a German, Manfred Worner, was also the NATO secretary general. He was the greatest advocate of our inclusion in NATO too. When he came to Warsaw, I hosted a dinner for him and his wife, a spirited blonde who spoke good English.

"Have you had the opportunity to look in your Stasi files yet?" I asked her in a lighter moment, alluding to the amazing revelations that were seeping out at the time from the archives of the East German secret police.

"Oh, yes," she enthused. "Manfred had always felt guilty about not keeping a detailed enough diary and now he is relieved. It is all there in the files, volumes of it. Even our conversations in bed are recorded. It's very useful now that he is writing his memoirs."

Worner was to meet President Wałęsa the next day and our military intelligence prepared an intelligence assessment of the Russian deployment in the Kaliningrad region and Belarus. The idea was silly to begin with because it implied that NATO did not know the Russian deployment better than we. I got an early look at the document. My dismay rose with every page. It was written in atrocious English, with words and whole sentences sounding as if translated word for word from a dictionary. Whatever the value of the intelligence itself, it was bound to make the worst impression, as if we were a banana republic unable to afford a good translator. It was a detail, but it summed up perfectly our predicament at that time. I was literally the only person in the entire ministry who could speak English properly. For years, officers had been discouraged from learning languages other than Russian and only a handful, in intelligence and those who had served in UN peace missions, had traveled abroad. Ignoring the proceedings of the military council, I corrected the brochure and sent it back to be printed again at the ministry's high-security plant. I wrote "shoot the translator" on the last page. I don't know if the order was carried out.

The following morning we held formal talks with Worner and his team at the defense ministry conference center near the international airport. During a break, a counterintelligence officer walked in, gaunt with tension. He made a report. Our radio monitoring station, whose sensors had trained on the conference center that morning, had just detected a brief electromagnetic burst beamed from inside the building— a bug. Modern eavesdropping devices record a long stretch of a conversation and then beam it out in a condensed form, which makes it harder to detect in the airwave noise. Clearly, some intelligence organization wanted to know what we were up to, and it wasn't a Western one, because NATO countries would be receiving minutes of our meeting through routine channels.

The detection of the bug concentrated our minds. Worner was sympathetic to our aspirations and went as far as NATO governments would let him in giving us encouragement. After lunch, he made a speech to an assembly of officers, which sketched out the conditions we would have to meet before admission. He stressed one sentence in particular: "The door to NATO is open to Poland." Naturally, it didn't mean that we could join right away if only we applied, but it was the first ever public statement by a NATO official that we would even be considered. Having suffered weeks of media attacks for supposedly "kicking at a closed door," we felt vindicated. Our drive for changing Poland's geopolitical orientation was beginning to bear fruit. I was jubilant.

It was now crucial to make NATO's position known to the public, both domestic and foreign. I had no authority to influence the state television news broadcasting at all but the head of the news department was an habitué of Małgosia's salon. I rang him in the early afternoon and pleaded to give Worner's words maximum exposure. *Of course, minister,* he replied without hesitation and I could tell from his tone of voice how gratified he was to be given a task to carry out. Success is wonderful for one's authority. All the news bulletins that day opened with the phrase "The door to NATO is open to Poland, said Manfred Worner, secretary general of the Atlantic Alliance." Repeated in Polish and international media for some days, it created the impression that it was merely a matter of time before we were really there. Soon, this indeed became official Western policy.

Mrs. Thatcher was even more supportive. I had met her several times over the years. The previous year I had helped her draft a speech she made to the joint houses of Polish parliament and was rewarded with a hearty lunch she cooked for me and her husband, Dennis. To my surprise, she was to acknowledge our conversations in her memoirs. Now, I took the first opportunity to slip away from the Foreign Office conference and the pleasures of hobnobbing with Uzbek generals, to her office at Chesham Place. It had the atmosphere not of the office of a retired politician but of a government in exile and reminded me of nearby Eaton Place, where the Polish government in exile had met during the forty-five years of Communism. Unlike the émigré Poles, however, Mrs. Thatcher still obviously had strong adherents inside the regime. She rose from the sofa twice during our hour-long chat to talk to cabinet ministers, rallying their spirits.

I did not need to argue our case. She anticipated it. Most other Western politicians, diplomatists, and bureaucrats still thought in terms circumscribed by the realities of the Cold War. NATO and the European Union had become cozy clubs for the rich and comfortable. Their kneejerk reaction was to defend the status quo. But while they thought bureaucratically, Mrs. Thatcher thought geopolitically and historically. The Soviet Union took on the world, and lost. It was now time to reclaim for Europe the lands in the East which enabled Moscow to threaten the West. She believed that international policy should have an aim—to extend the boundaries of economic and political freedom. At the end of the hour, she wrote a statement in support of an immediate withdrawal of Russian troops from Polish soil and of our integration into NATO, which made the front pages of Polish newspapers.

In 1992 she was, of course, no longer burdened by the responsibilities of office and one wonders what she would have done if she was still prime minister. My debut in print in the English language had been in 1982, when the *Spectator* published my letter criticizing her for her muted reaction to the imposition of martial law. But now, after eleven years in power, she was tougher and I think she would have been just as supportive in office. When freedom dawned in 1989, she had not hesitated. Within weeks she gave us a helping hand in stabilizing our currency and set up a knowhow fund to help our transition to the market. Had she not been toppled in the Tory coup in 1990, the West's handling of the collapse of Communism might have been more statesmanlike. She had influence over President Bush and might have prevented him from sounding foolish in Ukraine and elsewhere. She would have had the guts to tell Moscow the hard truth about its diminished role in the world and perhaps Russia would have channeled its energies into building a decent society rather than into neoimperial illusions. She certainly had the courage to oppose the entire political and diplomatic establishment of the Western world over Bosnia. The following year she visited Warsaw again, to open the Bristol, Poland's premier hotel newly refurbished by Forte. (Lech Wałęsa, through Mr. Wachowski, the former chauffeur, passed on the message that he does not receive failed politicians.) She made a stirring speech calling on the West to use air strikes to end the war in Bosnia. A standing ovation greeted her words, marred only by the sight of the British ambassador, no doubt under instruction from London, walking from table to table and saying to all who would listen "This is not the British government's policy. This is not the British government's policy." It was to take three years and 200,000 Bosnian corpses before the policy changed. Sarajevo and Warsaw each owe her a statue.

Back in Warsaw, I was beginning to get into my stride. My office was now ticking over smoothly. The secretariat was adorned with a framed quotation from Mrs. Thatcher on the theme of an ideal lieutenant, which she once applied to Nicholas Ridley, one of her cabinet ministers: "Others bring me problems, *he* brings me solutions." The chief of the secretariat only needed to point to it when someone wanted to bother me with details that did not require my attention. I took particular pride in the fact that my guests were no longer poisoned with the standard cup of tea—made by floating a tea bag in a cupful of Warsaw's famously polluted tap water. My tea was brewed properly in a pot with water from Chobielin's deep well, a container of which Pani Halina kept in the office safe. It was to amaze several Polish embassies which, due to lack of money, were receiving Polish newspapers only sporadically, that current press clippings about the ministry followed me by fax wherever I went.

We organized the first civilian department in the ministry, the Defense Policy Bureau, and soon a steady flow of analyses and reform proposals began arriving on Parys's desk. We negotiated a military confidence-building agreement with Ukraine under which troops would pull well back from our respective borders and officers would start being trained in the other country's schools. We selected a capable officer to be Poland's liaison officer with NATO in Brussels. Knowing how unpronounceable and difficult to remember foreigners found our surnames, I conceived and supervised the manufacture of several thousand name badges, which soon appeared on officers' uniforms, just as they do on American officers' uniforms. It made their contacts with NATO colleagues easier but there was a hidden agenda too. I have a terrible memory for names and constantly meeting people dressed in the same clothes made me terrified of giving offense by mixing them up. Also, I reasoned, people are generally more likely to behave themselves when their identity is always known.

One day, I inspected an exercise ground that was being vacated by the Russian army in Silesia. It was vast, covering tens of thousands of hectares. Seen from a helicopter at the height of several hundred meters, the earth was scorched black as far as the eye could see, in all directions. Hundreds of charred tree trunks lay on the ground. Only here and there a dead tree still stood up. It was the middle of spring but not a green shoot rose up. We flew over a base, really a self-contained town with barracks, rows of tanks and trucks, and blocks of apartments for the Russian soldiers' families. You could tell from the air which blocks had been abandoned. There were holes in the walls where doors and windows had been. Poland was never to receive a kopek toward cleaning up the environmental damage. Our predecessors in government had still talked publicly about perhaps "keeping the Russian troops in Poland as a hedge against the Germans." We were anxious for the Russians to clear out as soon as possible, compensation or no compensation.

Having been brought up in Bydgoszcz, the headquarters of one of Poland's three military districts in Communist times, I had thought I had a fair idea of the lifestyle of most officers—many of their children were my classmates. They were mostly somewhat better off than my parents, although this was largely offset in our minds by their inability to travel to the West. Now I saw what life was like at "green" garrisons, small towns in the middle of nowhere where combat units were stationed. There were usually no jobs, let alone entertainments for officers' wives, and the education of their children suffered. You had to love the army very much to put up with it. Never again was I to permit myself to question the basic patriotism of the regular Polish army officer, even if he had signed the Communist Party application form. The officers' families' biggest complaint was that, under the rigid Warsaw Pact system, readiness for action had to be kept up at all times, irrespective of the country's security environment. The result was that each family had a holiday in the sun only once every few years. There was no need for a permanent war footing anymore. We changed the rules at once so that more officers could vacation in the summer. If an adversary ever has the cheek to invade Poland at the height of the holiday season, Parys and I will be to blame.

I visited our staff college at Rembertów near Warsaw. In reality, it had served in Communist times only as a preparatory school for real general staff training, which our officers received in the Soviet Union. Despite the new governor's best efforts, its backwardness still showed. My journalist's laptop had a faster chip than the computers which they used for battle simulation. The school offered no teaching at all on irregular warfare, which should be a necessary ingredient of any Polish security doctrine. We encouraged plans for a NATO college to be housed there, so that the Ukrainians and others from Central Europe could be prepared for cooperating with NATO by visiting Western lecturers. In subsequent weeks I tried to squeeze some money to try to double the output of our college of languages.

There were also pleasant distractions. A particularly festive occasion was a party at the embassy of North Korea to celebrate the eightieth birthday of the Great Leader, Generalissimo Kim Il Sung. A couple of years earlier, a Polish cameraman had made a documentary called *The Parade* which received a film prize from the North Koreans as a particularly realistic depiction of the way in which the people demonstrated devotion to their president. The Cannes film festival subsequently also rewarded the film—as a biting parody about a totalitarian regime insane with self-adulation. I did not really have to go to the party—our relations with North Korea were cool and normally only a low-level Foreign Ministry official would have attended. But I was curious. I had never seen a proper Stalinist celebration. The Foreign Ministry cleared me to go and the North Koreans were delighted to have bagged such a dignitary. The ambassador welcomed me at the entrance and led me to a large square room, a miniature of one of those great halls of the people shown in *The Parade*. To my surprise, the room swarmed with our generals, particularly a few whom I specifically did not suspect of having a sense of humor. If they thought they were in for a cozy evening in the company of old Communist friends, away from a world outside which no longer loved them, they were surprised. I filed away their faces in my memory for future reference.

"One hears disturbing news from your country, ambassador," I said.

"If you mean our nuclear program, minister, then I wouldn't give much credence to reports in imperialist media," he replied.

"No, I mean I have heard that the leadership of the party has promulgated the doctrine of 'One country, two systems' as a path to unification. Don't you think it smacks of revisionism? Look at the mess Poland has landed in because of ideological slackness."

He was speechless for several seconds. I hope a report went out to Pyongyang the following day that Poland's first democratic government was not so reactionary after all and that Jimmy Carter was not the only foreign dignitary who showed understanding for the North Korean people's struggle.

My eye wandered toward a slender blond woman who was talking to several fat dignitaries, including a familiar figure with a straight back and dark glasses. We were soon introduced and I contrived to detach her from the rest of the company. The adjacent room housed a photographic exhibition of the triumphs of the North Korean revolution and was empty—the crowd clung round the food and the drinks on the central table in the main room. She was called Monika and we flirted pleasantly, strolling from a picture of a worker building a dam to a crowd of saluting young pioneers in red scarves. She was as bright as she was pretty and had character too. She had helped the Solidarity underground in the 1980s and now worked as a journalist in one of Poland's most successful new glossy magazines. I was sorry to have to drift past the last picture and back into the main room. I said:

"Will you please introduce me to your father?" I smiled mischievously.

"If you want."

He was in civilian clothes but his stiff figure and dark glasses were unmistakable—General Jaruzelski, the former dictator. We greeted each other politely and I told him about my recent inspection of the Silesian military district. He nodded with approval when I praised the order I found in a couple of units.

"Yes, we had reared those regiments for first-line duty. They are commanded by talented officers and you shouldn't persecute them for their former politics."

"I've marked them down for possible promotion."

The first ice broken between us, we reached for a glass of vodka from a tray that moved past. Jaruzelski had the reputation of being a teetotaler, but we downed them in one. Thus fortified, I said, "You probably don't know how much you changed my life, General."

"Oh, yes, how?" He seemed genuinely interested. There was a human being behind the mask. I told him about my eight years' exile in Britain, which would not have happened had he not clamped down on Solidarity. He said he was sorry to have inconvenienced me and seemed to mean it. We chatted away for a while yet.

A former Politburo member joined us and said to me: "You denounced us for taking our orders from the Soviet embassy and now you people go to the U.S. embassy to get yours. So what's changed?" Warsaw was indeed rife with rumors about Thomas Simons, the U.S. ambassador, a particularly arrogant State Department specimen, trying to dictate appointments inside our government. I itched to argue that there might nevertheless be a difference between being a protectorate of Moscow and that of the U.S., encapsulated for example in the difference between East and West Germany. But I bit my tongue. The party was beginning to wind down and we moved toward the exit to collect our coats. A couple of uniformed generals did so at the same time and I saw from the corner of my eye that the caps they collected were of the old, Communist design. They were round, like Soviet ones. It had in fact been Jaruzelski who had reintroduced the traditional square caps, but only for the guard of honor. We were making them compulsory for all officers.

"Look, General, they still haven't bought themselves proper Polish caps," I whispered to Jaruzelski before I thought. The implication of my words, I belatedly realized, was that while they wore those round caps for the forty-five years of Communism, the Polish People's Army had been, as one member of parliament famously put it, "a Polish-speaking Soviet army." Indeed, the majority of officers may have served with dedication but the top brass knew that they were used as a tool of Soviet policy. The generals knew the contingency plans and they realized that in time of war the Polish People's Army was to be controlled by the Soviets so tightly that our men would not even have been entitled to a Polish court martial. Whatever the state of mind of most of its officers, the fact remained that throughout its existence, the Polish People's Army had served Soviet, not Polish, interests. It might have been used to attack the West, although the average Pole regarded the democracies as friends and allies against Communism. General Jaruzelski had been a chief architect and manager of this arrangement. He was one of the Communist army's youngest-ever generals and served as the head of its political directorate. As minister of defense he had directed the Polish contingent in the invasion of Czechoslovakia in 1968 and carried out the order for the bloody suppression of the workers' revolt in Gdańsk in 1970. He ended up imposing martial law in 1981 and imprisoning thousands of Solidarity activists and dissidents. Jaruzelski was a latter-day janissary, but had not yet admitted it to himself.

In a flash, his amiability was gone. He gave me a mean look, turned on his heel, and left for the waiting limousine without saying goodbye.

The following week, photographs of me drinking vodka with General Jaruzelski circulated in parliament, prompting wild rumors. Were we selling out? Some former dissidents, upon discovering that he was not a monster, lost their heads and started defending his record. In fact, I sent Monika a copy of my Afghan book, with a dedication, but I did not change my view of her father. General Jaruzelski was personally decent and, by comparison with Lech Wałęsa's buffoonery, he had been a dignified president. But he was still a political criminal, guilty of helping the Soviets control Poland. His last chance to vindicate himself was after he had imposed martial law. Holding absolute power, he could have introduced bold market reforms and Poland might have entered the post-Communist period better prepared. Instead, he clung to power until the country went bust. He admitted to a bad conscience when he ordered the destruction of the Politburo transcripts from the 1980s. Some of our leading intellectuals may have been taken in by his military charm but history is more likely to agree with a peasant who met General Jaruzelski a few months after me. His farm had been ruined by Jaruzelski's commissars in the 1980s. Despairing of the dictator ever being brought to justice, he stalked the general to a book signing ceremony and put a brick in his face.

I was getting a grip on my job and I heard that my performance, most gratifyingly, was beginning to gain acceptance on the chauffeurs' network. This was a web that linked all the offices of state as reliably as, and more discreetly than, the secure telephone network. It worked like this: when I was in conference with the minister at his offices in Klonowa, or attending a function, my driver, Jarek, killed time by talking to other ministers' drivers and bodyguards, exchanging office tittle-tattle. The bodyguards, while changing shifts, gossiped with other bodyguards, who gossiped with officials from the cabinet office. Within a couple of weeks, the word was out whether a new official was a good or a bad egg. I heard my own verdict from Jan Parys's wife, who had heard it from the prime minister's wife. I was particularly relieved at the sympathetic judgment because I drove Jarek and my office hard. He was up at dawn to drive me to work at 8:00 and we rarely finished before 8:00 or 9:00 in the evening. In addition to serving as an informal vetting machine, the drivers' and bodyguards network also provided institutional continuity. While ministers came and went, they remembered back a long time. The only danger was that the drivers and bodyguards were even more badly underpaid than we were ourselves, so the temptation to leak to newspapers was high. The tone of the commentary about our team was also beginning to shift. Someone told me an anecdote he had picked up in the parliament lobby: "What do our two deputy ministers of defense have in common? One has already been to a victorious war [me], the other is yet to start one."

I may have been finding my feet in the job but, two months into my ministerial career, it became clear that the government of Jan Olszewski was dying. I had expected when I joined that it would not last long. It never commanded a majority in parliament and it failed to reach out to a centrist party called Democratic Union, which polled only about 10 percent of the vote, but had friends in the media. I had hoped for nine months in power, after which some results might have started to come through and we might have caught a second wind. It was not to be. Wałęsa was now implacably hostile to my boss and developed a habit of subjecting the prime minister to humiliating grillings on live TV. The feud came into the open over the question of civilian control of the army. The constitution gave the president the title of "head of the armed forces." He handed out promotions up to the rank of general, just as he bestowed decorations and professorships. But just as the right to nominate professors did not entitle him to run the Polish Academy of Sciences, so the powers over the Defense Ministry and the services were unequivocally the responsibility of the cabinet and the minister of defense. This was not just a matter of our internal political arrangement. Effective civilian, democratic control over the army was one of the preconditions for Poland's integration into NATO. But titular authority was not enough for President Wałęsa. Wachowski, the former chauffeur, took to inviting senior generals behind the minister's back and promising them preferment in return for political support against the government. Parys protested but nobody backed him. A parliamentary commission composed of the government's opponents ruled against him and he was sacked from the government under a cloud.

Events soon vindicated him. As we expected, the general who had defied him soon became chief of staff. A few months after that, he was in open defiance of civilian authority, several times prompting speculation about a possible coup. He was to preside over a bizarre dinner at which the senior generals, egged on by President Wałęsa, held a vote on whether or not they would continue to obey the minister of defense. The Polish model of civilian control over the armed forces became a joke in NATO capitals. Parys could have been more diplomatic in his language, although personally, I respected him precisely because he dared to call a spade a spade. It was the shortsightedness and cowardice of most of our politicians that was at fault.

In May 1992 the Olszewski government was tottering on the brink of collapse, but it still managed to chalk up one last achievement. The negotiations with the Russians on the withdrawal of their troops from Poland had been going on for many months and the date for their departure had already been set. Now, however, Lech Wałęsa was to go to Moscow to sign a Polish-Russian friendship treaty, which would seal the matter for good. Unexpectedly, the Russian Defense Ministry came up with an original idea. They proposed that their bases in Poland should be turned into Russo-Polish joint ventures. It was not explained how garrison towns in the middle of nowhere, military airfields, or lines of bunkers would make money, but we already had a fair idea. Many of the bases were vast, like the scorched exercise ground I had seen from the helicopter. Even when they were surrounded by a perimeter fence, scores of kilometers long, they were impossible to police. At the same time, traffic into those bases was extraterritorial, with no immigration or customs checks. It didn't take a genius to work out how to make money on the arrangement. You only needed to buy tax-free goods in Germany or Russia, transport them to a base in Poland, and then spirit them out and sell them in the Polish market. We were receiving reports of giant Russian transport planes filled with cigarettes, alcohol, and even cars landing at the bases, their cargo subsequently disappearing into thin air. The Polish state budget was losing millions of dollars every month in taxes. Pavel Grachev, the Russian defense minister, came to Warsaw and harangued our foreign minister to accept the clause. The Russian commanders were obviously sending a cut to their superiors.

The joint ventures would have been a gigantic financial scam at best and, at worst, a network of Russian spying stations financed by the Polish taxpayer. But President Wałęsa wanted to let the Russians have them. Wałęsa was about to go to Moscow and the matter was still unresolved.

That evening I gave a talk to military attachés and other diplomats, reaffirming our new, defensive security posture. The Parys affair was still rumbling on and the atmosphere in the room was charged. The diplomats hung on my every word. During drinks afterward, a slim man in his forties in a well-cut suit approached me. He gave me his card, took a cigarette out of a silver holder, and said, in English, with barely a trace of a Russian accent:

"Why do you insist in seeing us as the enemy? We mean no harm to Poland."

"I am sure you don't. But why do you keep 200,000 soldiers in the Königsberg region, with a striking force greater than our entire army?"

"Königsberg?" he said, and his face went red and strangely contorted with anger. "We prefer to call it Kaliningrad. At least for now."

It was a terrible gaffe on my part. After the Red Army conquered East Prussia in 1945 the ancient Teutonic Knights' city of Königsberg was renamed Kaliningrad, after a Stalinist speaker of the Supreme Soviet. When speaking English I often called cities, even Polish cities, by their German names simply because these were easier to pronounce for English speakers. Also, I liked baiting some of our superpatriots. But this was bad. He could kick up a diplomatic fuss and he would have been in the right.

"I mean Kaliningrad, of course." I tried to sound apologetic. "And please, understand that our NATO aspiration does not mean to threaten Russia. When Germany was unified and NATO came to the Polish border we did not feel threatened, because we regard NATO as a friend. So can you. Threat is in the eye of the beholder. Anyway, I hope we will negotiate the Russo-Polish friendship treaty eventually. I mean, the business about the joint ventures in the bases should be smoothed away somehow."

"Don't you know? That's all been agreed."

I did not know. I gave him a sharp gaze. Now it was he who was looking sheepish, as if he had said something he should not. He reached for another cigarette from his holder and, as he tapped the filter on the back of the case, I noticed that his fingers trembled ever so slightly. I also had a good look at the cigarette case. It looked sterling silver, in good taste. My interlocutor was too well groomed for an ordinary Russian diplomat. But before I got a chance to probe him further, he pointed to his empty glass and, pretending to get a new drink, disappeared.

First thing the next morning, I placed a call to counterintelligence, and gave them the name of my new friend: Valeri Poliakov, first counselor of the Russian embassy. Shortly, the answer came back. Poliakov was indeed down in our files as a serving officer of the KGB. I placed the second call to the prime minister, Jan Olszewski. He was soon on the line.

"I had a strange conversation with a Russian diplomat last night. Apparently, we've agreed to let the Russians have their joint ventures in the bases."

"Really?"

He knew nothing about it. I told him what had transpired.

"Please write it down and send me a memo as soon as possible." He sounded agitated.

My staff carried out additional checks on Poliakov and by early afternoon a memo went out to the cabinet office. A special courier carried an envelope with my large, round ministerial seal on the back. The cabinet was in session and, to his surprise, my courier found himself ushered into the room and handing the letter personally to Olszewski. The government was in uproar. Everybody thought the same thing: the foreign minister and Wałęsa had agreed to the treaty behind the cabinet's back. Wałęsa was already on his way to Moscow and now, upon inquiries, it turned out that the text of the treaty had indeed already been printed, including the joint ventures clause. It was classic Wałęsa. Promise whatever they want, and worry about how to get out of it later. But this time, he was way out of line. And he underestimated our determination. Olszewski sent him a cable care of the Polish embassy in Moscow, literally forbidding him to sign the treaty in the present form. The next day, ten minutes before the signing ceremony, in a tussle between Wałęsa's entourage and Yeltsin's on the steps of one of the Kremlin staircases, the offending clause was crossed out and an anodyne phrase inserted by longhand. We had won. Three and a half years later, in January 1996, Mr. Józef Oleksy, the first former Communist prime minister of Poland since our liberation in 1989, resigned office under investigation as a possible informer of the KGB. He was eventually cleared but not before it transpired that he was very friendly with a KGB spymaster in Warsaw. I was glad that by the time of his appointment there were no clauses in the Russo-Polish treaty which Mr. Oleksy could interpret in a light sympathetic to his friends.

But the sending of the cable to Moscow was the Olszewski government's penultimate act. I was going to leave the ministry whatever the fate of the government. I did not see eye to eye with Parys's successor, Romuald Szeremietew. It was another curious twist of fate. He did not know it, and I did not tell him, that his name had been on the posters demanding the release of imprisoned dissidents which I had plastered on the walls of Bydgoszcz in 1981. We agreed that I would delay my resignation until after a week-long conference at the Maxwell Air Force base in Alabama which I had long agreed to attend.

So I was in America during the affair for which the Olszewski government is now chiefly remembered. I was attending lectures and inspecting equipment—giant transport aircraft and F-16 fighters, discussing their merits with pilots, fresh-faced veterans of the Gulf War. I walked to meetings and cocktail parties past neatly cut lawns and immaculately tended officers' houses, but my mind was on events in Warsaw. The Americans must have thought me odd, checking my pigeonhole at the guests' lodge and asking for faxes with my press clippings several times a day. Every day, the faxes became longer and the typeface of the headlines bigger. Poland was going through its worst crisis since the restoration of democracy.

It had started a couple of weeks before, when the eccentric leader of a small, ultra-Thatcherite party, the Union for Realpolitik, moved a motion in parliament asking the interior minister to "inform parliament" about former secret police agents who still held prominent jobs in the government and bureaucracy. Unexpectedly, the motion passed. The former Communist Party, which could have blocked it, voted in favor, knowing that its members had rarely been recruited by the secret police because they had informed as a matter of routine, through the party channels.

I had always been in favor of exposing those who had made Communism last for as long as it did, the same way the civilized world dealt with Nazi criminals. In the 1950s, Stalinist prosecutors and judges had sent to their deaths heroes of anti-Nazi resistance such as Captain Witold Pilecki, who had volunteered to go into Auschwitz and had reported back to a world which would not listen. Communist terror in Poland may have been a pale reflection of what had transpired in the Soviet Union, but it still managed to claim the lives of several hundred thousand people. Political murders occurred as late as the 1980s. Such crimes should be punished where possible. Justice should be seen to be done, or else new scoundrels might think that they can always get away with it. At the very least, the truth should be revealed.

The question of what to do with people who had been informers for the secret service was harder. Some had done it for money, or advancement in their careers, or perks. Others were literally beaten into signing an undertaking to cooperate while in prison for opposition activity, and then blackmailed. Yet others played an elaborate game with the secret police—giving it some information, but trying not to harm anyone too much. Many, however, had been hardened misanthropes, causing by their denunciations untold misery over many years. Many stories of their activities that were now coming out would not be believed in a novel. One journalist had knocked over a flowerpot one weekend when his wife was away, and it had damaged his desk. A panel moved, revealing a secret compartment where he found his wife's report on him, ready for handing over to her controller. Another journalist, a friend, spent much of the 1980s in jail, sentenced for spying for the United States because he had had the temerity to cooperate with Radio Free Europe. While he was in jail, his wife sought solace in a medium, who proved extraordinarily prescient. Over a crystal ball, mumbling hocus-pocus, the medium said things like "Your husband is near, yet very far." She predicted "You will see him next week" or "In three days time, you will get a letter." Permission for a prison visit or a letter invariably arrived. The medium was even able to predict what the letter from prison would say. Needless to say, my friend's wife trusted the medium implicitly and told her all about the prisoners' plans and secret schemes. The medium turned out to have been a secret police informer, her knowledge of the timing of visits and of prisoners' correspondence derived from the authorities, who had controlled both.

I had also been targeted. A family friend, a brave man who had been sacked as dean of the Bydgoszcz Teacher Training College for his Solidarity sympathies, had come to see me at Oxford. On his return, he was interrogated about the meeting but he did what any decent person should have done: told my parents all about it. My time at the university seems to have held a particular fascination for the Communist authorities. Months after leaving the government I learned from acquaintances at the Interior Ministry who had carried out my security vetting that there were piles of reports on my progress. News of my anti-Communist speeches at the Oxford Union reached Warsaw within forty-eight hours. I was flattered that so much attention had been lavished on me. The secret police had obviously thought that I showed promise.

It would have been satisfying if the files were open and one were to find out who had ratted. Some people might react to the news by turning the other cheek. Others would spit in the informer's face. The choice, I thought, should be up to those whose lives had been inconvenienced or wrecked. Personally, I would just like to have had the satisfaction of knowing the truth.

But *lustracja,* as the proposal to weed out former informers was called, also had a more important, political dimension. Relatively harmless informers were now ashamed of what they had done and either came out voluntarily, offering explanations, or at least kept a low profile. But what was one to think of people who continued to be active in politics? Dozens of politicians, top civil servants, diplomats, and members of parliament had been compromised. In East Germany and the Czech Republic it had turned out that up to half of all the journalists working for the official state-owned media had been secret police informers or agents of influence too. All these people had a vested interest in preventing an honest reckoning with the past. They were also obvious security risks. Under an elaborate system of information exchange within the Warsaw Pact, Moscow had received detailed information from the Polish secret police. After many Interior Ministry files had been destroyed in Warsaw, Russia was now in possession of a full set of compromising material about these people. They could be blackmailed for years. It was a sickness of the body politic. The Germans had dealt with it by allowing everyone to inspect his or her secret police file and ruthlessly purging the army, the civil service, and the political class. The Czechs had likewise cut the Gordian knot and, Prime Minister Vaclav Klaus was later to tell me, it strengthened their democracy. In Poland, the disease was yet to be treated. As for me, I thought herbs were more appropriate than surgery. I had asked the British to supply us with a blueprint of their security vetting, and they obliged. If we had implemented their procedures, the informers could have been weeded out gradually, as a matter of routine, without raising the specter of a witch hunt.

It was not to be. The parliament's request to the Ministry of the Interior was vague and did not establish any procedures for dealing with dubious cases. Premier Olszewski established a commission under the chairmanship of the chief justice, but it never got a chance to start work. In the first days of June the interior minister, Antoni Macierewicz, delivered sealed envelopes to the heads of parliamentary caucuses which contained the names of those in the government, civil service, and parliament who figured in the secret police files as informers.

What happened next is and will remain a subject of bitter controversy in Poland. What is not in doubt is that *lustracja* proved a monumental fiasco. The lists of alleged informers were supposed to be secret, but of course they leaked out immediately. They contained the names of Krzysztof Skubiszewski, the foreign minister, Lech Wałęsa, several dozen members of parliament, and even the heads of parties that supported the government. Polish politics exploded. Wild rumors swept the city. The army was put on alert. The government was accused of trying to carry out a constitutional coup.

As I followed it from afar, my anger grew. First, at the incompetence and naïveté of it all. The public had not been prepared for *lustracja,* the government's case never laid out clearly. Support in parliament or the loyalty of the Interior Ministry troops had not been assured. Interior minister Antoni Macierewicz has since been portrayed in hostile profiles as a manipulator extraordinaire, who supposedly tried to knock out all his opponents with one elaborate masterstroke. My impression was, rather, that he was disarmingly innocent. He should never have imagined that anything can be kept secret in Warsaw for more than five minutes.

What angered me even more than the government's mistakes, however, was the attack on it, nothing short of shameless. The alleged informers, and their friends in parliament and the media, counterattacked. The interior minister was threatened with assassination. The media threw everything they had against Olszewski. "Politics of Hatred!" screamed the headlines. Before the week was out, instead of informers being purged, the government was finally recalled. The takeover by a new administration itself looked like a coup: armed units took over the Interior Ministry and ministers whom parliament specifically asked to remain at their posts were locked out of their offices. A videotape which has subsequently come to light, shot at a tense meeting at which Wałęsa plans the coup, shows the new prime minister, Waldemar Pawlak, objecting weakly to the "gangster methods" that were about to be employed. Thus was the first fully democratically elected Polish government for fifty years brought down: because it tried, however awkwardly, to do the right thing. Soon, everything was stood on its head. The government were portrayed as a bunch of psychopaths, while the secret police informers now basked in the glow of martyrdom, as if *they,* rather than the people on whom they had spied, were the victims.

Although I doubt my presence could have made much difference during those crucial days, I can't help somehow blaming myself for having been absent. Perhaps, if I had been on the spot, I could have influenced events. I had not known about *lustracja* in advance and would have objected to the form it took if I had. But once it started, it should have been carried through. The informers' coalition should not have been permitted to triumph. Olszewski's resignation speech to parliament was watched by half the nation, even though he made it at midnight. I hope I would have had the presence of mind to persuade him to make it earlier in the day, and instead of resigning, call on the people of Warsaw to picket parliament in the government's defense. The government might have survived; the judicial commission might have started carrying out orderly *lustracja.* Once the informers were exposed, the public would have been appalled by the extent of the elite's rottenness and by their attempt to wriggle out of it, and we would have been vindicated.

As it was, I landed back in Warsaw to find both the minister of defense and the prime minister already dismissed from office. Within a couple of days, I had cleared my desk and said farewell to my staff. They gave me a wonderful album of historic uniforms of the Polish cavalry. Some were, I fancy, genuinely moved.

Parys had wisely forbidden me to spend any government money on office decor, so I now took down from the wall a lamp which I had purchased with my own money. While fiddling with a screwdriver I noticed something odd about the picture of the white eagle, our state crest, that had hung above my desk. There was something on the reverse. I took the picture down and looked. It was the familiar bearded face of Comrade Lenin. Like a reversible raincoat, the picture could be changed with just a flick of the wrist. I don't know whether it was made that way as an economy measure, or for a joke, or as a sign of defiance but I now think that the picture encapsulates Poland at that time.

The battery of my jeep, which had spent several weeks parked in front of the ministry building, was dead from lack of use and so the army rendered me one last favor and two recruits pushed me on my way.

Three hours later, I was back in the solitude of Chobielin, and could take stock of what had been done at the building site in my absence. The roof was finished and the copper of the new gutters gleamed red. A meter of soil and sand had been cleared from the drive so that my tires now whirred on freshly exposed cobbles. Within a fortnight, I was in Washington, getting married, but I had the rest of the summer to organize my notes, take long walks, and think. Had it been worth it?

In the three short months, we had achieved quite a bit. Poland's Western orientation, which we had proclaimed, became a matter of national consensus. From then on, nobody ever dared to hark back to the Warsaw Pact anymore. We had focused attention on the need to reform the army and its intelligence branch and the seeds which we had then sowed eventually blossomed. The principle of civilian control over the armed services, the issue over which Parys fell, is now sacrosanct. The new department at the Defense Ministry which I had created was renamed, but continues to function. The contacts with Brussels and Ukraine eventually brought results. My proposal to rent out our spare exercise grounds to Western armies, dismissed as batty at the time, is now a reality.

If absolute power corrupts absolutely, then five minutes of power corrupts only a bit. I did not hold any orgies at the ministry's Helenów palace outside Warsaw, as the press hinted, but I did get used to sending Jarek, the driver, to pick up Anne from the airport. She would come in all smiles after the guards on the gate had clicked their heels and saluted "the minister's fiancée." More insidiously, I caught myself several times, even months afterward, scanning the papers for a mention of my name. At first, it was a reaction to the press onslaught. I had tried to size up the day's commentary first thing in the morning and react to it as fast as possible. But then, when the storm abated, I found I missed it, even the bad notices. I think I now know why politicians never give up. It's the delicious feeling of being in the center of the action, one's mind and body working at full throttle, journalists hanging on one's words, the feeling, however illusory, that one's words matter, that is addictive. I think I am now inoculated.

I had learned a great deal. Not only about the inner workings of the government machinery but, above all, about human nature and about my own journalistic profession. Most friends and acquaintances in general failed the test. The power of the printed word! People who had known me from the cradle were now giving me funny gazes and, while mouthing reassurances, obviously believed the idiocies they had read about me. It made me think of the scientific experiments that were supposed to have been carried out in America in the 1940s. Men in white coats told their subjects to turn a dial which was said to be the control of electrodes strapped to a patient on the other side of a glass pane. As the current increased, the patient was seen to writhe in pain. But the man in the white coat told the person at the dial that this was good for the patient. Disturbingly, it was found that most people obeyed the authority figure even past the point when the patient was apparently in danger of his life. The printed word, and the television news item, function like the men in the white coats, as sources of authority. I was the patient convulsing on the floor, except that I wasn't pretending.

When I now read political news I try much harder to sift propaganda and journalistic incompetence from the facts. Having been on both sides of the barricade, I now think that media nastiness, whether driven by circulation wars or political bias, is actually a threat to democracy. Democratic choice implies competition between politicians, parties, and their programs. But the choice can only be as good as the information on which it is based. If the information is distorted, democracy suffers. The winner is not the best or the least bad party or program, but the team whose friends in the media can most successfully smear its opponents. Personally, I am much kinder to politicians now. They are people too. Democracies need strong libel and privacy laws. Otherwise, nobody should be surprised that politicians become gray and uninspiring.

I have one final, lasting satisfaction from my time at the ministry. Every time I see a Polish officer in uniform, with his name tag above the breast pocket, I smile.

FULL CIRCLE

BY THE SUMMER OF 1993 the manor was half restored. The roof was back on, new windows had been installed, plastering of the outside walls was proceeding apace. Inside, bats still nested in the corners of the ceiling and pipes poked from the walls. But from a distance, looking through the trees, you could not tell that there were rough boards in the windows and that rude brick showed in places which ought to gleam with white paint. The eye focused on the bold triangle of the porch and the red roof with its solid, brick chimneys. If someone happened to be burning some rubbish in the cellar stove and smoke issued from the chimney, a passerby might suppose that the house was already inhabited. With every passing month, it took less imagination to see what the end result would be. I began to take pride in my creation.

But the news from the wider world was bad. That summer, a weak Solidarity government had been frivolously brought down when a few MPs proposed a vote of no confidence which they did not imagine would pass. It was the final act of folly of a parliament elected under a purely proportional electoral system, in which more than a dozen parties endlessly jostled for advantage. That parliament was hardly missed when President Lech Wałęsa had abruptly dissolved it. There was a moment of hope that with a general election under a new electoral law—which set a threshold of 5 percent and favored large parties—our politics might at last begin to straighten out. But by polling day it became obvious that it would be a disaster for the parties that had evolved from the anti-Communist opposition.

Opinion in towns and villages around Chobielin was probably typical. I asked Mr. Stramowski, our fat neighbor from the mill, how he would vote. He was angry that I would even ask. "Under the Communists if you borrowed a thousand zlotys from the bank," he shouted, "you paid back a thousand zlotys. Maybe you paid 3 percent interest. But under these bastards we have to pay back more in interest than we borrowed." It was no use arguing with him about the virtues of having an interest rate above the rate of inflation, which hovered around 40 percent at the time. I was relieved to hear that he did not intend to waste gasoline in his ancient Syrena to bother to drive to the voting station.

At the Chobielin farm a couple of people I spoke to said they would vote for the PSL, the Peasants' Party, which had been a faithful ally of the Communist Party. They had once worked for the collective farm and now were mostly unemployed, so it was hardly surprising that they supported a party which promised guaranteed prices and higher duties on foreign food. In Występ, our nearest village, I hoped to find some petit bourgeois spirit in the new shop by the asphalt road. I bought several things I did not need and asked the owner, a fierce woman in her fifties, who to vote for.

"Na komunę, proszę pana, tylko," she said. For the Commies, only them.

"Why?" I asked, puzzled. Hers was a new shop, clean and with a nice veranda, filled with brightly packaged goods. Its very existence was made possible by the economic reforms since Communism's fall. According to handbooks of political theory, people like her should be pillars of conservatism.

"Because people are poor and they need money. The Communists will give them more money. And when they have more money, they'll buy more from me," she explained. Clearly the debate between Keynes and Friedman, the arguments about the causal links between deficit financing and inflation, had not yet reached Występ. I didn't argue.

It was the same in Nakło, our local town. A policeman, a kiosk vendor, even people who walked into the polling booths straight from church, mostly said they would vote for post-Communist parties.

I even canvassed Pan Stasiu, our likable village drunk who was chopping wood for the winter.

"Who will you vote for?" I asked him.

"Oh, I don't mind," he said. "Stand me a bottle of vodka and I'll vote for whoever you like." His honest eyes pleaded earnestly that he would keep his side of the bargain but I didn't take up his offer. He had several minor convictions to his name so it was not certain that he was entitled to the vote. But his attitude suggested that apart from anything else, the poll would be low, which also favored the former Communists, whose electorate was more disciplined.

The defeat proved to be worse than almost anybody expected. The Communist Party, renamed the Social Democracy of the Republic of Poland, and its close allies polled just under 20 percent of the vote and, under a counting system which favored larger parties, gained about 35 percent of the seats in Parliament. Together with the Peasants' Party, its former ally under the People's Republic, the two post-Communist parties gained enough seats to form a government. The post-Solidarity camp polled a respectable proportion of votes but, because it was divided into several parties, most of them failed to make the 5 percent threshold. These various right-wing parties had splintered into factions of factions whose names even their activists could hardly remember, gained about 30 percent of the votes cast and failed to make it into parliament at all.

Some people vented their anger on the voters, calling the public names for being so ignorant. Others cheered themselves up with the thought that it was only the fragmentation of post-Solidarity parties that made the defeat so severe—as if the arrogance of our leaders in quarreling was not the best proof of their unfitness for office. Still others, speaking with bogus sophistication, maintained that politics no longer mattered because the economy had become autonomous and even a bad government would not blight our prospects. More curiously, underneath the humiliation of defeat and worry for the future, I also detected a mood of relaxation. It was back to normal, to the good old days before 1989 when the Communists were in charge and we, the dissidents, could mouth away against them with abandon. The strain of government was off our shoulders. We could sit back and watch them rule.

Personally, I thought the defeat was a just punishment for pride, incompetence, and hubris. For four years, the Polish electorate had watched patiently as the Solidarity politicians bickered and fumed, made and broke promises, displayed hypocrisy, arrogance, and graft. The sins of commission and omission multiplied. The warning signs that the fund of trust in the Solidarity elite was dwindling were numerous and frequent. Nobody had paid attention. The number of votes cast for parties led by former Solidarity activists dropped, while the former Communists steadily grew in strength.

Poland was not going back to Communism, of course—the renamed Communists became electable only because they genuinely embraced democracy and the market. But the outcome of that election was still a disaster, for two reasons, one measurable and one moral.

The first reason is prosaic. It is about money. In 1989 Poland faced an opportunity that was unique in the history of modern societies. In that year the Communist ideal of equality had been approximated in Poland—it was equality in poverty. Nevertheless, the First of January 1990, the official birthday of capitalism in Poland, was in economic terms a classic Day Zero, so beloved of intellectuals. It was a moment at which the vast majority of Polish families had almost equal, negligible assets to their name—perhaps a few hundred dollars in a mattress, perhaps the deeds of an apartment or a house. At the same time, the state, under various guises, still owned almost everything: factories, forests, town houses, office blocks, shops, even newspapers and publishing houses. At that moment we could have tried to distribute the state's assets more or less equally so that, forever more, those who failed in the subsequent rat race could not complain that they had never had a chance. Our capitalism could thus have been fairer than that in the West, built as it would have been on the solid moral foundation of equal start and equal opportunity.

Two things were required for this sense of fairness to take root: a fair distribution of assets accumulated by the state under Communism, and the tough execution of laws, so that nobody could cut corners in the great national marathon to prosperity. The 1993 Communist victory dashed the last hopes for either.

Western commentators assumed that the former Communist Party would metamorphose into a Polish SPD or Labor Party. In fact, the former Communist Party embraced capitalism in more senses than that. It could claim to be the party of enterprise. According to public opinion polls, about half of businessmen voted for it. Some were no doubt sufferers from what Marx would have called false consciousness, like the bewildered shopkeeper in Występ, but most made a more realistic calculation: in a country still dominated by a corrupt bureaucracy it is better that one's political friends sit on top of it. The old *nomenklatura,* having swapped their Party membership cards for checkbooks, wanted its friends in charge of licenses, subsidies, and tax breaks. The point that Western pundits missed was that the battle was never about trying to restore Communism. It was, rather, about which sort of capitalism we would have: the liberal, Anglo-Saxon model where free competition is at least an ideal to aspire to, or the kleptocratic, Italian or Latin American model. What our political scientists call "concessionary capitalism"—where private businesses thrive on corrupt deals with dishonest politicians and bureaucrats—can be pathologically stable for decades.

In the five years after the fall of Communism, my native Bydgoszcz gained the reputation as the corruption capital of Poland. The biggest crooks came to be known collectively as the Magnificent Seven. Rarely has so much ingenuity been applied in so short a time to such dishonest ends. One budding entrepreneur, remembered from Communist times as the boss of a network of hard currency dealers, was notorious for crossing puddles by walking on the back of his bodyguard. In the early months of capitalism, he miraculously acquired a letter from a deputy finance minister stating that his company need not pay excise duty on imported alcohol. Truckloads of spirits gave him fabulous profits, from which a regional mini-empire called Weltinex sprung: office blocks, a distribution network, a bank, a newspaper. It supported charities and a soccer team, and drew up bold plans for restoring Bydgoszcz's historic city center. For a couple of years, it seemed as if almost everyone in town was either working for or had business dealings with Weltinex. My mother's friends at her old construction design partnership were under contract to make plans to screen an ugly, Communist-era café in the old town square with a row of quaint town houses. My friends from school worked in the Weltinex-owned Apple Macintosh dealership. An architect advising us at Chobielin was designing an extravagant residence for the Weltinex chairman. Even the keeper of listed buildings dealt with Weltinex, concerning an old manor house whose grounds the chairman wanted to turn into race horse stables.

In 1993, by the time the authorities began catching up with "Schnappsgate," the company chairman was evading justice in Moscow. But things might still have worked out fine for him. From Moscow he launched a campaign to be elected senator from our region, which, incidentally, would have given him immunity from prosecution. Unfortunately, our ungrateful people only cast about thirty thousand votes in his favor—only a third of what was needed for victory.

Another pioneer of our march toward modernity was the owner of a regional banking network. Branches were set up in most towns in our region, including Szubin and Nakło. The company's English name, Loan Banc, prominently displayed, added to the company's prestige. The c in the name, far from a misspelling by some benighted provincial, was the crux of the entire operation. Loan Banc looked like a bank and behaved like a bank: taking in deposits and, at the beginning, paying out huge interest earnings and capital. Finance Ministry officials accused the owner of running a bank without the appropriate license. But, the owner protested that his company was not a bank at all; it was a banc, pronounced in Polish as bantz. People loaned him money but in a free country such as we now were, he argued, that was surely a private matter. Apparently satisfied with the explanation, officials left him alone, until the classic pyramid scheme he was running collapsed on its own.

My favorite scam originated in Paterek, a village not twenty minutes' walk away from Chobielin. Its author was a classic chłopo-robotnik, a peasant-worker. During the night he worked as a guard at a nearby railway repair yard. By day he tended a small landholding: a few hectares of poor land, some cattle, chickens. His assets also included a worn leather briefcase, and it was the briefcase which turned his fortunes. The briefcase sufficed for his branch network, his bank vault, his computers, and his cashiers' desks. Stacks of notes disappeared into it, only to reemerge miraculously multiplied. The countryside around us was rife with rumors of his triumphs: profits from the stock exchange, property speculation, fabulous deals in faraway countries. Actually, nobody ever saw a deed to a property or a share certificate, nor a trading contract. Nobody dared ask about details. For, as his fame spread, and more and more people saw their money coming out of the briefcase doubled and trebled, the wily peasant became choosy. He would not take deposits from just anybody who happened to find his tumbledown cottage. One had to be recommended into the deal.

This was a brilliant piece of post-Communist psychological analysis. Conditioned by decades of queuing to think that anything that was in short supply must be desirable, eager clients besieged the cottage in ever greater numbers. Soon, the briefcase could not hold all the cash, and bundles of notes rose up in the corner of his room. Depositors did not even demand a loan contract. A receipt was all that was needed. The peasant's word was his bond.

By the time our enterprising neighbor was arrested at the Polish-German border trying to flee the country, he owed hundreds of people about a million dollars. The hoodwinked included several parish priests, top brass at the Pomeranian military district headquarters, and senior doctors at Bydgoszcz's largest hospital—which is the best illustration of the depth of ignorance about the market economy, even among so-called educated people.

Scams at the national level were, of course, on a much bigger scale. There was the ART-B affair in which a couple of bright young men milked the banking system of millions of dollars by kiting checks around dozens of accounts and receiving interest on account balances many times over. The ruble affair was even simpler. If you had an export contract signed with a company in the USSR (this was 1990), and a friendly customs officer who would stamp your forms to testify that the goods—computers, potatoes, whatever—had left the country (even if they never existed), you could collect an instant profit of several hundred percent when the Polish government exchanged your rubles into zlotys at a grossly inflated exchange rate.

Then there was the little matter of the FOZZ, the shadowy fund which the Communist authorities set up to illicitly buy up Polish debts on the cheap in international markets. Its accounts were never reconciled but people who ran it now own and manage huge industrial and banking conglomerates. Further tens of millions of dollars were pilfered out of state banks as so-called "bad loans," a misnomer since they were very good loans for those who took them. It was similar to the American savings and loans fiasco in the 1980s. A flexible friend on the board of a state bank sufficed. You set up a company to which a friend lends without security. The loan is unpaid, the company goes bust but, given that the bank is state-owned, who loses? Only the taxpayer who bails out the remaining depositors.

Poland's archaic commercial code did not even bar directors of bankrupt companies from serving on company boards in the future; let alone make it possible to recover the fruits of fraud from their personal wealth. When *nomenklatura* privatization is added to the list of abuses—a process whereby thousands of Communist-era bosses, under the noses of their bewildered workforce, became the owners of the enterprises they managed—it is amazing that capitalism still commands any support in Poland at all.

Naturally, not all the corruption of the transition period could be attributed to the former Communists. Early Solidarity governments talked about corruption as "the inevitable price to be paid for the transition to capitalism," which made it sound as if the thieving was natural, and therefore okay. But the Communists went a step further and sanctioned it. The portly figure of Ireneusz Sekuła, a deputy prime minister in the last Communist government, personifies the issue. Temporarily ejected from politics in the twilight of Communism, Sekuła used his connections to launch himself in business. By 1993 he was back in politics—running the Customs and Excise—but allegations of fraudulent loans from his interval in business continued to follow him. Eventually, even his party colleague, a former-Communist justice minister, ruled that there was indeed a case to answer. A prosecution was announced, but the Communist-dominated parliament voted to refuse the lifting of Comrade Sekuła's immunity, presumably because his fellow former-Communist members of parliament did not want to establish a dangerous precedent. That vote can be taken as the moment of Poland's rite of passage from an errant democracy to a nascent kleptocracy. Only our political scientists are surprised at low voter turnouts and scant respect for democratic politicians. As for Mr. Sekuła himself, he was last heard of helping to finance the presidential campaign of Aleksander Kwaśniewski, the post-Communist candidate.

Fraud and corruption occur everywhere, of course, but in Poland the game was about more than who gets to buy a large house or a fast car. It was about who gets to belong to the new Poland's upper and upper middle class, and who will become the proletariat. The question has largely been settled. The Communist *nomenklatura* is the new

upper class, whereas those who made it possible for them—the workers who brought down Communism—remain the proletariat.

It is likely to stay that way. Corruptly obtained economic power is
easily transformed into political power: in the 1995 presidential campaign Mr. Kwaśniewski drove about Poland in a Western-style high-
tech campaign bus; his chubby face smiled from thousands of posters
and filled television screens in professionally produced advertisements.
One of his non-Communist rivals, Poland's chief justice, Professor
Adam Strembosz, came to stay at Chobielin during his election tour.
He was traveling by public transport and struggled to pay the phone
bill.

That the former Communists are becoming the new ruling class is
particularly visible in the countryside. My own class position is secure:
I am a peasant. It happened quite suddenly, in November 1994, when,
after a three-year battle, I acquired a ten-hectare field adjacent to the
park. Along with the land around the house, I now own about fifteen
hectares. Given that the average landholding in Poland is about six
hectares, this makes me quite a wealthy peasant—though far from a
landowner. In fact, I seem to be a classic *kulak,* a rich peasant, the very
definition of a "counterrevolutionary element." Fortunately, my landholding is almost identical to that of Mr. Waldemar Pawlak, the former
Peasant Party prime minister, so I should be fairly safe even if the post-
Communist coalition starts having bold ideas.

From my middle position I am watching some of my neighbors
rapidly rising in fortune, while others stagnate. The largest landholder
in our district, for example, is someone I shall call Mr. Kędzior. He is
the former collective farm manager about twenty kilometers from Chobielin, and ably manages a thousand hectares. When I saw him for the
first time in 1989 he looked and spoke like the *nomenklatura* specimen.
He was typical of the ambitious young peasants who traded in their
principles for the opportunity to become a collective farm manager.
Ten years before he would have been a keen Communist, denouncing capitalist tendencies, joining party-ordained, anti-imperialist campaigns, and preaching the merits of collectivized agriculture. But, in
1989, with the Communist regime on the way out, he was sounding
sheepish, and was probably worrying that he had made the wrong
choice when he had signed up for the Party back in the 1970s.

Today, Mr. Kędzior is a changed man. To begin with, he is no longer a mere state employee. I now call him *Pan Prezes*—Mr. Chairman. Two years ago, together with some of his former farmhands, he set up a company with himself as the majority shareholder. Under the privatization plan, the company has leased the farms from the state Agricultural Property Agency, which disposes of the old collective farms. He complains, as farmers are wont to do, of the weather, of foreign competition, and of high interest rates, but in fact his business seems to be thriving—partly as a result of the Peasant Party government having retaliated against the European Union's trade barriers with duties of its own. Mr. Kędzior's company has doubled in value in just over a year; it has just bought new German machinery. It's a testament to the wastefulness of the Communist economy that the same manager on the same land now gets the same work done with fifteen instead of 130 men. Another few years of hard work, good fortune, and high tariffs, and he can start turning his lease into a freehold. If other *nomenklatura* types were as hardworking as he is, one wouldn't begrudge them their wealth.

I suspect Mr. Kędzior still votes for the old Communist Party. But, as we sipped Scotch one evening, I detected a new tone in his voice. The workers, he complained, had become obstinate. In the old days, when a few lads had a fight at a local dance hall, they would come to him the next day to apologize, just on the off chance that he might hear about it. Moreover, the mere mention of the People's Militia, as the police used to be called, was enough to stop the thieving of hay and potatoes from the fields for a week. Children knew that they would work on his collective farm when they grew up, and they took their caps off from afar. But today, with all those unemployment benefits, sacking is no longer the threat it used to be. Discipline has slackened, youngsters don't care to acknowledge him, and criminals at the local prison watch porn movies in their cells between weekends off. There's supposed to be unemployment (I nodded energetically as his voice rose in indignation) but he cannot find hands to collect the sugar beet crop. Nor are any of the so-called unemployed jumping at the opportunity to look after his herd of cows. On the other hand, there is little he can do when such layabouts refuse to pay their rent or electricity bills. These people are so ignorant, he laughed, that they don't understand how he, one man, can outvote the rest of the workforce at a shareholders' meeting.

A reactionary camaraderie developed between us as he spoke. But when he left I felt that I had heard his tale before. I reached for my copy of George Orwell's *Animal Farm,* and there he was, the perfect pig, one of the ruling caste who direct the farm when the human owner has been chased away. In Orwell's satire, the pigs start by appropriating for themselves apples and milk taken away from the other animals. Then, they break every taboo set up after the anti-human rebellion: they sleep in the farmer's bed, they drink beer and whiskey, they handle money and even send their fellow animals to the slaughterhouse. The pigs end up walking on two feet, cracking the whip on their former comrades, and socializing with the local squires. After all the blood, toil, and disappointed hopes, the leaders of the animal rebellion become indistinguishable from the animals' old tormentors. What even Orwell did not predict was that the pigs would stay in charge, even if the human owner came back one day.

Mr. Kędzior is not quite at that stage yet, although he has already hinted that he does, in fact, come from a landowning family. As a precaution, he had concealed his aristocratic genealogy under Communism. In a few more years, provided the business continues to flourish, he might change (change *back,* that is) his name to the more genteel-sounding Kędziorski, send his children to a Catholic private school, and dazzle his farmhands with a brand-new signet ring. Who knows, perhaps one day he might even get around to restoring the manor house in which he resides (it was the office of the collective farm) to something like the old style: replace the linoleum floor with parquet, get rid of the fake leather sofas, and clear the porch of concrete flowerpots. If, that is, his fellow shareholders don't hack him to pieces one day when they finally work out that their company is less like the co-op they thought they were joining and more like the old estate on which their grandfathers used to work for the old squire before the war.

In the countryside, as in the city, our social structure has come full circle. A century of revolution and war has achieved little.

The other reason why the Communist victory in the 1993 general election was a disaster, the moral reason, is even more important. The election victories of the former Communists mean that there will never now be a clean break with Poland's totalitarian past, the sort of break that Germany made after the Second World War. Scoundrels of the old regime will go unpunished. Heroes of the resistance will not be acknowledged. Good will not have been seen to triumph over evil. The world may be ruled by appearances but people need morality tales to keep them good. The police do not need to catch all the criminals all the time for most people to submit to public order, but they need to catch a significant proportion. Nothing encourages lawlessness more than the sight of villains getting away with it, living off their spoils, and laughing in the public's face.

Communism was too great an evil—and lasted too long—for it to be buried quietly with no one noticing. The Czechs were wise to bring it down in a revolution, with crowds in the streets, a moment or two of heroism, followed by dancing in the streets. In Poland the chances for making a new beginning were never great. Communism ended by negotiation, which avoided the perils of violence, but the negotiators went to the other extreme and fraternized with the enemy. You only need to look at photographs taken during the secret negotiations between top Communists and top dissidents at the Magdalenka manor in early 1989. The elaborate menus of their meals, the beaming faces, the backslapping, and the vodka toasts tell the story more eloquently than any transcripts could: there would be no de-Communization in Poland.

In short, the Communists and their allies among the former dissidents have finally proven that it does not pay to be decent. Those people who had gotten ahead by collaborating with the Communist regime—receiving apartments, cars, and other privileges at the expense of their fellow citizens—have been allowed to keep their apartments, their dachas, and control of their businesses which they had fraudulently acquired. While maintaining their ill-gotten gains, they can posture as true Europeans, sophisticated and superior, at least by comparison to the vengefulness which allegedly drives their opponents. They will use an esoteric example or two to show that the victims and the executioners were often the same people and are impossible to tell apart. Gullible Western journalists will affirm poetically that, under Communism, unlike under Fascism, the lines of complicity ran like veins and arteries inside the human body.

What about all the men and women who sacrificed their careers because they would not collaborate—the millions of ordinary people, like my parents, who were never seduced by the ideology and never joined the Party for the sake of a career? From today's perspective, they were just dumb. They should have been swine, compromised their consciences and gotten ahead, for today they would be building on their privileges with a condescending smile at the simpletons. Evil is seen to have triumphed over good and now rides arrogantly on top. This feeling, of virtue unrewarded and evil unpunished, is the chief reason why Poland still suffers from a post-Communist hangover. The sense of truths suppressed and spades not called spades—our own Vichy syndrome—is what makes the politics so messy and so nasty. Poland continues to wallow in acrimony. The language of public discourse has suffered—in the words of Zbigniew Herbert, our best living poet—"semantic collapse." The most basic concepts from which societies build their hierarchies of values have been debased. Most intellectuals have betrayed their calling—to search after truth—indulging instead in ever more sophisticated casuistries with only one aim in sight: deflecting attention from their own murky pasts. The 1993 Communist electoral victory ensured that the boil of lies and half-truths would swell bigger and bigger. One day, it will burst.

Fortunately, politics does not control our lives as much as it did in People's Poland. Corrupt as the neo-Communist administrations have proved to be, they never snuffed out the eruption of creative energy that was released by the removal of central planning in 1989. Their economic iniquities are no worse than those of any populist regime in the more prosperous parts of the Third World. With luck, Poland will turn out to be no worse than an Italy without the sun. It may be disappointing to one's public spirit but, of course, life can be perfectly tolerable in a kleptocracy. Governments come and go, one more laughable than the previous one but the economy continues to grow. Institutions do not work but, equally, they are usually too sluggish to interfere in most people's lives. Some of the wealth trickles down to the masses. Shining office towers rise up in city centers, condominiums fill the suburbs, bright shops line the shopping malls. Most of the side effects of rising prosperity are already part of our daily lives. Growing up in Bydgoszcz I never saw a traffic jam. In a block of apartments housing thirty-six families, my father's car was one of three or four parked on a minuscule parking lot in our street. Now, guarded car parks are the biggest creators of municipal jobs. All those who complain that living standards have not risen since 1989 only need to drive through any Polish housing complex counting the number of satellite dishes gracing the balconies.

Moreover, a new class structure, based on skills rather than money, is beginning to cut across the one established immediately after Communism's collapse. A new divide is forming in politics, economics, and culture. The children of Communists and the children of dissidents fall on either side of it irrespective of their parents' politics. "Us" and "them" will hardly tolerate each other socially. It has not been articulated yet, but it is already visible: the one category of people tend to move briskly, love their computers and mobile phones, vote for free-market political parties, use pithy language, and go on vacations abroad. The other seem sluggish, are suspicious of the telephone, let alone the computer, wear gray clothes, and vote for socialist parties (national-socialist included).

In short we have our own yuppies now, who have joined the global division of labor, are beginning to earn Western-level wages, and will perceive Poland's integration with the West as a great national and personal opportunity. The distinction between them and the rest of the population is not just cultural, it is linguistic. Just as noblemen in the Old Commonwealth, however poor, spoke Latin, so today the new Poles speak English. And just as the old Sarmatian nobles ended up speaking a curious mixture of Polish and Latin, so our yuppies, even when they speak Polish, translate English idioms.

I hope that once the novelty of joining the civilized world wears off, our yuppies, just like yuppies everywhere, will tire of their airport-to-air-conditioned-office existence. When they become truly cosmopolitan they'll start longing for the provincial and for the particular, going back to the villages which they or their parents had repudiated. For myself, I don't know whether I belong to the old-fashioned, improvident Poles, or to the new capitalist-inspired ones. On the one hand, I have built a house without first making the fortune to keep it up. On the other, I hope I anticipate the future in creating this refuge from the modern world.

The English language and capitalism, going hand in hand, are changing not only our lifestyle but our very national character. Insofar as national character is definable at all, ours seems to have been amazingly constant through the ages. Perhaps because Poland grew territorially in the fifteenth and sixteenth centuries with comparatively little effort—or perhaps because the predominant economy, the lore, and the life rhythms have been, for much longer than in the West, those of the country rather than the city—the average Pole still has the virtues and the vices of a seventeenth-century minor nobleman: hospitality and impulsiveness, courage and a short attention span, nimbleness of mind and unruliness, readiness for sacrifice and laziness. We have changed in the last five years faster than at any time in our history.

So far as influence on national character goes, Communism can be regarded as the last phase of feudalism. We talk in Poland about *restoring* capitalism, but in truth, unless we reach back to the long-forgotten period in the Renaissance when a bourgeoisie of sorts briefly surfaced, Poles hardly ever bore bourgeois values. There has been a Polish middle class since the nineteenth century—but it was a professional and administrative elite, not an entrepreneurial one. Particularly in the small towns, where the soul of the nation dwells, commerce, industry, and finance were culturally mostly foreign, Jewish, and German. Poles, at least in the self-image of our cultural elites, remained unsullied by trade—and Communism prolonged this blissful detachment. Penniless intelligentsia remained at the top of the social hierarchy, as noble in opposition to Communism as their gentry grandfathers had been in opposition to the czars, and just as inept. Writers, actors, artists of every sort—whether officially sanctioned or, even better, dissident—continued to consider themselves prophets, not entertainers. Money was an awkward subject for them. Tales of such Western habits as sharing a gasoline bill or paying for a telephone call made at a friend's house, or bringing one's own bottle of wine to a dinner party aroused curiosity tinged with disapproval. To this day, any Pole from the intelligentsia who was over thirty when Communism ended finds it difficult to haggle over a fee or demand his dues. A Polish journalist friend of mine created consternation at one of the large dailies in London when it was realized that he had worked for six months as a stringer before even alluding to fees and expenses, which had not been paid due to a bureaucratic oversight. It was attitudes like that which made many former dissidents so ineffectual at running bureaucracies or businesses.

Today Polish cities are rapidly developing a bourgeoisie for the first time. Twenty-five-year-old advertising executives or thirty-year-old bankers and company managers no longer elicit much surprise. Discouraged by the farcical politics, a whole generation of young Poles has channeled its zest into business. For better or for worse, for the first time in living memory—perhaps for the first time in Poland's history—financial success is becoming a yardstick against which people are beginning to measure one another. While producing instances of fantastic nouveau riche vulgarity—the houses with more towers than a medieval castle, the courtesan-look-a-like wives, the mobile phones ringing during dinner—it is a necessary dose of realism. For the first time there are no excuses: no Russians, no Communists, no Jews can plausibly be blamed for failure. The Communist old boys' network may still function, particularly in banks and local government, but not so efficiently as to entirely stifle a competent man with a good idea. Those who fail have to look to their own shortcomings for the cause. Polish businessmen remain Poles while doing business: our national vices, self-centeredness and megalomania, can be a handicap. Foreign bankers report, for example, that the greatest number of business failures in Poland occur in the second and third years of running a business, when the entrepreneur has made his first serious money and, instead of consolidating, embarks on an empire-building spree. In the past, such follies would have led to acts of recklessness, whether in politics or the economy, for which society as a whole usually footed the bill. Now, the market is beginning to discipline behavior, rewarding and punishing roughly on the basis of merit. At last, the most competent, rather than the least scrupulous or the most eloquent, are beginning to rise to the top.

I now meet local businessmen such as Rafał, once a couple of years below me at secondary school, who has transformed an old canteen in a nearby village into a textile factory in which a hundred local women make garments on a state-of-the-art production line. Łochowo, where my father's family spent the war, is the base of a company belonging to Karol Pawlak. My grandparents and parents used to buy flowers from his father's greenhouses in Bydgoszcz. Today, he runs a multimillion-dollar business which includes nurseries and two large estates. Wojtek, Stefan and Krakus, my comrades from the National Liberation League with whom I had once pasted leaflets on the streets of Bydgoszcz, continue as a team, building gas stations for a Western corporation. Such businessmen, who are seen to do something useful, are beginning to lift the odium from private enterprise.

Thanks to people like them, Poland has undergone a civilizational revolution. Coffee, for example, is no longer served the "Turkish" way—that is, boiling water poured on top of a spoon or two of coffee grounds at the bottom of a glass. Elaborate coffee machines have become standard equipment in most homes and offices. Teapots have also made a reappearance, replacing the Communist-era tea bag in a cup. Along with satellite dishes, garden gnomes, musical greeting cards, and a score of other gadgets, which on their own could be dismissed as cargo cults, or ascribed to our showy character, the quiet revolution has touched matters that are mostly hidden from view. Among competing definitions of civilization I have always liked the most tangible standard, that of lavatories. Clean lavatories = civilization. Filthy lavatories = barbarism. (This standard even tracks the ups and downs of particular cultures over time. In its prime, Britain gave the world modern drains. At Łańcut, Poland's best-preserved aristocratic residence, tourists still admire British-made brass bathtub fittings. In today's Britain, owning a modern bath is often thought to be flashy.) In 1989 I saw a Japanese businessman in the lavatory at Okęcie airport in Warsaw, fossilized in a posture not so much of disgust but, beyond that, of disbelief, staring at a pool of urine filling most of the floor. Today, he would not only find the lavatories at the new Okęcie terminal perfectly adequate; his luggage would be handled faster than at Heathrow. The most obscure gas station on a side road, the tackiest fast food bar, will now have a plasticky, but clean and functional, lavatory. By unspoken national consensus, we decided that we could not go on as before.

Similarly, just as a polite waiter or sales assistant was an aberration under socialism, so today they are the norm. Much of the economy may still be state-owned and inefficient but that part of it which affects most people's daily lives most often—services of every kind—has changed beyond recognition. The change in the appearance and manners of what jargon calls in-person servers is a scientific proof of the responsiveness of human nature to economic stimuli. Before, people were quite rational in treating one another as enemies because they competed for a pool of scarce goods. Today, they smile and chat because they prosper by serving one another.

Above all, when we travel in the West, we no longer feel like beggars. When I went to Britain in 1981, the $400 I carried in a chest pouch represented my family's life savings. The maximum you could save on an average Polish monthly salary represented a single meal at McDonald's. Buying a cup of coffee or an ice cream during a vacation in Greece was an extravagance which, we joked, "made your palate go green" from the thought of the precious dollars. Today a cup of coffee costs about the same in Bydgoszcz as in London. My mother manages to save enough from her modest pension to go on a yearly vacation abroad, on which she does not have to deny herself ice cream. We still cart things from the West to Poland. Twice a year my father crosses the Channel and returns with the car sloped low on the suspension from the weight of goods. But we no longer smuggle banned books or gadgets that the system of progress was incapable of producing. He carries mostly paint, grass seed, and electrical fittings, which tend to be better and cheaper in Britain than in Poland.

The changes are particularly striking at Chobielin. In 1989, when we bought it, the manor house lacked an indoor lavatory and had a telephone line possibly dating back to Kaiser Wilhelm. (In Wierzbiński's *Freedom* Chobielin is already equipped with a telephone at the time of World War One.) Calls went through a manual switchboard and audibility fell to zero if wind swayed the open wires, or if a flock of birds landed on them for a rest. The house had barely entered the age of electricity: a few weak bulbs threatened to explode prewar cables. By 1995, we had obviously entered the twentieth century because the hall of the keeper's lodge bristled with a high-tech security alarm (we had been burgled four times already). I can now dial direct anywhere in the world and no longer think much of hooking up to the Internet and browsing the *Washington Post* before it hits the streets in America.

Thanks to the Internet, I stay in touch with friends around the globe. We compare notes and send articles to and fro. I am better wired up at Chobielin than I was in London a few years ago. Nakło, our local town, has a world wide web home page. The idea that exchanging information with the outside world, such as sending a few pages of text to a Western newspaper, was once something which may have required weeks of scheming and carried the risk of a jail sentence, now seems bizarre—such tales are like the hardships of crossing the Atlantic by steamer. As proof for posterity that it was really like that, my mother keeps the receipt for a copy of George Orwell's *1984* which was confiscated by customs officials in 1984—it was found concealed in one of the parcels of washing powder I sent her from London. For the same reason, I keep a collection of street signs which I had the presence of mind to collect in 1989: Red Army Street, Dzierzyński Street, Polish United Workers' Party Square.

Even the local bureaucracy has improved. Replies to my occasional letters—a suggestion for repairing the road, mending a road sign, or replanting an avenue—are now addressed as *Pan*—Mr.—in place of the Communist *Ob,* short for *obywatel,* citizen. Their tone is less that of an official form and more and more like a coherent answer to another human being. In more optimistic moments I even fancy that this change of attitude is general and not just because they have seen me on television.

So have I achieved my aim, that of restoring Chobielin to a state in which my visitors might be deceived into thinking that somehow Communism spared this remote spot? Perhaps. I have certainly cleared up these few acres of Poland. Bounded by a neat wall, the trees in the orchard stand in regular rows where once weeds grew taller than a man. The beehive among them gives us our own honey. A row of outdoor lavatories with a capacious cesspool underneath has given way to a flower garden. Lawn spreads where once there were pigsties. A sheet of green—a grass tennis court—covers the foundations of an old stable. A row of chestnuts, still small, has risen up along the cobbled alley. In the park, once dark and dusky as a primeval forest, shafts of light streak through and birds sing where once dead branches creaked.

There is still much to do. The ground floor in the house is barely begun—renovated doors swing above cement rather than parquet. An expanse of tar covers the terrace—it begs to be covered over by the glass roof of an orangery. (I thought of surrounding the park and the field on the high ground, fifteen hectares in all, with a two-meter fence inside which deer could graze and multiply but I gave up when a neighbor's deer herd dispersed after local louts stole twenty meters of fence.) The old *lamus,* a Tudor-style outhouse, needs repair but for the time being houses an old-fashioned motorbike on which I like to scour the countryside.

All in all, the plaque in the drive, under which visitors like to photograph themselves—official-looking white letters on enameled red: *Strefa Zdekomunizowana,* De-Communized Zone—is no longer a complete boast. Half a century's filth is gone. The white paint, the mowed grass, the regular paths proclaim that the land has a master again. Money permitting, I will print a postcard, divided into sections, with Chobielin's pictorial history and dates in the corner of each photograph: the squalid ruin we purchased in 1989, an aerial view of the bare outside walls when we took the roof down in 1991, the rough, half-built bulk in 1993, and today's gleaming jewel. I have already experimented

258 · RADEK SIKORSKI

with those photographs. They shame even the most envious into respectful silence.

Life is good here. We eat tomatoes and cucumbers untouched by chemicals and drink a hard, delicious mineral water from our own well. We heat the house with renewable energy—dead trees from the park. The preindustrial and the information ages happily cohabit. My wife's American friends get excited and take snaps of themselves in front of a real haystack. Working at my computer, I gaze out the window to watch old Mr. Erlich potter about the park with a wheelbarrow. His fat, talkative wife—from whom I buy eggs which have yolks the color of ripe mango, even though Mrs. Erlich probably never heard the word "organic"—has told me that he becomes restless and impossible when a long weekend or a spate of bad weather separates him from the manor around which his whole life has centered. A trip to Bydgoszcz, to escort his son Jacek to a conscription point, was a traumatic expedition for both of them. The Erlichs would probably never recover if uprooted from this, their native patch of countryside, with their relatives, friends, and enemies in neighboring cottages. I love joining them in manual work, chainsaw in hand, breaking sweat to the sound of trees falling on moldy undergrowth. There are signs that some of our workers and neighbors may like us. When Pan Stasiu and his drinking friends steal wood from the forest, they take it only from the state-owned part, even when they think nobody is watching.

I take particular pleasure in receiving as guests those who have been through Poland's twentieth-century horrors, but have lived in truth, proving that it pays to be decent after all.

When my uncle Klemens, the Gdańsk gunsmith, takes a walk around the building site and the park, he invariably finds an object which the rest of us, passing the same spot dozens of times, have overlooked. A dirty stone poking out of the ground proved to be the wheel of an ancient sword sharpener; a hole in a tree trunk hid rifle bullets. When Communism fell, Uncle Klemens hardly noticed. He still talks to workers on his daily meanderings through Gdańsk's Old Town in search of buried treasure—they are now more likely to be laying fiber optic cable than dredging the canals—and will harangue anybody who will listen on the superiority of craftsmen over advertising executives. There are two differences in his life. First, his antique collection is now worth a fortune. Second, retired colonels and generals—his army contemporaries—occasionally turn up at his workshop at odd times of the day and apologize for having been swine.

My great-uncle Roman, the one who spent five years in Buchenwald and Dachau, spent the forty-five years of Communism helping to restore a Romanesque church in Inowrocław. He still drives to Rome to make a pilgrimage most years. In May 1997, shortly after his ninetieth birthday, he is due to officiate at the blessing to mark our move from the keepers' lodge to the house.

In fact, one has to wonder at the toughness and longevity and good health of that generation. My maternal grandmother, though poorly now, still comes to Chobielin when the weather is good and delights the company by singing a song she learned at school before World War One to celebrate Kaiser Wilhelm's birthday.

Her elder brother, my great-uncle Stefan, the one who fought the Bolsheviks in the victorious war of 1920, passed away the other day but not before he had visited us at Chobielin. Robust, and with a full head of white hair at ninety-one, he took a walk along the riverbank and found the stump of a tree from behind which he used to peep at the enemy on the other side when he was a sixteen-year-old volunteer. What we had taken to be an irrigation canal turned out to have been the 1918 Polish trench. He wrote in his fine, old-fashioned handwriting the following note in the manor's guest book: *After seventy years I have visited the place for which I had the honor to fight in Poland's only successful uprising as a soldier of the 9th Regiment of the Wielkopolska Fusiliers. Radek, I could do this thanks to your excellent project....*

We now need to perform a rite of passage or two—a wedding anniversary party, a birth, or at least a conception—to feel we truly belong here. The manor house, just like my life, and the country around it, has made a full circle. Whatever happens, there is now something in the world I can point to and say: "I did this." I have found a patch where I want to see the trees that I have planted rise tall, where I want my children to roam, where I can take pleasure in growing old.

Notes

1. Translated by Kenneth Mackenzie (London: Polska Fundacja Kulturalna, 1986).
2. I was reminded of the story of *Matołek the Goat* and used the research from Violetta Bukowska's article in the August 1994 issue of *Słowo,* the Catholic daily.
3. Robert Skidelsky, *The World After Communism* (New York: Macmillan, 1995), p. 144.
4. *Przewodnik po Ziemiach Dawnej Polski, Litwy i Rusi,* by the pioneer of modern Polish tourism, Dr. Mieczysław Orłowicz (Kraków, 1914).
5. *Starożytna Polska* (Warszawa, 1843), p. 319.
6. *Historia Bydgoszczy,* Vol. 1, ed., Marian Biskup, PWN, 1991: *Dzieje Zakonu Krzyżackiego w Prusach,* by Marian Biskup and Gerard Labuda, (Gdańsk: Wydawnictwo Morskie, 1988).
7. Congressional Research Service Report for Congress, *NATO's Military Enlargement: Problems and Prospects,* December 1995.

Index

Communism (*cont.*)
  in post-Communist Poland,
    232, 240–43, 246, 249–50
  25th Party Congress, 41–42
  see also Poland, Communist
compensation for confiscated
    property, 172, 174, 176
concentration camps, 127
  Auschwitz, 147, 149, 153–54
  Buchenwald, 108–9
  Dachau, 109–13
  Potulice, 147–49, 154
  Stutthof, 148
concessionary capitalism, 243
confiscated property, 173–76
  see also Chobielin
consumerism, 49–51
corruption in post-Communist
    Poland, 243–47, 251
craftsmen of Gdańsk, 48, 258
currency allocations, 50
customs officials, 51–52
Czech dissidents, 218
Czechoslovakia, invasion of
    (1968), 226
Czech Republic, 234, 250
Czerski, Jan, 189

Dachau, 109–13, 147
Danzig, *see* Gdańsk
Defense, Ministry of, 205–7, 215,
    237
  civilian department in, 222
  offices of, 211–12
  Wałęsa's interference with,
    228
Defense Policy Bureau, 222
Democratic Union party, 228

deviants, in Potulice concentra-
    tion camp, 149
Dołgie lake, 93
dwór and dworek, 23–26
Dzierżyński, Feliks, 166

East Germany, 218, 234
eavesdropping devices (bugs),
    219
education in Communist Poland:
  landowners' children, 175
  patriotic occasions and, 40–41
  primary, 35–45
  school elections and, 40
  secondary, 45, 69–72
elections:
  of 1992, 205
  of 1993, 239–42, 247, 249, 251
English language, 50, 252
  military intelligence's use of,
    219
Erlich family, 31–33, 174, 198–99,
    203–4, 258
Estonia, 218
European Union, 218, 220, 248
Evangelical church, 189
Evening Standard, 209
evictions, 33

factories, students' "voluntary
    works" in, 44
Falkenberg, August, 196–97
Falkenberg, Friedrich von, 181,
    197, 200
family claims, to property, 172–73
Farmers' Solidarity, 77–78
farming, 28, 248
Filipowicz, T., 41

Polutice internment camp and,
150–56
prices in, 46
property rights in, 172
prosperity in (1970s), 49
secret police in, 234
shortages in, 28
Spain compared with, 168
television in, 37–38
travel in, 50–58
"Volkswagen Deutsch," 198
Poland, post-Communist, 144
class structure in, 251–53
Communists and allies in, 232,
240–43, 246, 249–50
corruption in, 243–47, 251
defense in, 206
economics and business in,
240–43, 251–55
Germany's attitude toward,
199
journalism in, 208–10
labor issues in, 248
living standards in, 251
local bureaucracy in, 256–57
military intelligence in, 207
1992 elections in, 205
1993 elections in, 239–42, 247,
249, 251
Polish-Russian friendship
treaty and, 229–31
post-Solidarity political parties
in, 241
Russian troops in, 216, 221–23,
229
state ownership in, 242
tax-free goods sold by, 229
telephone service in, 205, 212

travel in, 255–56
Western orientation of, 237,
252
yuppies in, 252
Poland, pre-Communist, 91–92
first partition of, 186–87
German domination of,
187–91
Kościuszko uprising in (1794),
187
kulturkampf in, 96, 190
nineteenth-century population
growth in, 190
post-World War I uprising in,
160, 191
Swedish occupation of (1655),
192
in World War I, 190–91
Yalta and Potsdam agreements
and, 150
see also World War II
Poliakov, Valeri, 230–31
Polish army, 223
civilian control of, 228, 237
in World War II, 103
Polish-Bolshevik war (1920),
48–49
Polish language, in German Empire, 189
Polish-Lithuanian Common-
wealth, 91
Polish military police, 140
Polish national character, 122,
252–54
Polish People's Army, 226
Polish People's Council, 191
Polish-Soviet Friendship Society,
41

About the Author

Radek Sikorski was born in Poland in 1963. He played an active role in Solidarity and was granted political asylum in Britain in 1982. After studying at Pembroke College, Oxford, he worked as a freelance journalist, contributing to the *Observer,* the *Spectator,* the *Sunday Telegraph,* and *Encounter.* He is the author of *Dust of the Saints: A Journey to Herat in Time of War.* He served as a deputy defense minister in the first entirely freely elected government in Poland after Communism. Sikorski has written for *The National Review, The Wall Street Journal, Foreign Affairs,* and *Rzeczpospolita,* Poland's newspaper of record. He is married to Anne Applebaum, the journalist and author.